The Classical Rider
Being At One
With Your Horse

SYLVIA LOCH

Trafalgar Square Publishing

First published in the United States of America in 1997 by Trafalgar Square Publishing,
North Pomfret, Vermont 05053
Reprinted 1997, 2000
Printed by Dah Hua Printing Press Co. Ltd., Hong Kong

© J. A. Allen & Co. Ltd., London, England, 1997

Library of Congress Catalog Card number 96-62094

ISBN 1-57076-084-5

Designed by Nancy Lawrence
Cover illustration by Jo Taylor
Illustrations by Jackie Mallorca
Typeset by Textype Typesetters Ltd., Cambridge, England

Disclaimer of Liability
The Author and Publisher shall have neither liability nor responsibility to any person or
entity with respect to any loss or damage caused or alleged to be caused directly or indirectly
by the information contained in this book. While the book is as accurate as the author can
make it, there may be errors, omissions and inaccuracies.

Sylvia Loch was born in Edinburgh, the youngest of three children, to Barbara and Alexander Cameron. She grew up in a rural world filled with animals, stories of foreign travel, art studios and country sports. By fourteen she had started her own small riding school at home in the foothills of the Pentlands where she began to discover a natural bent for teaching.

Leaving Scotland at 21 to work in the wine industry and later the editorial world in London, Sylvia found herself as a young company director in Portugal in the late sixties. She was soon to be enveloped by the horse culture of the Iberian Peninsula after meeting her future husband Lord Loch whose family had also originated in Scotland. Henry Loch, much influenced by a friendship with Ernest Hemingway, had moved from Britain first to Spain and later to Portugal to study tauromachy, the art of combat on horseback. Those heady pre-Revolution days were filled with horse fairs, visits to great studs and always the schooling of their Lusitano stallions in between long hours of teaching.

In 1979, the small dressage school which the Lochs had established at Quinta das Esporas, near Loulé, moved to England. The Lusitano Stud and Equitation Centre was founded near Henry's old Suffolk home at Stoke by Clare and was the first classical academy of its kind in the UK.

In 1982 Lord Loch died suddenly leaving Sylvia with a baby daughter, Allegra. To carry on their commitment to the Portuguese horse, Sylvia founded the Lusitano Breed Society of Great Britain and became involved in writing to spread the word outside the Peninsula about the wonderful horses her late husband had loved so much.

Now married to Richard Hawkins, an international environmental lawyer, who supported and encouraged her work, Sylvia's first book *The Royal Horse of Europe* was published in 1986 to be reviewed in *Horse and Hound*, as the 'book of the year'. A year later, *The Classical Seat* followed which, now in its fifth edition, has become a bestselling video with a 1996 sequel. In 1990, another definitive book, this time on the evolution of dressage, *Dressage, The Art of Classical Riding*, was published in English, now translated into French and German.

In 1995, Sylvia launched The Classical Riding Club, to encourage a higher standard of horsemanship and a more philosophical approach among dressage riders. Now in its third year with over 600 members worldwide, the club is run from her home in Scotland. Today Sylvia teaches and lectures all over the world, but is happiest of all when riding her beloved Lusitanos with her daughter in the *manège* at home in the Borders, overlooking the Cheviot Hills and the River Tweed.

From his first day, the horse in all his glorious freedom knows how to move correctly. It is we riders who have to be educated to understand this movement.

(Photo: courtesy Jim Goff)

Contents

v

The classical rider

Dedication

To Palomo

While this book is written for the benefit of all horses everywhere, there is one horse above all to whom I make this dedication.

Palomo Linares, in so miraculously finding me (when I was not looking for another horse) and then coming to live with us over a decade ago, changed our lives. Not only did he bring me back to teaching and from thence to writing, but he also taught me to think, to feel, and above all to listen to horses – not only to him but to all horses.

My students tell me he has touched and changed their lives too, not only the few, but the many. Clearly he is a unique and special horse.

I often think he was sent by God – one of those 'angels unawares' – to touch and mould the lives of others and to bring a little glimpse of heaven into our world.

We swing ungirded hips,
And lightened are our eyes,
The rain is on our lips,
We do not run for prize,
We know not whom we trust
Nor whitherward we fare,
But we run because we must
Through the great wide air.

from the Song of the Ungirt Runners by
Charles Hamilton Sorley

Author's preface and acknowledgements

You could say I came to my present understanding of horses in a somewhat unusual way. To understand the author of this book, a bird's eye glimpse of our family shows we were not always mainstream, so perhaps the individualistic approach and yearning to explore beyond the established parameters was inevitable.

Despite passing all his law exams, my mother's father became an actor; my father's father, underage, ran away to South Africa to join the cavalry and fight against the Boers. While Mummy's other relatives were lawyers, doctors or clergymen and lived ordered lives in the Home Counties, she made the most of our romantic, but often unconventional Scottish homes, generally miles from the nearest neighbour, cheerfully fitting in her poetry and piano between bringing up children. Always game for anything, she gave each one of us love and support in all that we did. I once came home from school to find her lying stretched out across the huge oat bin in our barn in order to prevent a client's hunter, which had broken out of its field, from pushing a greedy nose under the lid. A gentle, dainty person, she was not strong enough to lead him away, but her gallant and resourceful attempts to prevent him from gorging himself certainly saved the day.

My father, who had been an accomplished athlete in his youth and who ran an exhibition race with Eric Liddell (cf *Chariots of Fire*) was, like his father, lured away from home by foreign fields. Underage, he sailed to India and soon managed the south coast offices of one of the great shipping lines. Years later, after malaria struck, he returned home and took up farming but eventually gave up everything to paint. His degree had been taken at Edinburgh where the majority of his colleagues were embracing modernism but, against the trend, he turned to classicism. His watercolours and his oil portraits, mainly of men in uniform and Highland dress, are still to be seen all over Scotland today.

My elder brother, a 400 metre sprinter in the army and a keen hill climber, went into teaching. Fluent in Russian, he now runs a training consultancy from home in Berwickshire, in between being a lay preacher. My second brother went from the navy to deep-sea diving, preferring the discipline and silence of the deep to the easy camaraderie of the mess. Even as a boy he had enjoyed danger. Today he is converting a Suffolk barn singlehanded, sails his own boat and his passions are the bagpipes and the fiddle.

Looking back, I had a wonderfully free and unusual country childhood, although, at the time, it seemed far too normal. Holidays were the kind people read about in books – galloping over the moors with picnics in saddlebags, exploring quarries and ruined houses and skating on frozen ponds before the days when people became so rightly concerned about allowing children out for long hours, unsupervised and alone. At school, alas, I scribbled horsy derring-do stories, liberally interspersed with drawings, at the back of exercise books in the maths and science lessons, but worked hard at the things I understood and enjoyed. In this way, I struggled through A level English, history, art and history of art but failed higher biology three times. Failing that exam prevented me from getting into the university of my choice, so I went off to learn how to type and run a business instead.

My only break from horses came when I was offered a holiday job, with officer status, as the first disc jockey at sea on a Union Castle ocean liner. Longing to travel, I seized the chance. The SS *Reina del Mar* carried a crew of 300 and numbered over 900 passengers. As the installation of a discotheque in the mid-sixties was nothing more than an experiment which no one seriously believed would work, I determined to prove them wrong. Aware that the job would end after a fortnight unless the discotheque could compete successfully alongside the ship's band, I took the challenge very seriously. As a result, for a wonderful year the position remained and grew while I travelled the world. Later, I spearheaded the sale of sound systems to several of the world's great shipping lines – the rest of that story is history.

During my time at sea, we visited Rio de Janeiro, Buenos Aires, Capetown, Cannes, Lisbon, Madeira, the Azores, Cadiz, Barcelona, Mallorca, Naples, Malta, Tangier, Tunis, Athens and many other magical places. In this way, I became fascinated with different cultures, different ways of life and just being abroad. As Lisbon was nearly always our first port of call once out of Southampton, I grew to love the elegant city with its magnificent baroque architecture and charming people, determining one day to live there.

The chance came when, as a young director of our company, I returned to open a Portuguese office. Despite impossible hours and a peppercorn salary, this brought me back to horses in an indirect way and introduced me to a way of riding and scholarship that I had never dreamed possible. The rest of the story, particularly how I fell in love with the Lusitano, unfolds in these pages. As for the people, whose kindness was overwhelming, I still have as many friends overseas as I do at home in Britain and many of our Portuguese friends are mentioned in these pages.

Horses are not only levellers but also bonders of friendship and, through them, I have met some exceptional people over the years. Some individuals I would particularly like to mention, as they were always behind one in one's work, offering enthusiasm and encouragement at different times in one's life, are Yvonne Marchant and Arsenio Raposo Cordeiro in Portugal, and Veronica Ward and Liz and Madeleine McCurley in Britain. Tragically, courageous Maddie is no longer with us so she cannot share in the happiness of publishing this book, although some of her photographs are included.

Another special friend is Pat Quinn who believed so much in what my late husband, Henry, and I were doing with our school of dressage horses, that when we brought our entire Lusitano stable to England in the late seventies, she enabled us, with an interest-free loan, to build the first classical academy of equitation in the south east. This was a particularly noble gesture at a time when few had heard of, or were even interested in, the concept of classical riding. We were also much supported by Manuel Sabrino Duarte and his wife Lourdes in Portugal who often stabled our horses in transit and took care of so many details. Later, Bernardo Vasconcelos e Sousa was generously to make it possible for me to transport my own horses in comfort and I owe all these extraordinarily kind people a huge debt.

As for my dear supportive mother, husband and daughter, for whom no praise is sufficient, I am sure there would have been no books over the years without their patience and understanding. Writing makes it hard to keep up with friends and relations and so often one must appear selfishly hermitlike.

Indeed, throughout my equestrian life, there have been scores of understanding people at my side, not least my students who mean a great deal to me and who continue to inspire me with their support and shared beliefs in the classical ethos. It is hard in a book like this to include everyone but, even unnamed, I hope they will know who they are. From as far away as Australia, New Zealand, Kenya and Canada as well as the Isle of Man, Anglesey, the Channel Islands and of course this country, the many people who have ridden my horses or invited me into their homes on far-away clinics has meant a great deal. I feel humble and grateful to every one of them.

Thanks go for help in my office to Clare Lodge and Zoe Harrison and especially to Sue Tuck for all her enthusiasm and making me learn the Apple Mac WP. As for hardworking, so reliable and regardless of the weather, Ruth Fiddler and Melanie Scully, I would not have been able to write this book without their conscientious guardianship of my horses. Mel has been with me and my family for six years now and since no writer can operate fully without peace of mind, I cannot thank her sufficiently for all she has done.

Thanks also go to Jackie Mallorca, another student from faraway San Francisco, but who, curiously, unrelated and at a different time, was a pupil at my old school in Edinburgh and who has since become a dear friend. Her clear line drawings for this book show some classical riders, but concentrate in the main on those who have clearly missed the point. With her deep understanding of equitation it has been hard for her not to draw perfect posture and to show instead the common faults I wished to demonstrate. Nevertheless, despite the pressure of a tight deadline, she has produced just what was required and I thank her wholeheartedly for somehow making the time possible across difficult distances.

Photographers Alan O'Neill and Terry Burlace have been most supportive and I am very grateful to Jim Goff in Kentucky for his wonderful pictures of his Spanish youngstock. Thanks are also owed to Classical Riding Club members Simone Brooks for an important historical reference, to Peter Feaster for some last minute thoughts and to Jackie Ockenden who found that wonderful piece of prose for the last chapter. Often, pausing for thought in between writing, those words have inspired me, as have so many books past and present. One of my reasons for quoting intermittently from other authorities is to prove the point that so much of what I have said has all been said before. Yet people still insist that this more philosophical and academic approach to riding is somehow inapplicable to this day and age. But how can this be when we and the horse are just the same as we have always been?

In this context, I would like to thank Eva Podhajsky from the bottom of my heart for writing the foreword to this book. I first met her several years ago in Vienna when I visited her wonderful apartment in the Hofburg and touched with reverence some of the many exquisite and moving mementoes from the time of her husband, the great Colonel Alois Podhajsky who saved the Vienna School of the Lipizzan from virtual destruction, and certainly preserved it in the form we know and revere today. Later, Eva came to visit Richard and me in Suffolk, staying with us for a few days and observing close at hand the work with my own horses and pupils. Since that time we have kept in constant touch. She is a great lady and it is an enormous privilege to have her name on my book.

A heartfelt tribute is owed to my publishers and editors over the years. Caroline Burt of J.A. Allen deserves a special mention for believing in my first book and also, by her continued encouragement, commitment and occasional gentle bullying, making it possible for me to write this one. By that token and for all their support over several years, I would like to thank Marion O'Sullivan, her daughter Kate Austin and present editor Alison Bridges at *Horse and Rider Magazine*. Lesley Young has been a very assiduous, patient and sympathetic editor with whom to work.

Author's preface and acknowledgements

Last, but not least, I want to thank those fine experts in the veterinary and biomechanical field of horses and humans who have travelled through these chapters to guide and correct me over the use of medical and veterinary terms when describing the movement of horses and people. This knowledge has come to me first-hand through my own riding, teaching and observation. Nevertheless, through general reading and discussion with medical practitioners over the years, I have been able to confirm that what horses have led me to believe is scientifically correct. As I am certainly not an expert in the field of biophysics, it has been interesting to complement the scientific overview with my own personal understanding of the subject. I am deeply grateful for proof-reading, time and some fine-tuning of anatomical terminology by sports physiotherapist Anne Gerard; equine chiropractor Dana Green BSc; and especially fellow writer and former researcher in biophysics at Manchester University, Dr Averil Cox. Thanks also to Doctors Michael Monk and Michael McBrien, both of whom supplied me with food for thought through discussion as well as some valuable reading matter. Finally, a tribute to that *primus inter pares* equine vet, Robert Lees of the Taylor and Lees Practice, Sudbury, for all his interest and support over the years.

As well as Palomo this book is dedicated to all horses who have been my constant teachers. First and foremost it is written to help people who may not have had as many opportunities as I have been fortunate enough to enjoy to understand their own horses better. Nobody knows all the answers, especially this author, and there is much still to learn and always will be. Nevertheless, if everyone throughout our long history had tried to please everyone else and waited until they themselves were perfect, no book, no poem, no piece of music, no stirring opera would ever have been written.

Foreword
in the form of a Personal Letter

Dear Sylvia,

When you asked me to write this Foreword, I felt very honoured. We had first met in Vienna and later I came to know you, your husband and horses in England.

In the context of your book, understandably, I had to begin by quoting Colonel Podhajsky as whatever I may know about horses and riding I learned from working on his books and watching him ride and deal with horses and riders.

In his *Complete Training of Horse and Rider* he stresses the importance of studying the available classic equestrian literature. 'Theory without practice is of little value,' he states, 'whereas practice is the proof of theory . . . Theory is the knowledge, practice the ability. Knowledge, however, must always take precedence over action.'

You have written a very special book, every page of which gives proof of your knowledge and understanding of the horse. As there are nearly always several sides to a problem, you give at least as much space to the training methods of the rider as you allot to schooling the horse, along with asides to the judges.

It is the technicality of your explanations which struck me. This was particularly notable in Chapters 8 and 9, 14 and 15, where you discuss the matter from all sides and lead it back to the sources of the old masters. Shortcuts may bring about temporary success but generally have to be paid for by relapse and loss of direction mainly at the expense of the horse.

The encompassing thoroughness of this book can only be achieved by years of intense studies and by a philosophical approach. The structure and the logical sequence of your chapters dealing with age-old concepts and misconceptions interspersed with very personal reflections and anecdotes naturally lead up to the one and only basis of correct training which you obviously take most seriously. That is, the respect and the love for the Horse.

Eve Podhajsky
Vienna, November 1996

CHAPTER 1
The circle of life
– the quest

The term 'classical riding' has been much misused and, in consequence, much misunderstood in recent times. Most people recognise that classical equitation implies a purity and correctness of practice, yet today there are many people who believe they are riding classically when they are not. Even if the final result is technically accurate, anything achieved under duress and force in a manner which looks contrived, heavy, tight, domineering or aggressively thrusting can scarcely be termed 'classical'. R.S. Surtees[1] wrote, 'there is no secret so close as that between a rider and his horse', illustrating the undeniable truth that many a hunting man was as aware of the classical ethos as most of today's dressage riders, and arguably more than some.

Neither is the pursuit of classical riding about pomp and ostentation, although this aspect may enter into it. In essence, classical riding is simply that which appears natural for both horse and rider as well as flowing, light, unconstricted, soft, harmonious and effortless. Indeed, it could well be described as common-sense riding. If this seems a little dull, one cannot help remember what Ralph Waldo Emerson wrote: 'Common sense is genius dressed up in working clothes.'

The centaur, the concept of horse and rider merged together as one, should be the ideal for which we all strive if we love our horses and take our chosen equestrian sport, of whatever discipline, seriously. The centaur was the mythical figure created by the Ancient Greeks who were the first people to write about horsemanship as an art and whose whole philosophy of classicism concerned working with nature, never against it. Whether this was applied to life's more practical aspects, such as agriculture, town planning and architecture, or to the more aesthetic spheres of poetry, music, sculpture or literature, the ethos remained – that only by submitting to the laws and rhythms of the universe would we begin to find that perfection

---

[1] R.S. Surtees, *Mr Sponge's Sporting Tour*, 1853.

1

The myth of the centaur grew up in the Classical Greek period and
has remained an inspiration to many generations of riders.
(Engraving from *Ecole de Cavalerie*)

and purity of balance and form with which the Creation itself was so
magnificently endowed.

How different, therefore, is the idea of the centaur – man and horse
perfectly joined – from the following statement which creeps in with
startling regularity in an abundance of twentieth-century equestrian
publications: 'The horse was not made for man, nor the man for the horse.'
As this short pronouncement is not ascribed to any particular writer,
yet so many modern authors deem it worthy of repetition, one cannot
help but wonder if its prominence provides a powerful excuse for
failure. For, indeed, so many have failed not only to ride better but
also to understand the horse, this extraordinary and most wonderful of
animals.

Is it not this same failure, this same cussedness, which has caused the
human race to make inexcusable excuses for defacing and despoiling so
much of our natural environment? The excuse that it could not be helped or
it has to be done that way, when, in fact, it could be done another way so

much better if only more respect and thought were applied, is simply not good enough.

Only now, as we reach the twenty-first century, are we beginning to pinpoint and blame that lack of care as we assess the extent of the damage which has been wreaked on certain areas of the planet and on certain species of wildlife. Those countless follies performed by so-called civilisation over many decades and particularly over the last 60 or 70 years could simply not have happened had there been more awareness, more imagination. Even more than greed, it has been ignorance and insensitivity which have combined to pollute, tarnish, contaminate, even lose forever some of the most precious gifts of the universe. With a gross lack of respect, generations have gone far beyond simply using these assets responsibly. Too often 'civilised' man has taken without returning, reaped without sowing and, in the case of so many animals, including the horse, exploited and abused without understanding.

Yet there is an alternative way if only people were prepared to make the effort. Access to past ideas and inspirational philosophies is more accessible today than ever before but we have to want to grasp this knowledge. 'Send imagination forth!' implored W.B. Yeats. If we want to change the world, it must start in our minds, with a real desire for a better alternative.

There is so much to learn from the past. Over the centuries, while educated man had grown to recognise in the horse powers that could be harnessed for a variety of uses and, indeed, upon which one's life depended, he also acknowledged an innate quality which, if nurtured, could prove enriching and ennobling for the human soul. Kings did not merely have their portraits painted while sitting on a horse to look greater; they felt themselves personally touched and enhanced by the grandeur of the horse beneath them and through their improved horsemanship. It was these very monarchs who were largely responsible for the setting up of centres of learning where an understanding of equitation could take place and grow. A beautiful but balanced charger could transform the most insignificant man into a noble leader almost by osmosis. It was the nobility and forbearance of the horse which lent the man his air of dignity and majesty.

Somehow we have got to return to a desire for these virtues which marked the classical age. If we continue to ignore them we risk losing the spirit of self-improvement which is the hallmark of a truly civilised society and, in the context of equestrianism, the horses themselves will suffer. Already there are signs that many of today's riders have ceased to care; too often the horse is regarded as a tool, a piece of merchandise

The nobility of this Van Dyck horse appears to enhance the monarch Philip IV who is grandly enthroned on its back.

(Courtesy Prado Museum, Madrid)

which is bought, swapped, changed, spoiled and even chucked away if he has not come up to scratch. As with the environment, too often the despoiling of the horse has been the direct result of ignorance.

It was the desire for self-improvement that made a silk purse out of a sow's ear for all horses in the days of the baroque and classical riding academies. The practice of scientific equitation not only led to more useful and obedient horses being rendered available for use in the realm, it developed from being a pastime for noblemen into a rich and noble art in itself. Indeed, centres of excellence, such as the Spanish Riding School of Vienna, were noted for making silk purses out of people as well as horses. The strict discipline and codes of practice led to refinement of the mind as well as the actions of the body so that the crude artisan could aspire to become a sensitive artist.

As the words of Ancient Greek scholars were translated, published and made available to all scholars, men of learning repeated, added to, embellished and incorporated these philosophies and ideas into their own riding manuals and academic tomes. Thus a golden age of enlightenment in riding dawned across Europe. From Hanover to Copenhagen, from Versailles to Budapest, from Lisbon to Antwerp, from Madrid to York, whatever the city, whoever the writer, always the dedications and inscriptions which heralded these *oeuvres* concerned 'the illustrious art', 'the gentle art', 'the noble art' of horsemanship. From the onset of training, therefore, it was incumbent on the rider to respect that art for the sake of the horse and for the sake of art itself.

In this spirit of understanding, the relationship between horse and rider was no longer regarded in the eyes of equestrians as that of servant and master. The horse was elevated in rank and the idea of partnership reintroduced. As Xenophon[2] had first acknowledged around 400 BC, the horse had a personality; he too had his pride and his feelings, so training must take account of both. Xenophon's advice, incredibly modern in context, was to work with the horse's natural instincts and allow him to do what the horse himself glories and delights in. This not only encouraged kinder training methods but created an atmosphere which promoted a profound overall respect for the horse. Thus the idealism and philosophy of the Greeks was rekindled and pursued throughout seventeenth- and eighteenth-century Europe, inspiring even the most hardened cavalrymen to pursue a more thoughtful, humane way of training their horses. Barbaric ways of riding would only cease when the perpetrators of such barbarism became educated and enlightened themselves.

So where has this inheritance of ideas gone? To what remote corner of the globe have fled the aspirations, the strivings and the desires to rise above the mediocre, the rough and the crude, and to soar? In the past century, so much of the classical philosophy has been lost not only from equestrianism but from our daily lives. Look around! Everywhere the script is being rewritten, the Creator's rulebook rejected and overturned. In art, literature, sculpture, music, theatre, we have welcomed in, even honoured, the banal, the ugly, the hideous, the distorted, the unnatural. Standards have dropped; the second rate and tawdry become acceptable. Everything, even language itself has suffered; boring, nauseatingly repetitive, mediocrity has become the norm. The fine, the gracious, the dignified, the courteous are considered to be élitist and no longer have their place in a world of political

---

[2] General Xenophon, *The Art of Horsemanship*.

correctness, a world turned sour. As Albert Finney said in the film *The Schoolmaster:* 'When the classics master goes from the schoolroom, we lose the classics, wave goodbye to culture. Civilisation drifts away and we give in to barbarism.'

As it is now, so it was then. Indeed, it was none other than political change sweeping alongside the ravaging Napoleonic Wars which laid waste those centres of excellence built around the cavalry and the courts and which caused the demise of classical riding. Riding as an art was deemed to have no place in an atmosphere of egalitarianism. Thus the time-honoured disciplines became fragmented, although some few pockets of learning remained, particularly in lands influenced by the old Austro-Hungarian Alliance. Those dedicated adherents who remained took their message to new lands, to America, Australia, South Africa, or married up with existing small schools which had struggled to survive among minority groups scattered throughout outlying parts of Portugal, France or Spain. Indeed, it is interesting to note how today's most learned and inspirational instructors tend to be those who have been influenced by those countries which retained a continuity of philosophy from that golden period of classical study which burned through Europe after the Renaissance.

Somehow we must bring back this sense of idealism to the everyday rider, particularly those who go out to compete. There is nothing wrong with competitive equestrian sport, but success must never be gained at the risk of dropping standards, particularly those of humanity. If we do not imbue our students with a yearning for self-improvement and self-discovery as well as for red and blue rosettes, our horses will continue to suffer as too many have in the past. Riders must be educated to see beyond the muscle and might, the smooth sheen of the athletic machine in their care. Today, in the technological age, through further knowledge and all the educational means at our disposal, including videos, televisions, the Internet, lecture demonstrations and endless laboratory research into animal behaviour, we have every opportunity to treat the horse once again with improved understanding of the classical ideas and to bring up our young riders to work within that framework.

Sadly, in the decades since the last world war, this has not always happened. In many circles, the material aspect of horses far outweighs the aesthetic approach; the idea of riding horses for physical and spiritual pleasure being forgotten in the rush for self-gratification. Motives for riding have changed; too often horses become just another commodity in a way of life where success is measured by what a horse has won or what you paid for him rather than how much personal effort you put into him, how well you ride and how much he gives back to you.

This sculpture echoes the idea of the centaur. The rider appears to be joined to the horse, spiritually and physically, and the hands are outstretched to receive the horse's energy, almost as a gift.

If all young riders embarking on a course of study of equestrian qualification were to have the classical ethos briefly but succinctly explained to them prior to their entry into college or in the riding school itself, we might look forward to a radical change in the attitude of riders not only towards the horses in their care, but also to life in general. At the 1995 Seminar of the International League for the Protection of Horses, one of the speakers, Major Charles Lane, who heads equestrian studies at the University of Warwick, remarked that most people recognised that work with horses constituted a vocation rather than just another job.

As with all vocations, such as nursing, life-saving, firefighting, the medical profession and the clergy, it is generally considered important to imbue students with a sense of awe concerning their chosen profession, to make them ponder and take time to think so that nothing is treated too lightly. Hands-on contact is not always sufficient; in the rush to get jobs accomplished within a tight timetable, people are often denied the opportunity to pause, take stock and appreciate the true nature of the career in which they are involved. Space must therefore be made for inspiring talks and lectures to encourage a more thoughtful and humane approach. In medical spheres, it would not be considered unusual for a senior practitioner to take the novice on one side and to place things into a philosophical and moral context at certain points during their training. When this is sensitively done, it can create a strong feeling of awakening and pride in the work ahead and it seems sad that this aspect is so often neglected in the modern equestrian world of education and training future teachers.

Taken to its logical conclusion, an explanation of the classical ethos should lead not only to a greater awareness of the environment but to a rejection of force and a positive submission to all that is good, balanced and harmonious. The young often yearn for excitement and inspiration in their lives but when there is no obvious source to follow it is all too easy to turn to negative influences. Yet horses, riding and their training can be enormously stimulating and challenging – if only this could be made clearer!

While the modern teaching schools have taken enormous strides forward in day-to-day care and tending of horses, all of which involves a certain amount of mundane, routine, hard work, the spiritual side of equestrianism is so often neglected. On the scientific side, students will be encouraged to understand the chemical aspects of nutrition and the biological effects of disease, but too often they are not always made aware of the science of riding itself. It is this which can be so rewarding and lead the student to a realisation of the marvellous complexity of their subject. Wisdom therefore grows not from cleverness and knowing all the answers, but rather from an appreciation that we and the horse live under the rule and sovereignty of the universe and that even with the latest technology no one has yet cracked all the mysteries. Only from an awareness of our own fallibility can the mental side of riding be developed.

To make a positive start, it should be impressed upon riders from the beginning that training the horse on classical precepts requires a thorough understanding of the basic laws of gravity and locomotion. Comparisons should be drawn with other disciplines which involve a supreme understanding of symmetry and balance as required for dance, gymnastics and the martial arts. This, coupled with an understanding of the mechanics of the horse's body, as well as those of our own, should govern every rule written, every method handed down from past and present instructors. If not, they can be thrown away. People should be taught that received truths or fashionable doctrines in equitation can only have a basis if they comply with the laws of physics as in any other activity. From this we may conclude, therefore, that there is far more to riding than gritty determination. Mastering athletic co-ordination requires theory and pure logic and this is as important in equestrian sport as in any other. Later in this book we shall discuss how controlled movement will stimulate the psyche.

Just as important, however, students must learn that to succeed in riding, a vital added dimension is required, something far greater but far less obvious than an understanding of the physical alone. Equitation necessitates a heightened perception of feel, tuning into the animal and the environment around us. Once the students can shrug off any idea of the horse as a vehicle for their own sport and achievement and begin, instead, to regard the horse as an intelligent living creature with his own needs and place in the scheme of things, perception will grow. As the horse is as super-sensitive and complicated in his mental make-up as, indeed, we are ourselves, to understand him better will require a very real and consistent development of our own mental faculties and powers. Indeed, when this mental aspect is lacking, the physical will suffer.

To appreciate these things better, we must understand that the nervous system of the horse is one of extreme complexity involving voluntary and involuntary responses carried to and from the brain through a highly efficient but sensitively charged telegraphic system. Although the equine brain is smaller than our own, the spinal column, which houses the central nervous system, is far longer, and the signalling system, which runs the length of the spinal cord, is highly refined. This can cause intense reaction, often deemed as stupidity due to the mere fact that it is different from our own, but which is actually nothing more than a miraculously swift response to external stimuli. Sometimes this is so extreme that the horse will appear to operate as though by extra-sensory means but it is, in fact, merely indicative of his highly developed sense of smell, touch, taste and hearing. While his sight is not as all-embracing as our own, it is more stimulated by motion; very small fluttering movements, which we would not notice, may cause an immediate reaction, generally for flight, which forms part of the strong survival instinct of the horse.

The old cavalry schools took account of the way in which the horse's nervous system worked and recognised the need to address the psychological aspect of training from an educated overview. One

We should never underestimate the sensitivity of the horse, or forget for one moment his flight potential. It is hard to believe that this beautiful Hanoverian can be transformed into a highly disciplined dressage partner.

(Photo: Bob Langrish)

particularly good book, written by Colonel Reginald Timmis[3] of the late Canadian Royal Dragoons, published in 1915, devotes much space to this subject. Rightly, the author points out: 'The intelligence of the horse increases rapidly with education. An intelligent master or trainer can make an intelligent horse. It is a stupid trainer that makes the so-called stupid horse. A horse develops in a marked way the characteristics and intelligence of his trainer or master.'

Among horse people, there will always be those who say the horse is stupid and this, of course, beggars the obvious question. There are also those people and no doubt always have been, who learn to sit on a horse and follow his movements, and those who not only become riders but who are part of that movement. The latter, by taking the trouble to understand the physical and mental aspects of horses, and in particular how to initiate

[3] *Modern Horse Management*, Colonel Reginald S. Timmis DSO.

and control movement, are the thinking horsemen and horsewomen. This way of approaching the whole subject of riding holistically is far more demanding and exciting to young people than learning by repetition and rote as though one was dealing with an inanimate object.

The marvellous thing about horses, and life itself, is that everything is always changing. Nothing is certain. Every day, every new experience should be accepted as a fine, transient gift. Indeed, we all need to remind ourselves of the ephemerality of life. When we can accept that nothing is permanent, that the horse himself is merely on loan to us and is not a possession, attitudes change. By self-examination and by broadening our attitude to ourselves and to our riding, we enlarge and flourish. The old masters were right when they promised that the noble art could make noblemen of us all.

The psychological approach to riding involves two superficially opposing, but in reality complementary, stances. First, it is important to believe in ourselves and to try at all times to think and act positively. 'I want to do this; I will do it; I'm not nervous; I love my horse; I want the best for my horse, so I will learn how to ride better so that he understands me; this is right for me and my horse'; and so on.

Second, in addressing this positive aspect, we should not forget that in order to realise our full potential, we need sometimes to make space, become inwardly quiet, and allow the senses to open up, absorb and receive. We can do this as we ride and it involves listening to our horse at all times. In his thoughtful book *The Art of Contemplation,* Alan Watts writes: 'The individual is an "opening" through which the entire energy of the universe becomes conscious of itself – a whirlpool of vibrations through which it manifests itself as man, animal, flower or star.'

There is nothing mystic or New Age about such thoughts. It is simply a question of becoming more receptive, more aware – recognising the need for reflection and study. The car or train is a good place to think; I have often solved physical equestrian problems with thought rather than action, off the horse's back. However busy our lives, such time out will be time well spent; it will makes us strong and lead to greater purpose when we do act. Often, this involves a relinquishing of ego which, ultimately, should imbue us with a sense of humility. The horse will give his life-force to us, but do we give our life-force to him? The least we can do is try to understand him better; 'centaured' riding is about partnership. Far from setting us back, such an attitude will empower us as riders.

Whatever our religious beliefs, it is important also to recognise that there is an order, a pattern, about the Creation, about life itself, which governs each one of us. We cannot escape it. As the Japanese author Taisen

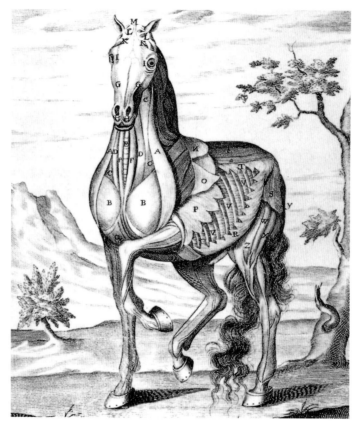

The classical masters regarded the horse in the context of the natural world around them, which led to a universal respect for balance and harmony throughout nature.
(From: *The Anatomy of a Horse, 1693, Andrew Snape, courtesy Paul Mellon Collection, Virginia*)

Deshimaru[4] writes: 'Everything in the universe is connected, everything is osmosis. You cannot separate any part from the whole; interdependence rules the cosmic order.' However much we may think of ourselves as free spirits, each one of us is bound by the same rules, the same disciplines of the universe which bring balance and symmetry out of chaos, light out of darkness and, carried to their ultimate conclusion, understanding out of ignorance.

Once we can accept this natural order of life, appreciating that everyone and everything has its place in that never-ending journey, that circle of life, we can then learn to harness the disciplines and laws of the world around us and work with them. This can only be to our advantage. Indeed, it is this realisation which provides the key to the door behind which stretches the

---

[4] *The Zen Way to the Martial Arts*, Taisen Deshimaru, published by Arkana, Penguin Group, USA.

path of learning and enlightenment. Once we have stepped over that threshold, life will never be the same again. With a profound respect for nature and all that we encounter on the way, the path opens up to us. It asks questions of us, challenges us and becomes a quest. The stimulus of testing ourselves, learning something new, and finding that one discovery leads to another will be enormously exhilarating. The way may not be strewn with glittering prizes but the rewards will be those of increased confidence and deep fulfilment in the quest itself.

In opening our eyes, we see there is perfection about everything in nature. Every blade of grass, a swan's feather, the claw of a wild cat, a hair on the back of the hand or in the mane of a horse, all viewed carefully or microscopically through a lens, will reveal a host of wonders, a design which is unique, suited and finished for its purpose. In the words of the poet Davies, we should find the time to stop and stare. The eyes, however, form just one of the senses with which we have been endowed. Touch is equally important and there is a very different feel between the inanimate and the energy of the living. Thus the leaf on the tree feels quite unlike the dead leaf underfoot, a living stem quite different from a piece of charcoal. Whether we are conscious of it or not, there is a pulse which permeates through to us from the lowest form of life and which, through touch, connects our own body rhythms and energy to the rhythms of the universe itself. It is this awareness which is an essential element of riding and, indeed, of all the arts.

I have often wondered at the inspiration that drove the great artists to achieve works of such unbridled excellence that they must, in the end, have surprised even themselves. Where did their incredible motivation come from? How many of us question our own drive? What drove the ailing Handel to compose his great *Messiah* even as he grew blind and slow, unable any longer to pen the notes for his own music? What desire burned through the discomfort and pain, allowing Michelangelo to forget his cramped body as he worked day after painful day slung in a cradle against the roof of the Sistine Chapel? These murals vibrate with energy, they burst out at you, they resound with unspoken glorias to the Creator and they affect all who have seen them; there is a pulse that throbs within – a huge outpouring of passion and energy. Mozart's great *Requiem,* one of the most haunting, stirring pieces of music ever written, was composed when the composer himself was at his feeblest and weakest, wracked as he was by tuberculosis, with destitution knocking at his door.

Tamer may seem the efforts of Wordsworth, yet if you read his *Prelude,* again it bursts with a passion and profound feeling for nature which leaves images on the mind long after you have closed the book. Years later, one may arrive in the Lake District and the words come flooding back – you feel the glowering foreboding of the mountains; even on a calm sunny day, you can see the frozen lakes and the swirl of the skaters; and when a shadow passes over the sun, you are transported back into a time when communication with nature was recognised and sought, when artists, poets and musicians submitted as one body to the rhythms of life. Clearly, William Wordsworth felt the urgent heartbeat of the earth.

Today among the rush, the whirl, the turmoil of the city, the traffic and of everyday life and how best to survive it, it is often hard for us to embrace nature as those creative men did. Often we can't hear the pulse, remaining unaware of the never-ending circle. Yet there are those who will set themselves apart, who determine to respond to the drive within and who are prepared to take time, to retune, to open, to question, to look beyond, even to take a step back and to stoop or humble themselves in order to conquer.

Then suddenly, having desired it all along, the force is there and we let it in. Who can explain what drove Claire Francis to sail singlehanded round the world; who can denounce Alison Hargreaves for assailing the monstrous K2 after her conquest of Everest, even though it claimed her life? The pulse may be harder to resist for some than for others. Pity only those who do not feel it at all. How much richer their lives could be if they opened themselves in however small a way and let that life-force come in.

In today's everything-for-nothing society, it is difficult to stir passions in the same way as in former years. There is so much to distract, so much trivia threatening to engulf us. Fortunately, however, there is a new word which today's youth find easy to accept. They may sneer at 'inspiration' but 'buzz' is acceptable. From buzz comes self-challenge and to dare is OK. Yet if we are to analyse a little, we may conclude that this sensation emanates from none other than the pulse that we spoke of earlier, the very force that has always inspired and driven the human race to transport itself from the mundane towards the special, the extraordinary; to reach for the stars. This phenomenon is not exclusive to the arts; it is the dominating factor in the new challenges in sport for those who pit themselves against the elements in a struggle to combat the impossible in nature. All say the same: 'There was something inside me which took over and made me want to do it.'

As a teacher, I see this push, this drive, this force as inherent in each of us if only we would receive it. The child of this universe is not such a modern concept as the gurus of the sixties would have us believe; this idea has been around as long as the human race has yearned for something better, tested itself and striven for the common good. The beautiful poem 'Desiderata' was written by a seventeenth-century nun, but the Greeks wrote in a similar vein two millenniums earlier. To be in tune with that universe, we must understand that the special powers it offers can only be ours if we have the imagination to let them in. We also have to believe all things are possible. For affirmation, we do not have to look far. The pulse of life runs through all our veins, the heartbeat of the world keeps us all turning; the circle of life is always there. Creation itself is a constant miracle.

Children often display something of this awareness because they are closer to the natural world than most adults. A child cannot be expected to discipline themself or to understand to the same extent as an adult in a chosen sport or art, but in physical activity, in particular, the child may learn much more quickly through a heightened sense of feel and a greater connection to the primitive earth around us. How else does a child learn to stand other than by trial and error; yet once that child has mastered their balance, why is it that the five or six year old will have a more perfect form of posture than a young adult of 25 or 26?

Although natural awareness and empathy may seem poles apart from academic study and a disciplining of the mind, I believe that the one cannot exist without the other. While the child is closer to feel and the adult more capable of logical thought, the ideal will arise when both concepts unite. The thinking rider, the centaur, is a feeling, rounded, empathetic rider with a huge awareness of both the wonder and the disciplines of the Creation. To understand those forces, which exert their influence on both the rider and the horse beneath, the rider must take the trouble to explore them further. Drive comes from striving towards perfection – looking always for further enlightenment.

We hear much these days about how to psych oneself into winning – becoming number one. There is no doubt that this attitude works for many, and by imagining ourselves excelling in a situation, we may well do this. But life is not just about winning; the goal in itself is not everything and, life being savage, there will be massive disappointments if we set too much store by material triumphs. To win is often a no-win situation for there is always going to be someone better coming up to topple the winner off their plinth. While this is acceptable to some, to others it can lead to a feeling of failure. More rewarding, perhaps, is to regard each day as a window, an opportunity for further discovery. If we are to rejoice daily in that opportunity and enjoy reaching out and finding more, then we will receive more. It may not be what we expected but therein lie the challenge and unpredictability of the path ahead. Travelling often into the unknown leads to a far greater respect for one's subject, while the whole pursuit is imbued with integrity.

Once respect is established, one can never again ride a horse without remembering that, like a tree or a flower, he is a miracle of Creation. No matter how we dress up our horse in travelling boots and rugs made of manmade fibre, no matter that he lives an artificial nine-to-five existence in a stable, is ridden in a concrete riding school and travels in the latest power-steered lorry, he is still a creature of the wild. He comes from the herd and his instincts are essentially primitive although deeply intuitive and complex. The fact that this essentially wild creature allows us to ride him should ensure our humility for all time. We should appreciate that, in his natural state, the creature beneath us is as perfect in his formation, his design, his engineering as the latest hi-tech aircraft. Similarly, he is perfect in dynamics and locomotion, until, that is, we clamber on his back and upset the balance. When a beautiful horse no longer looks magnificent, then it is likely that, somewhere along the line, someone or some people have robbed him of that natural beauty.

Generally, most imbalances in the horse, physical and mental, are manmade. As with some people, however, there will always be horses which are genetically difficult in character or conformation from birth and they require even more understanding and patience. In trying, however, to understand the horse better, we have to ensure that we ourselves are aware of the whole structure, appreciating that each small component part affects the entire mechanism. This gradual awakening should eventually lead to us being able to ride in such a way that we learn to feel where corrections are to be made so that we can give the horse back that roundness of form which we may have interrupted.

When we ride we should remember, too, that every component of our own bodies has a part to play. The horse is incredibly sensitive to our weight, thus the action of the rider's little finger can be as important as the action of the arm, the ankle joint as the whole calf. We should not forget that the skin of the horse is delicate; if he can feel a fly on his back, he can feel our every move. The horse has a way of picking up little signals and ignoring the big or the obvious, the forced, the contrived. The most beautiful combinations are those when the rider appears to do nothing and the horse works round and soft as though everything comes from within.

The student who wants to ride in this way will have an enquiring mind, one which searches and quests. They will not be disappointed, for, once they start the quest, answers come from the most unexpected quarters, which may or may not have anything to do with the actual subject in hand. There is a balance and roundness to every discipline which affects us all, whatever we are doing. The quest is there for us all to follow if we are only prepared to open up and to work.

CHAPTER 2
The generosity of the horse – an awesome gift

It is not often that I go out to the stables, take a lesson, watch people and their horses walking calmly down the road past seething traffic, observe a horse jump a testing round, load trustingly into a trailer, perform an intricate dressage test, see liberty horses dancing in the circus ring, driving horses in an endurance test, racehorses in full flight, polo horses turn on a dime, ponies in a bending race, police horses on duty outside a football match, without feeling a deep sene of awe. For where on earth can such a partnership be found as that of a human being with their horse? How can any creature allow us such minute and demanding control over its entire being? How is it the horse, above all the animals, offers us so much?

Now, as I reach my half century, I realise I will probably never know the answer, never know half the answers, not even if I was to enjoy another half century with horses. What I do know is that the submission of the horse to the human being is beyond compare. It is truly awesome. Not only does he allow us to become master of his slender limbs, but of his entire muscular system, his massive power, even his mind. The better trained the horse, the more he puts his own fine sense of balance in our hands which ultimately means relinquishing all self-preservation. What trust! What sacrifice! It is hard to believe that such a sensitive creature, with so much awareness of danger and suspicion of the unknown, can endow us with so much generosity that he will willingly make the final gesture. Yet this has been proved and repeated a million times over down the centuries – the horse, in all his nobility, will even die for us.

Ironically, it is this unconditional giving of himself that has led all too many people to abuse him. The cynic sneers, others are unimpressed, unmoved or allow themselves to believe the horse has no reasoning powers, no sense of imagination. Yet the diaries and true accounts of travellers and cavalrymen over the ages tell a different story. Horses have saved lives; horses have journeyed through unknown territory for days to bring help and to lead rescuers back to the fallen and wounded; horses have

People do not always appreciate the sheer physical effort made by the horse as he lifts himself into the *levade*. Only horses of a particularly generous nature can be trained to make these High School movements correctly.

(Photo: Elizabeth Furth)

refused food and water to stay with the dying. In short, the horse has not only saved man in times of need but has shown an extraordinary capacity for loving man over countless generations in good times as well as bad.

None of this love, incidentally, has anything to do with the hand that feeds them, for often it is reserved for the rider and not for the groom. It is clear, however, that a horse will not love back if he is not first shown love and consideration. Generally, how a horse treats his rider inevitably reflects how the rider has treated him.

How strange that in an age where knowledge and opportunity abound, we still need to be reminded of the Greek concept of the centaur – man and horse joined together in partnership – if we are to focus on the positive side of riding. Once we are ready to acknowledge that such a bonding is possible, however, we should be halfway towards achieving a better relationship with our horses all round. We may then be ready even to admit that if the horse can offer these human qualities of trust, fidelity, partnership and sacrifice, it would be logical to assume that he also experiences other 'human' emotions. We might then come to appreciate that the natural courtesy he extends to us simply by allowing us to ride him in the first place should at all times be reciprocated.

It may sound insignificant but one of the most disquieting attitudes I have ever come across was brought to light recently when I was teaching at a clinic in Hampshire. A pleasant horse ridden by a pleasant enough looking woman entered the *manège* for the first lesson of the day. After ascertaining the pupil's name, my next priority is always to ask the name of the horse before finding out something about its history. On this occasion I was told that the mare, a six-year-old warmblood, did not have a name. 'How long have you had her?' I asked, assuming it to be a new relationship.

'About six months,' was the answer.

I was profoundly shocked and immediately named the horse for her. I could not contemplate working with an animal even for half an hour without giving it the security and identity of a name. By the end of the lesson, the horse was responding to her name. I told the owner to continue with it. Horses, like people, need names. Only with a name can you feel singular, unique, special. How can a relationship blossom and grow if there is no sense of identity?

I have heard too many times not to be thoroughly angered by it that the horse is an animal of low intelligence. Along with all dumb animals, we are told, he has few emotions, no sense of right or wrong, and no ability to work out solutions for himself. If this were truly the case, we should tear up every riding manual, every article that has ever been written on the subject of schooling and go and ride a bicycle. Every aid we teach our horses has

19

both a mechanical and a psychological effect. It is the association of ideas which involves memory and reasoning powers and which makes it possible for the horse to interpret what we want and, more important, to remember it for the next time.

In addition to this, I find it remarkable that this, of all animals, will try to mould himself to our every movement and obey our every whim. If he were not bound by emotions of courage, fidelity and duty, why else would he allow us to mount him, why would he enter zestfully into every sport, accompany us on our journeys, and what would motivate him to try, and to *want,* to follow our every movement both at his side and on his back? For follow us he does and here again is found one of the great misconceptions of riding.

There are those who teach us to follow the horse – yet they have failed to grasp one important thing. The horse actually wants to follow us! At all times he tries to come under our weight so that he can carry us more easily, and in classical dressage it is not he who leads the dance but us, although if we are clever we will allow him to feel that we are equal partners. As Xenophon teaches, we must always make him think it was his idea in the first place.

Wanting to bond is scarcely the instinct of a stupid, unthinking creature. Rather, it involves desires and expectations and we should recognise that this is the act of a creature which has become voluntarily dependent through his own need for reassurance and friendship. In the same way that a wild horse respects and focuses on the herd leader and wants to be part of the hierarchical system, so the horse in our stable is anxious to be aligned with us, to become part of a symbiotic relationship. In riding, therefore, the horse earnestly wants to join with us – like us, he too desires to become a centaur.

If all this sounds sentimental, I make no apology. Romance and sentimentality have been responsible for some of the greatest pieces of music, art and poetry ever created. There can be no passion, no desire to reach new height without some degree of dreaming and sentimentality and riders should be the first to recognise that the concept of the horse has impassioned some of the strongest men that have ever lived, to the extent that whole nations have moulded their culture and ideals upon the nobility of the horse. It was the horse, after all, which led the conquest of unknown lands and territories. It was the horse which crossed new frontiers; the horse which bore peoples of the civilised world into the unknown, bringing light and education to the barbaric.

Only by recognising this power within the horse to move people, both literally and emotionally, can we begin to understand the animal in our

Trusting each other: Beauty and myself, aged nine.

care. Once we have taken this step towards understanding him and humbly. recognised those qualities which, for too long, have only been accepted as 'human', we may then be closer to understanding ourselves.

I am glad to say that I was brought up at a time when ponies and horses were still a way of life to most rural people and we accepted them as they were. When I was a child, I thought like a child. I knew nothing of high ideals and noble art, I merely accepted. Horses came seriously into my life at the age of eight and having, like so many children, dreamed of owning a horse for as long as I could remember, one accepted everything that came one's way in that amazing way that children do. But what is even more incredible, looking back after so many years, was that those horses or ponies accepted me. How, with my extreme lack of knowledge was I able to succeed at all with the odd variety of horses and ponies which passed through my hands between the age of ten and twenty?

I say this with no trace of vanity or pride for we never progressed beyond the most basic level of training. How could we without a mentor or tutor to teach and inspire? Now that I have become more educated in the understanding of the classical principles, it shames me to think what I may or may not have inadvertently done to make life difficult or unbalanced for those animals once in my charge, despite having had the best intentions in the world. Yet here is a curious thing! What I now believe sustained us and led to modest success, which included backing some difficult animals and turning the more truculent into sound and safe mounts, was my unconscious psychological approach. Always wanting the very best for one's horses could bring about extraordinary changes; more important, this was done for the best of reasons – one simply loved them. Obviously, through their own highly intuitive powers, this was recognised and eventually reciprocated.

Today there are many people who have never received a formal education in horsemastership but who enjoy unqualified success in terms of rapport, handling and partnership with their horses. Again, their great strength is their love of the horse. At the same time there are also many who enjoy competitive success but who may not actually like horses. In a recent television interview with a great racing trainer, I was astounded, when asked if he loved his horses, that the answer came in the negative. He loved the sport but not the animals. Like many viewers I suspect, I felt let down, quite cheated. I suppose, however, that if you are not brought up to love, it is hard to feel love.

His success came more from working with the people who rode his horses, than from his contact with the horses themselves. He had an eye for what was right, he could match horse and rider together and work on each particular partnership through his insight into the sport. Had there not been love at some stage in the process, however, I doubt if he would have enjoyed such success. It is as important to employ the right stablehands as it is the right jockeys, and behind every famous racehorse or showjumper there is generally a story of genuine love and caring at some level. We hear of a horse that relies on the support of his stable companion or the same groom in order to perform. You cannot quite take love out of the equation without losing out somewhere along the line.

It is the same with children. I was fortunate enough to grow up with a bounty of love all around. In this way, my parents, both artistic and sensitive people, enabled us to love back as well as to appreciate the creation around us. There was so much love in everything they did – from the way in which my father picked up his palette or handled the amber to polish his violin strings, to the way my mother's voice softened when she called the geese and hens in at night from the paddock or sat down to write poetry at the kitchen table after we had all gone to bed.

Family holidays were taken in the West Highlands around the magnificent glens and lochs of Fort William, in the deep, scented forests of New Galloway or camping as we watched the salmon leap by the clear peat-brown waters of the River Tweed. If you surround the psyche with beauty and stimulate the senses with smells and sights and sounds, it has to rub off on you somehow. Thus, I guess, from the earliest age, my brothers

My mother, Hannah the goat, my two brothers and myself in the arms of a nanny.

and I were unconsciously filled with a sense of awe and love of nature. This, in turn, led to respect for every living creature. Family prayers included prayers for any sick or injured animal on the farm. It may sound simplistic but often if we believe something will get better, it will get better. I believe we can carry this further and say that when we look for good in someone or something, we often find it.

When I think back to how I began with my ponies, everything – well almost everything – seemed to be governed by one stroke of luck after another. Yet now I know it was not luck. As Louis Pasteur wrote, 'Chance favours only the mind that is *prepared*.' Despite the fact that one knew so little, relying time and again on the generosity of the animal with which one was dealing, things did indeed turn out all right on the night because one deeply wanted them to. I see now that this innocent confidence was similar to what is nowadays recognised as the power of positive thinking, a phenomenon which not only gives people the vision and will to achieve, but which, unconsciously, can be exerted upon and felt by the people or animals which come within one's orbit.

Nevertheless, the saying 'ignorance is bliss' falls short of the truth. Things will not be bliss if we start off with a flawed attitude. The influencing impact of a positive frame of mind is not yet fully understood, but many papers, theses and books have been devoted to the powers of suggestion. I now believe it was this which influenced my own early life and which, over many centuries, has made it possible for certain uneducated people to handle and to train horses and other animals with amazing success.

I believe also that out of an awareness of the inherent good in animals, in an appreciation of their beauty and dignity, we, in turn, learn to handle them properly, with kindness and respect. As far as I am aware, there have only been two occasions when I personally broke the rules under which I had been raised. Looking back, they could scarcely be rated as instances of abuse but they were sufficiently against the ground rules for me to remember and to be ashamed.

It is nonsense to say that a young child has no conscience. I was only six when I treated an animal with a thoughtless lack of dignity yet I can remember it to this day. It was late autumn and I can still picture the exact spot in the garden where it happened, smell the fetid smell of dying leaves, feel the wet drizzle on my bare arms and legs. The flashback is as clear as a film; I am standing on a path between tall, wet, dying chrysanthemums, some taller than me, with red, orange, russet heads, weeping their petals on to the earth. Weeping at me? I was being rough and unfair to a helpless creature and although one is told children do this sort of thing all the time, I definitely knew it was wrong.

What was my sin? As the youngest of our family and desperately keen for a little sister, I had dressed up a young cat in doll's clothes and was making it walk on its hind legs up and down the garden path. By make-believing that if I made it walk like a human, jerking its paw to keep it upright, it would become a human, I had allowed myself to abuse its patient nature. I can still remember the warning bells sounding in my six-year-old soul and I chose to ignore them. Half of me was in a fantasy world, but half of me already knew that what I was doing was wrong.

So strong was this sense of discipline that every motion of that long-ago scene is still etched on my brain with shaming clarity. I did not actually set out deliberately to hurt the patient cat, but my treatment was unreasonable and I became rough and cross when it did not conform to the demands I was making on it. Yet adults, who should know better, all too easily become rough and cross with a horse who, like my cat, cannot give them what they want. They too are in make-believe world but ought to know better.

The second time was less excusable. I was about sixteen and it happened a few months after Mercury, a beautiful Thoroughbred hunter mare, had come to live with us. Again, guilt sharpens the memory. It was a glorious evening in May or June and I was riding her after school with the sun glowing gold over the splendid policies where it had been my privilege to ride over the years we had lived at Kaimes Cottage. I remember the rhododendrons were in full bloom, always a little later in Scotland than elsewhere, and we had cantered the whole length of the smooth park and were now ascending the gentle hill which would take us up to the northern side of the gully which overlooked our old farm, Hill House, nestling in the valley beside the burn. As I turned to take the slope, Mercury began to pull. She was still hunting fit and had been pulling too much lately for my liking. Despite a long pipe-opener, she had plenty left in reserve and I felt aggrieved at her determination to set the pace.

It had been my intention to achieve a nice, slow hand canter up the hill, not this headlong race on the forehand, and I grew annoyed. I remember circling her, to try to achieve a steady equilibrium, but she was no sooner out of the circle than off again, hasty, strong on the rein and impatient. I pulled back on the reins, to no effect. I circled again; the same thing happened only faster. I became angry, to no avail. This little charade went on for quite some time until I did something I had never done before or since – leaned backward, standing in the stirrups and putting my full weight against the rein. The snaffle must have dug deep against the bars of her mouth and, of course, it was counter-productive. By now she was agitated and had worked up a real sweat. So had I. In the end, exasperated, we got to the top of the hill and then I made her do it again and then again. I did not beat her and I never rode with spurs, but I booted her angrily and was as close to losing my temper as I had ever been. When she took the hill a third time and began to tire, I made her do it once more. Valiantly, she obliged but, although slower, she still pulled. I realised then how useless the whole process had been. My ignorant disciplining had not cured her, it had only upset us both and put us into unhappy disharmony one with the other.

Riding home, stroking her sweaty neck and trying to say sorry, I vowed never to take my own inadequacies out on an animal again.

I am glad to say I have stuck to that promise – although I did once bite a horse back who had bitten me, but that, under the circumstances, was fair at the time and he knew it. Now, I make it a rule to give every animal the benefit of the doubt, making even more allowance for those that have had a difficult upbringing or an uncertain introduction to life. It is quite possible to work horses within proper guidelines in a fair and humane way. This means never blaming them when they do not understand you and often having to take longer to establish parameters of acceptable behaviour. I know there are some who think this is a sign of weakness but they are wrong. It takes far more strength of character not to lose one's temper, not to blame everyone except oneself. It is not always easy to be calm and patient when things go wrong but keeping cool inevitably pays off. It is very often the horses who stretch you the most that reap the greatest rewards later when you least expect it.

A few years ago I wrote a series of articles concerning the backing and schooling of young horses for a well-known magazine. The editor called the series 'Softly Softly' which was a fitting title in this instance. I later learned that a fellow trainer had subsequently begun to refer to me as 'Softly Softly Sylvia'. I think this was meant in a mildly derogatory way and he was highly embarassed when I commented on it the next time we met. As a matter of fact, I would much prefer it to be this way round than the other.

Too many teachers lose pupils, rather than gain them, because of their harsh ways; today's more enlightened riders want understanding and consideration not only for their horses but themselves. Those who have to prove a point, who cannot concede and who cannot occasionally admit defeat or say sorry, risk losing trust with friends as well as with horses.

Many years ago I watched a breeder of top competition horses school one of his young stallions at a big show where I was a fellow competitor. It was a magnificent creature of sixteen or more hands, but with its greatly developed neck and chest it looked bigger and much older than its years. I was horrified to see he was not only riding the horse in draw reins but with a severe curb bit and some form of martingale as well. Unable to go freely forward, the horse plunged and humped its back. The owner was clearly afraid of its boisterous power and rode it in the most aggressive but nervous way possible, spurring it forward in one instant only to punish it in the mouth the next. The horse, not unnaturally, was bottling up, looking fit to explode as, in this mode, the two progressed haltingly around the arena.

Anguished, I called his assistant over. She was young like me and looked equally pained. 'I can't bear this,' I said. 'Does he always do this? I want to say something, but feel I can't, he's so much older! Moreover, we're competing in the same class and it will seem I'm interfering for the wrong reasons. It might make things worse.'

She agreed, 'I've tried to tell him,' her voice was weary. 'He seriously believes that what he's doing is right and he certainly won't listen to the likes of me and you – small beer for him. His horses hate him. I'm the one who has to try and sort them out after he's finished with them. He gets them into a terrible state – it's awful.'

Two months after the event, I heard that one of his stallions had killed him. It was the horse that I had seen. I wasn't surprised. They called it an accident in the stable; they had to call it something.

One hopes there are few people as shortsighted as this. As the majority of horses sold for competition are gelded, the risks are obviously limited. Some stallions are so humiliated by bad treatment, however, that they turn in on themselves rather than on the perpetrators of their discomfort. I know one horse who self-mutilated himself so badly after being sent away for intensive dressage schooling with a harsh trainer that he was eventually put down. Even castration failed to change the way he felt about himself; yet he had been a wonderfully calm and talented horse previously.

In the short term, gelding male horses diminishes both their personality and ardour. It also takes away the pride that makes a stallion want to fight back. A gelding will generally submit to bullying tactics, which is why aggressive riders generally prefer them to mares. Mares will rarely fight but can be moody and easily upset and yet a good mare can be a most wonderful horse to ride, although only a tactful rider will bring out the best in her.

While the average rider is not actively cruel, it is all too easy to become pedantic and fault-finding; to forget to give praise can destroy a horse's confidence. Sadly, the power of positive thinking can so easily be replaced by the power of negativity which exercises its influence with deadly effect. Horses are quick to pick up on either force, which accounts for the fact that many horses experience nervous breakdown if trained in the latter way. These are the ones that are quickly sold on and which one rarely hears about.

When a rider or trainer finds or looks for too much fault in a person or animal with which they are working, a deleterious effect is exercised. This can cause minor problems to become major. Just as children will become hamfisted and awkward when scrutinised by an unsmiling and critical teacher, horses too can become ill at ease and stiff with a tight-lipped, negative rider. Physical movements well within their grasp may become rigid and stiff as they lose confidence and fluidity and proceed to tense up.

I believe this is one of the reasons why some sensitive people go to pieces in an examination or a dressage competition. Highly aware of the critical factor, they become awkward, their positive potential stymied. In a dressage competition, the whole system of marking is based on the finding of faults. If the rider starts their test in a defensive frame of mind, this will have an immediate downward-spiralling effect, both on their own performance and on that of their horse. Looking for faults will cause faults; looking for what is good and pleasing to the eye will bring out the best and help to promote a picture of harmony. It takes a very singleminded approach to be able to put these factors aside and go into the charged atmosphere of a public arena determined to succeed without compromising one's standards or ideals. Although few and far between, such individuals do exist and I am filled with admiration for those few special riders who are able to combine competition with art.

One of the reasons why people receive so much enjoyment and inspiration from watching the Spanish Riding School at Vienna or the National Schools of Equestrian Art in Portugal and Spain is because they arrive there with a yearning and expectation in their hearts to see something beautiful, graceful and aesthetic. Simply by being there, positive energy will be radiated outward. Waiting patiently in their gilt chairs for the performance to unfold, the spectators will already have a mental picture of something essentially noble and wonderful in their minds so, naturally, they exude warmth and admiration. As they are not there to look for faults, it is doubtful, therefore, that they will find any. The difficulty for dressage competitors is the knowledge that the judge in the box *is* looking for faults. Peering sharply out, he or she is unable to do their job unless they can spot where the horse is going wrong. How helpful for all concerned if the rider could only canter down that centre line believing that the judge at C is willing them to present a picture of beauty and harmony.

There are many animals which are capable of offering their owners love and loyalty. It concerns me that so many people, including riders themselves, have been brainwashed into believing that a horse is incapable of giving back love and that because of this we must treat him with more severity than, for example, a dog. Indeed, I well remember my first riding teacher saying that a dog will love you, a horse can only respect. What a shortsighted view! More accurate might be that a dog will love its master unconditionally, but a horse will love you if, first and foremost, you treat it fairly and, secondly, if you allow yourself to develop a relationship with it in the same way as you would with a human partner. It is quite illogical to assume that any partner will love us if we are not agreeable in our own behaviour and always put something back into a relationship. How many riders think like this? There are too many who will look after the horse's material needs but put nothing back into the partnership itself. It is very much a question of 'Since I feed you I can take, take and take again.' No wonder love does not enter the picture!

Both love and respect require rather more than a generous smattering of both virtues from ourselves if we are to be rewarded in kind. As with all things, no relationship can be built in a few days. Time, patience and effort will always be required but the rewards speak for themselves. There is a look in the eye of the horse which is quite different when his gaze falls on the person he loves. That 'look of love' is similar to what we would find in the human who loves. A loving look means soft eyes, warm eyes, deep, slightly unfathomable eyes, but there is no mistaking it. It is a very different look from the anticipating, interested look of a horse expecting his food, of a horse watching another horse or the arrival of someone new on the yard. Like people, you can read a horse through his eyes.

Respect can exist with or without love but, of course, as with all close relationships, so much more will be given where love exists. Far more

Building up trust with Palomo. He had been in England about 12 months when this photo was taken and, having been let down and retired, it had taken all this time to develop some muscle tone again.

(Photo: Madeleine McCurley)

numerous than the relatively few who love, there are many horses who respect their owners. They have no complaint for they have been fairly treated and, in return, they give respect and do their best to please. Nevertheless, much more could be attained if love entered the picture. As with children, horses will neither respect nor love people who punish them unjustly. In his book on Ahlerich, his Olympic horse, Reiner Klimke tells a marvellous story about the time Ahlerich would not work with him for weeks after he had punished the horse for something which was essentially not his fault.

Respect in a horse is quite different from fear or apprehension. True respect comes only from trust, knowing that he will be treated in an even-handed way at all times, something which will be discussed at length in the next chapter. In the final analysis, the horse gives most when he feels that the rider is steadfastly on his side.

Writing this chapter reminded me of a radio interview I recently heard concerning the work of one of our greatest British actors, Sir Anthony Hopkins, recently turned director. The interviewer wanted to know how he approached the subject of bringing the best out in people from a position of power coupled with enormous responsibility. The question addressed the subject of how far you push people to get what you want, and whether some degree of furore was acceptable to whip up the adrenalin of the performers. I thought Sir Anthony's reply was pure poetry and should be circulated to every riding school teacher and trainer of horses in the world as a 'thought for the day' and for every day of their working lives. 'This is not the way to promote good work,' he replied quietly. 'Art does not require anger and angst. I like to work with my actors, not against them . . . People should be allowed to enjoy themselves as they work. You see, I am interested in directorship, not dictatorship.'

After my parents, the person who exerted the most influence on my own approach to horses was my late husband, Henry Loch. A man who was slightly dyslexic and had had a difficult childhood, he often found horses easier to deal with than people. I think this was because once a horse has learned to love you, he remains emotionally constant. For him, people were more difficult to love unconditionally for they could let you down. Henry was so quiet with horses that you could scarcely hear him, yet when he entered the yard every horse came immediately to his door, every head and every pair of eyes followed him around the yard and if ever anyone was herd leader to his horses, he was. Each horse that came into his orbit adored him. Stallion, mare or gelding, each one knew he was on their side.

Looking back, I still marvel at the lessons he took. He was one of the few people I know who could command a ride of up to eight horses, including stallions and mares working in formation with relatively inexperienced riders, in perfect harmony. One order, clearly given, and they would respond as one, a file of horses trotting down the centre line in a disciplined shoulder-in or *renvers*, flowing, soft and together. It was as though they obeyed from his sheer presence, mentally united to him, unquestioning. The riders sat there, following, doing things they never knew were possible, mesmerised, like the horses, into making things happen because he made it seem possible for them. If a horse stepped out of line, one word from him would resolve the situation; he never shouted, never became angry in a lesson but he exuded discipline and respect. It was a wonderful way for people and horses to learn together.

Henry spent a great deal of time in the stables and liked to touch his horses, but he never overdid it. No great hugs or exclamations, just small gestures, light caresses, a few words. He always said the same few words to each horse: 'Hello, old thing, how are you?' It was a greeting and it was a question and it was almost inaudible but horses responded to it. They were immediately interested, even the dull or the lazy. It was as though, because he asked the question, they felt flattered and wanted to respond, to reciprocate. It was the same if a new horse came to the yard for a private lesson. He would go first to the horse and quietly greet it: 'Hello, how are you?' Often, to the surprise of the rider, the horse would turn its head and look at him with real interest. They seemed to know immediately that here was someone who was on their side.

What a positive way to start a lesson! It taught me a lot and for years I believe I have unconsciously copied Henry, to be rewarded by horses that really try for one throughout their lessons. Even when the rider is not competent, the horse will work with you as instructor if you can make that first contact, arouse his interest and reassure him that you are there with him every step of the way. Sometimes, when teaching with my own horses, they look at me as though to say, 'Help, things aren't too good up here. Can you sort it out?' I know then that they need to re-establish contact at base camp and call the rider over. We talk things through, I talk to the horse for a moment, maybe give him a mint – but not always – remind him one is there, always with him, and then everything resumes with a far better chance of succeeding. This natural courtesy with horses is part of the discipline of good manners and it is important for the horse to know that you are not blaming him when the rider makes mistakes.

One of the reasons why people have lost the ability to communicate with their horses better is because, too often, the horse is regarded as a pet, a vehicle or, at worst, a plinth. None of these role models helps the owner to understand just what it is they have out in the stable, field or paddock. Many horses are pampered materially, yet little understood psychologically. I am always a little suspicious of people who are forever buying new boots, new rugs, new headcollars, new buckets and so on for their horse. Of course, we all like to spoil our children sometimes and our horses, but too much preoccupation with the material often suggests a dearth of psychological input. It is often the least loved children who have the most expensive toys!

Like children, horses deserve better. They all thrive on time, trouble, physical contact, talking to, understanding and praise. Horses deserve friendship. They can do without new toys but if you deny them time and communication they and their work will suffer. In Chapter 3 we shall be discussing the role of the horse in the herd; if we do not enter into these aspects of social behaviour which horses require, the relationship so

31

Opus, the legendary Lusitano bullfighting horse, is set free in the ring at Jerez. This was a
mark of respect for his great generosity and courage over many years.

(Photo: Jane Hodge)

necessary for success in training and handling will always be lacking and
we risk losing half the personality of the horse. This generally means he
will realise only half his potential in terms of output, generosity and the
endeavour he makes on our behalf.

Finally, it is important also to regard the horse in a historical context and
to learn from it. Whether or not we are naturally attracted by the past, I
believe we owe it to the horse to remind ourselves of how closely he has
co-operated with man over the many centuries since whole nations first
took to horseback in battle. We should understand that different modes of
horsemanship evolved for different reasons and that, unlike today, the
horse was once the most vital link in man's progress towards increasing his
power and broadening his horizons.

If human beings had been more peaceable creatures, like horses, the individual horse's lot would have been a much happier one. Yet the horse gave himself willingly in most cases to fight in our battles and, if necessary, to die for us. Such was the awareness of great leaders of their horses' generosity, for example, Alexander the Great for Bucephalus, El Cid for Babica and the Duke of Wellington for Copenhagen, that these horses became immortalised in history and are still remembered by schoolchildren today.

Even today's bullfighting horses are willing partners in the *corridas* of Portugal and the *rejoneo* fights of Spain. People may sneer but, setting aside the moral arguments, it is simply not true that these horses[1] have been beaten and coerced into this work as has been suggested. Fighting horses are highly schooled and cherished horses and they could not and would not be used if they were not willing and ready to fight. A faint-hearted horse is a dangerous horse, as any event rider will agree. A horse which does not enjoy his work will lack the zest and willingness so needed for these highly public spectacles.

I shall never forget the look of pride on his master's face when Opus, the great fighting horse of Alvarito Domecq of Spain, cantered, unbridled and free, around the arena after the great man's last fight in the bullring at Jerez in 1985. But the horse was not so happy; firstly, he did not want to leave his master. Finally, when, after much waving of hands and hats, he was finally persuaded to move off, he looked lost and bewildered, all pride had gone – despite his great beauty and physical power. It was when he was under his master and they fought together as a team, in partnership, that his face filled with pride, his eyes shone, and the great grey stallion gloried in the work for which he had been trained. The fulfilment of a task undertaken together was the culmination of his generosity.

---

[1] Fighting horses are quite different from the *picadors* of the unmounted Spanish bullfight – see *The Royal Horse of Europe* by Sylvia Loch.

CHAPTER 3

Training the horse – discipline or abuse?

There seems much disparity nowadays concerning people's understanding of the word 'discipline'. In the context of horses, too many riders believe that to administer discipline means only to punish their mount, even to 'beat him up' – an increasingly populist expression which one hears much too often from the lips of a surprising number of public figures when talking about schooling.

Yet the interpretation of 'discipline', when applied to the teaching of children, to the arts or to sport, has a much more positive meaning than the perceived Victorian one of repression and penance and it is the progressive aspect of discipline which is not always sufficiently recognised in equitation. For the noun, the following interpretations are offered by both my Oxford and Penguin dictionaries: 'the maintenance of order and obedience among pupils, subordinates, etc', 'the acceptance of authority'; a 'system of training in obedience, orderliness, efficiency' – and so on. As for the verb, the general definition is: 'to promote discipline, control, train'. There is no mention of chastisement.

Even if words are manmade, the enforcement of discipline or order in the animal world is innate and important to the survival process. To understand what it means to horses in their natural environment, there is no better way forward than to observe the herd system and to appreciate that, alongside other herbivores and creatures of flight, each horse's welfare in the wild depends upon an instinctive submission to the discipline of the herd. Learning respect and acceding to authority starts, therefore, on the first day of life for the young foal. Born into an atmosphere of family, with other mothers and foals around him, while the stallion exerts a sense of powerful superiority from a distance, the young creature soon learns what is acceptable behaviour and what is not. He learns, too, that there is a pecking order and that when the leader of the herd indicates 'Move on!' there is no loitering about. The instinct is for immediate action. Indeed, to the horse action *is* survival.

34

To understand our horses better, we should try to observe them in freedom, noting their inherent way of moving as well as their natural pride and desire to express themselves.
(Photo: Kit Houghton)

The great wildlife photographer and writer Robert Vavra has studied herds of wild horses in Andalucia and his books give us a very clear idea, both pictorially and textually, of the structure and hierarchy that the senior members of the equine family bring to their pastoral lives. From this, one can begin to understand how, when he leaves his mother, the horse born in captivity will identify with an alternative provider and companion.

The natural focus will be his handler, later his rider, but it is important for any healthy relationship from the beginning that trust is coupled with respect, fondness with compliance and a desire to please. Just as the herd leader is the disciplinarian who makes the decision where his subordinates will graze, leads them to pastures new, protects them from danger and provides a safe haven, so the domestic owner will be expected to play out a similar role.

It is this last requisite that is very often forgotten in the relationship between riders and their horses. Clearly it is not enough to provide a dry stable, food and water. Emotionally and mentally, all horses need to feel they have their own space, a certain amount of physical freedom, as well as the security of continuity and knowing where they stand. All this combined constitutes a safe haven and if any aspect is denied, horses will suffer mentally.

How sad for those horses whose owners never provide that safe haven, particularly as dysfunctional behaviour is generally blamed on the horse. Firm but fair school procedures and discipline around the yard should establish respect. The one area which should be totally inviolate is the horse's stall or stable. No horse should be threatened in his own space; it must also be remembered that if he is to be denied physical exercise on his own terms, free and at liberty in the field or paddock, his psychological development may be stymied.

It is almost impossible nowadays to give the domestic horse ideal conditions such as the wide open spaces enjoyed by the herd, but horses adapt and have conformed well over the centuries to a manmade environment. There will be times when the horse wants to browse, roll or play and even a pocket-sized paddock is better than none at all. Of all the most difficult horses I have ever been asked to work with, all without exception have improved with routine turning out in addition to exercise on the lunge or under saddle. There is no doubt that a horse grows in confidence when a pattern of life is established. This is scarcely surprising when we consider nature's own clearcut daily run. Just as the sun rises, peaks and sets in the same place each day, so horses thrive on an ordered routine. They like to start the day at the same time, know when they will be fed, turned out, exercised and allowed to rest. They need a time to play as well as to work; they need peace as well as bustle and activity.

In a well-ordered yard, horses will anticipate certain events to the last second, their inbuilt time clock being extremely sensitive to a regulated timetable. Not everyone can organise matters like clockwork but if there is a rough routine for a horse to follow and the main issues are addressed, he will learn to cope and happily comply when certain aspects are changed. What disconcerts horses and turns them into anxious individuals is the constant concern of not knowing when the next meal is coming, when they will be exercised and how they will be exercised. All of these uncertainties can stifle the horse's psychological development.

Most big yards start the day with rattling feed buckets, banging of doors, general noise and activity and the inevitable radios blaring at the behest of the staff. There is nothing wrong with this but I remember one trainer at Newmarket switching off all the radios after morning exercise. 'The horses need to be quiet now,' he would say firmly and only at evening stables were

An ordered yard gives security to the horse, provided there is plenty of activity going on and constant companionship all around.

(Photo: courtesy Promark)

they allowed back on again. He was so right. Horses' ears are far more sensitive than our own, and a horse can be driven to distraction with permanent noise, particularly of a metallic timbre, jangling all day.

As with children, the security of familiar guidelines in a familiar environment leads to confident, happy horses which thrive and blossom. While changing hands may prove a mentally scarring process for some horses, particularly if they have bonded with a particular rider or another horse, others sail through this with never a backward glance provided the old safe haven is replaced with another. More upsetting for a number of horses is the lack of continuity they feel concerning their training when they enter a new relationship. They may cope with things being done at different times and in a different routine but when they are unfairly blamed because the disciplines and ground rules have actually changed and they do not understand, they feel threatened and defensive.

When it comes to riding, it is the familiarity of certain procedures which calms and reassures the equine mind. In jumping, methods tend to be the same worldwide, the Caprilli method or the forward seat being the norm, the idea of following through over jumps, universal. In racing and polo yards again there are no huge discrepancies; although there will always be degrees of emphasis and style and, as with all disciplines, some riders are pleasant to carry while others are not. Nevertheless, horses generously learn to comply and adapt.

What is worrying in dressage is the variety of schools, styles and seats which exist. Some people like to think they are riding in the German seat; others in the French, still others in 'a competition style'. If you asked the horse, he would beg for no style, just one way – the correct way – correct, that is, for him and for the way in which he and we are conformed and how we are made by nature to function in space.

This is where the classical seat and classical training enter the picture. There are no geographical or cultural barriers but every horse understands them for they involve the same language, the same principles, the same feelings of being directed through the same physical means. As I was putting the final touches to this chapter before my manuscript went to the printers, I read an article in *Horse and Hound* about the talented Gerard Naprous, a stunt rider whom I have known off and on over several years. Gerard, who travels all over Britain and abroad with his jousting and circus horses, has prepared horses for television and countless films, such as *Braveheart* and *Black Beauty*, as well as pageants and pop videos. What were the requirements for teaching someone to be a good stunt rider, he was asked in the interview. The reply was unequivocal: 'Learning the basic classical seat which can take anything from six months to several years to learn, and only when that is achieved does trick riding come on to the agenda.'

Whatever the country, wherever the horse and rider, whatever the agenda, the same methods should apply. Once horses become acquainted with firm, unswerving guidelines and understand the framework within which they are to work, they respond easily and comfortably to new challenges and further input. Indeed, they enjoy discipline provided the lines of communication are always there. Foundations which have been properly laid and understood in the first place can be added to and built upon by new craftsmen, provided the structure continues on the same lines.

What frightens horses and destroys their confidence is when there is no firm grounding to their work. When, metaphorically, the rug is swept from under their feet and when they are required to do things for which they have not been adequately trained or prepared, with something done one way one day, then overturned and done another the next. For any horse, suddenly to find that the goal posts have moved is bewildering and unsettling. It is this unwarranted lack of disciplined routine which sweeps away their personal safe haven and will lead to difficult or problematical behaviour.

Recurring mental anguish of this nature can be as painful for the horse as a physical beating or spurring. Many horses have to endure both mental uncertainty and physical abuse, which makes for a very dangerous horse through no fault of his own. Were it not for the generous nature of the majority of horses and the fact that most male horses used in sport are gelded nowadays, we would no doubt hear of more fatal accidents concerning horses who seek their revenge on the perpetrators of such misery. One of the great tragedies for the horse is that, unlike the cat or the dog, he cannot vocalise his terror. He can neither scream, nor moan nor whine. In short, he is a silent prisoner whose quality of life lies in our hands. It is therefore incumbent on us to learn to speak a language that he can understand. It is also important that we should encourage others to speak it too or there will be more silently screaming horses.

It is encouraging when special people promoting special methods towards further understanding of communication are featured in the horse magazines. Anything which raises public awareness and teaches people to treat horses more thoughtfully is to be welcomed. Enthusiastic editors sometimes make the mistake of suggesting that some of these methods are new and revolutionary but as horses have been around as long or longer than humans, there is very little that is new. What is new is that certain methods are being brought to the notice of the general public so that people who have had no previous access to horselore are now being given the chance to reach out and grasp it. I have witnessed demonstrations showing the talented Californian Monty Roberts with his join-up method, the late Barbara Woodhouse and her breathing method, Linda Tellington Jones and her Tellington Touch and a number of practitioners who teach the Alexander Method for horses. All these people had or have a genuine desire to help and a natural talent with horses, some more than others, but each would probably be the first to admit that their methodology is as old as the hills.

Over the years, I have learned as much by being with and watching old grooms in Portugal and Spain moving quietly about the stalls of highly charged, hotblooded stallions and bringing about a sense of calm. I have noted the way the Scottish ghillies deal with the ponies that will carry the dead stags back from the hill to the great lodges of the Highlands, and observed Irish boatmen put horses to sea. I have watched Brazilian gauchos and African syces and Moroccan warriors and have come to the conclusion that all those who love horses and have enjoyed years of experience with them use very much the same methods, the same universal language. All involve gentle disciplining with the voice, touch, body language and the age old practice of moving in such a way around horses that they know instinctively that you are the boss but also a friend.

As for learning about pressure points and blowing up noses, these things come with time and understanding. As a four year old brought up with farm horses, I was taught to breathe up the noses of our two working Clydesdales from the time I was tall enough to offer them apples and no one thought anything about it. It was just something which country folk had always done and common sense would tell you not to do it to an obvious nipper or biter. While acupuncture is a specific science, the Chinese are not the only ones with sensitive fingers. The more one gets to know a horse, the more he indicates to you just where he would like to be rubbed, tickled and massaged and a sensitive handler will soon discover the pressure points if they take the trouble to feel and to study their horse. Areas of tightness, of muscle spasm can be felt and explored; gentle manipulation with the fingertips can disperse tension and smoothly free the muscle fibres again. It is all a question of feel.

In the schooling of horses for dressage, we are always hearing that many roads lead to Rome. Whether all these roads are correct and acceptable for the horse, however, is open to question.

There are trainers who teach by use of voice commands and rewards which is perfectly proper provided this, in itself, is not the method. Their use can complement the method, but if used in isolation will result in the horse learning to do everything by memory in the way that a dog learns new tricks. What happens later, when the horse changes hands and the new owner says things in a different way or in a different language and there are no instant rewards? The horse will feel lost and bewildered.

Less effective, and worse by far, are those who train through punishment and pain. Here again the trainer relies on the horse's memory, the idea being an association of ideas. The horse is expected to work in a particular way otherwise he will be beaten or spurred or so stifled in his movement that his muscles ache because there is no respite. Whether the horse can analyse in his brain that he is being punished for the work itself or the way in which he worked, is anyone's guess. The trainer may not even have decided this for themselves either but as the criteria are based on the horse having a memory of a bad feeling, the whole method has to be counter-productive. Bad feelings and bad memories are not conducive to producing good, expressive work, although in certain circumstances the release of adrenalin associated with fear can make a horse appear to have greater impulsion and be more forward going. These punishing methods may work in theory but in practice they generally result in failure unless the trainer has other means of training at their disposal.

Overforceful, harsh riding can make life very painful for horses, particularly when the rider's position disallows the horse's own natural carriage.

Taking the fear element further will result in the brainwashing method. It was shaming to read recently in a leading dressage magazine[1] how a top competitor in this country has faith in her trainer mainly because, 'in that stable horses never go back to their boxes sweating and shivering wrecks as they do in so many places'. If this can be stated in public, what else is not stated, what more goes on behind closed doors? Even as I write this book, a former pupil has told me firsthand about the 'latest new method' for instant obedience and success at the highest level in dressage. The method comes from Western Europe but is already being slavishly copied in Britain and many other countries.

On my pupil's course, only two out of ten horses appeared to benefit in any way from the three-day clinic where this new method was employed and taught by an international rider of repute. The rest were het up, even traumatised, and months of work and accumulated trust were spoiled. My pupil pulled out after the first day. There will always be survivors in the most wretched of circumstances but who wants a horse which has become a robot? Nevertheless, this particular trainer's method, which has taken certain horses to the very top, constitutes nothing more or less than the most appalling abuse of the horse's mind. It reminded me of a method used during the Cold War to extract obedient submission from captured spies,

---

[1] *Dressage*, Cecile Park Publishing, London, February edition, 1996.

which often led to despair and suicide at a later date for those who complied and survived. Wait for the equine stars to crack when training has been incorrect and forced! Tragically, they generally do, later if not sooner. These are the horses which may tough it out initially, then quietly disappear. Their fall from the dizzy heights rarely makes the headlines.

For the sake of explaining unacceptable discipline and in the earnest hope that at some stage these methods can be exposed and publicly denounced, I shall attempt to describe this particular system which caused so much disquiet. Conducted in two stages, the first phase involves teaching the horse to become totally dependent on contact by eliminating all freedom of the head and neck and working the horse on a fixed, short draw-rein which brings his head behind the vertical and into an unnaturally deep outline for several days or even weeks at a time without respite.

As a result, despite the obvious discomfort, the horse becomes so reliant on the bearing-down effect of the rein that, when it is removed, he feels disorientated and afraid. Now he is easy prey for the second stage which, unbelievably, is practised in an indoor school from which the horse has no escape and which, by its extreme restriction, is terrifying to the horse. This involves throwing the reins at the horse so that he has no contact in his mouth, and he is then kicked and spurred into very fast forward movement at the gallop. This sudden freedom alarms and terrifies him and the idea is that every time he seeks the contact of the rider's hand to balance, the reins are chucked back at him and he is beaten forward again. Round and round he is made to go, reins flapping, legs kicking, spurs digging. He is not allowed to stop, every time he flags he is beaten on and on until he has no strength left. At the end of days of this procedure the horse's spirit is totally broken. In the words of the female disciple who has brought the method to Britain, 'The idea is that the horse is '*so grateful*' when you take up the rein again, he will never again refuse to submit to the contact. Neither will he ever refuse to move sharply off the leg.' Did she blush, I wonder, as she said it?

Unbelievably, this method is now being taught to many levels of competition riders as the way to success. Previously decent, if not very intelligent, riders have themselves been brainwashed if they truly believe such a method is acceptable.

Yet, such a system could be used in a positive way and, as with all things, there is often a fine line between the acceptable and the unacceptable. The method of warm-up I had so admired in Portugal also requires contact but this is never done through artificial aids. It is achieved by working horses through various suppling exercises in collected walk for about ten minutes at the beginning of schooling, to bring their hocks under more and to flex their joints before they are asked for the work proper. Then the horses are allowed to let off steam by having a liberated canter or, if they want, a short gallop, round the arena on a loose rein. One moment discipline, similar to 'exercises at the bar', the next a little fun, freedom and stretch – and finally the horse is ready for the real work. The results achieved are similar to those required by the cruel method: respect for the hand and forward impulsion, but there is a world of difference as to how they were achieved.

Thankfully, more common by far than those harsh, ambitious people are those who train through trial and error. Misguided they may be, but generally they are well intentioned as they try something one day, one way and, if it does not work, they try it another day, another way until eventually – they hope – something clicks. Most riders, including myself, have been through this situation at some time in their lives, but for those who are seriously aiming towards dressage, they owe it to the horse to become properly informed. Sadly, it is too often those people with no method at all who will buy a young horse and 'school' it on in the vague hope that a method will appear as if by magic along the way. This truly is a case of the blind leading the blind.

To understand the classical method, the only humane, logical and natural way forward, we should again take time to view the horse at liberty. We should note how he moves of his own volition, particularly when he is aroused, happy, playful, alarmed or parading himself before another horse.

Even the youngest baby learns to push off with his hind legs and raise his forehand in play and in flight. This is the way God made him.

(Photo by kind permission of Jim Goff, USA)

43

Ground-covering ability in the young foal relies on freedom and elevation
through the head, neck and shoulders. Note the flexion at the poll and
the pushing-off ability of the hind legs.
(Photo by kind permission of Jim Goff, USA)

We will note that, in movement, his poll is always the highest point of his body and that he flexes his head from the poll but never brings his chin behind the vertical. We will see that, when he turns, it is always from his hindquarters, pushing off with the hocks. Never – unless very old or stiff or about to graze – will he lead himself forward by the forehand.

We will observe also that for all forward movement his neck needs to be extended, either arched up and forward or more horizontal and forward so that the wither is higher than the croup and he is afforded ample free movement of the shoulder and the back. The whole frame will need to stretch at speed but the general outline through the wither and back will become more raised and rounded when he is collecting himself, slowing down or starting off. We will see that when he stops out of fast movement, this is achieved by pushing under with the hocks while his back appears to shorten and lift with the croup tucked underneath. Clearly, we can see that, as with all the vertebrates, movement stems from the mobility of the back and, in the case of the horse, from the powerful action of the hocks beneath.

A maturing foal, full of energy and vigour, will demonstrate this spontaneous behaviour better by far than the older horse who, too much influenced by the various riders in his life, may have lost many of these natural impulses due to stiffness in the relevant joints. Nevertheless, an old stallion, for example, who has been classically trained may still look magnificent at liberty and use himself as correctly, if not as freely, as a young, unbroken colt.

All of these observations should give us clear guidelines as to how and how not to ride our horses. The most important matter to address first will be exactly where the rider should sit if their weight is not to place undue stress or interference on the horse's back, particularly where it is at its weakest. It is therefore necessary to have an understanding of the horse's skeletal system and to understand that between the twelfth and fourteenth vertebrae the ribs are at their longest, creating a strong 'bridge' as the back is most supported here. Not surprisingly, it is also recognised that the horse's centre of balance, power and motion occurs just below this region. Nature is not stupid!

As to what we may fairly expect of our horse in his schooling, there should be no argument if we follow nature's laws and allow things to take shape in their own time. We must never make unnatural demands, appreciating, therefore, that is not correct to pull our horse's head behind the vertical, to restrict his neck or to allow him to work with a 'broken' crest which will occur when the poll is no longer the highest point. Worse by far is to allow the horse to work with a hollowed back. There is no excuse for this, even with the most novice horse, if we have always sat light and in the correct place and are highly disciplined in our own balance.

To teach the horse to march on, we must aid him with our legs. If they are applied in the correct place, he will use more hind leg than foreleg. If he does not respond to the leg, a light encouraging touch with the stick on the quarters is much more inviting that heavier leg aids. As it must be counter-productive to teach a horse to turn by pulling his head and neck round so that his body has to follow, we should eradicate all thoughts of riding the horse from the forehand at the very onset of training. This does not mean that the horse will not be on his forehand; the young horse will find it very hard to come into a correct and natural balance when he first carries the weight of a rider on his back. To allow him to succumb to this unbalance, however, is neither kind nor helpful. We must encourage him to listen to our body aids from the first day and help him to move more naturally again. Only by being attuned and counter-aiding with our balance will the horse learn to move correctly, pushing from behind.

As every single body aid we make is felt by the horse through his back and sides, this form of aiding is as natural to him as those we employ to move him about in the stable. A little push here and he steps aside, a little nudge there and he goes forward or back. Even the greenest horse reacts to this way of riding and it is flawed thinking to believe that the horse relies

The idea that a horse will find it easier to turn from a backward-pulling rein is essentially flawed. The only truly natural aids for the horse are those of the legs and body, which should act on the trunk and the hindquarters.

on a pulling rein for turning, moving on to the track in the school or changing direction. Instead, the rein keeps him together so that his energy can be chanelled between those mild physical guidelines but the direction and drive are determined from behind. By encouraging the horse to respond to our weight, we allow him to move as one with the rider and as though it was his idea in the first place.

Perhaps now the reader can understand that there is rather more to classical riding than meets the eye. Not only must the rider take account of the horse's natural instincts but also of his balance and his physical make-up. There are no ifs and buts about correct practices. Only one method complements the way in which the horse moves naturally so the rider must know how to sit over his centre of motion and to act on those parts of his body which are capable of making a mechanical response. While the conformation and temperament of every horse vary slightly, every equine under the sun is governed by the same laws of balance and locomotion as we are ourselves. For this reason, the principles of riding remain the same, whatever the horse and whoever the rider.

How fortunate for today's riders that these well-tried and tested precepts have been thoroughly explored and developed over so many centuries and laid down in writing for us all to follow. As there is not the excuse that we have to puzzle them out for ourselves, we should apply ourselves diligently to their pursuit, accepting their worth and learning to become disciplined ourselves.

Sadly, it is a fact of modern life that the more freely available information becomes, the less some people seem to wish to take advantage of it. Too many modern riders reject the traditions of the past, seek quick solutions and sincerely believe they know better. Not only is this arrogant thinking, it is essentially flawed and ignorant thinking. We should never forget the correlation between dressage and the art of hand to hand combat and remind ourselves that those who defined the classical principles enjoyed more practical experience of horses than any of us will ever know.

Up until the twentieth century, horsemanship was a serious way of life. It has become fashionable to sneer at the ways of the cavalry schools, yet the preparation of horses for war was not an idle pursuit but a practice connected with survival. Methods were tested in the field and only those which worked were handed on. Just as, today, car manufacturers are aware that in the building and testing of the latest model of car they are playing God with people's lives, so the men who broke, schooled and trained horses for combat were aware that anything which was incorrect or flawed imperilled the person who would ride that horse.

Moreover, those men who applied themselves to the theory and science of riding were not concerned with fame or success, theirs was a mission of service to others. They studied and shared their knowledge for the common good so that others who came after them might benefit and understand. As adversity and defeat taught lessons which would never be forgotten, conclusions were never arrived at lightly. Nothing was left to chance. The classical method was one which would endow the rider and his horse with the only possible chance, the best practical option in the most dangerous of situations.

Whatever happened, the horse must be placed in a position of balance to enable him to react at a moment's notice. He must be swift, supple, agile, stoppable, turnable and, above all, at the end of training, reliable. He must have the spirit and fire in his belly to cope with whatever was asked of him and this required his co-operation. The cruel methods of certain practitioners from the Middle Ages had to be rejected as they removed any desire on the part of the horse to work with the rider. A frightened horse is a dangerous horse; a trusting horse is a partner, even unto death.

It is sad that the art of passing on the classical principles has become so fragmented. Perhaps it is an aspect of modern life that we have to over-complicate everything so that the fundamentals are forgotten.Overembellishment can cloud the picture, distort the original message, lose the truth. Today, although most riding manuals still stipulate the basic principles, an alarming number of trainers seem to ignore them, embroidering their language with needless jargon which conceals the basics.

Adherence to the idea of art is often shelved for economic and practical reasons; shortcut methods are introduced, with gadgets used to circumvent days and months of solid training. Yet these so-called easy ways rarely work for more than a few weeks. Nearly always there is a downside to crude work, which accounts for the thousands of difficult, resistant horses which appear daily on the equestrian scene. If people wish to ride dressage, they must take time for the sake of the horse, otherwise they would be better by far to pursue some other less academic form of riding such as hacking or long-distance work.

One of the real difficulties nowadays is to find instructors who are truly versed in the art. There are many who do not speak the same language because they have not studied the whole spectrum. As in music, it is important to find a teacher who has struggled up through the stages to reach academy level or who has at least been taught by someone who has done this. Only then can continuity flow so that everyone retains an idea of the end product, a goal of perfection. It is too easy for teachers as well as pupils to be sidetracked along the wayside of mediocrity. Looking in front of the nose is important but we must also be able to look up and beyond!

While instant experts abound and will no doubt always do so, exploiting the naïve and giving classical dressage a bad name, I believe people are less easily fobbed off with slipshod methods today than they were ten or fifteen years ago. As more opportunities to watch correct riding are presented by regular visits of the Spanish Riding School and others from overseas whose horses work in easy harmony and without any visible aiding from the rider, the public become less inclined to accept crudeness.

With the growing realisation that much of what has been taught in recent years is misguided if not downright cruel, handfuls of teachers who have always adhered to the classical principles are finally being drawn out of the woodwork. Many had gone to ground when competition became so prominent and pupils became greedy for quick results. Now that the public has shown itself more discerning, those private masters of technique are more willing to pass on their hard-earned secrets to aspirants who care enough to find the time to look, watch, feel and listen.

At the end of the day, the justification and proof of classical training is that a horse taught in Italy will feel the same as a horse trained in the USA; a horse schooled in Paraguay responding to the same language as a horse in Germany.

It is odd how those who claim in the most strident terms to have discovered 'the' method, as though unique to themselves, are often those who have no method at all. Too often, what they purport to teach is based

It would be wonderful for the horse if everyone could ride like this. Sadly, only a few are sufficiently disciplined themselves to achieve such lightness.

on vague feelings and mood and there is no bedrock of practical knowledge built up from years of understanding and practice in the field. Neither is there any real awareness of those scientific principles structured around the physiology of the horse and that of the human being. However well intentioned, goodwill and empathy are simply not enough to teach the half-pass, or even the rein-back, correctly so that it becomes easy and comfortable for the horse.

Following the aids parrot-fashion is also dangerous. A few natural riders, who spend years in the saddle and enjoy a highly practical working relationship with the horse, may well have arrived at the proper conclusions without ever having read a book – they have struggled there by trial and error but teachers have a responsibility to teach in a way that is clear to horse and rider from the start. The classical system is therefore one which precludes something being taught only to have it untaught at a later stage. Classical riding is built on laid-down, solid foundations which will remain the same from the first day of training to the last. Progress can only be made step by step over that consolidated base.

Ironically, it is the good nature of horses and the honest desire in them to please which often count against them and allow people to try to ride without attempting to acquire this knowledge. Novice riders buy novice horse and are lulled into a false sense of security as they attempt to 'train' simply because the horse himself is often too polite to object. Frequently,

49

they will get away with their mistakes until one day their horse is put to the test. Suddenly, rather like a house built of straw, at the first puff of wind everything falls apart. Unfortunately, in the case of the horse he is more often blamed than his trainer. In that amazing arrogant way of humans, the lesson is not learned; one horse is sold off to be replaced by another; that one in his turn is deemed unsuitable and yet another unfortunate will be brought in. The same chain of events may continue *ad infinitum*, with riders never realising that the faults they found in their horses all stemmed from them.

Then there are the romantic practitioners of the art of riding. They buy a schoolmaster horse and believe they can learn to ride it without further study. 'The horse can teach me,' they say blithely and full of optimism. Sadly for the horse, his task is made impossible because there is no common language between them. Such a combination can only work if an instructor can interpret for them both, at least until the rider has learned to communicate with the horse himself on his level.

With considerable sadness, I remember a horse who, with his owners, was enrolled for a clinic I took not so long ago in the north west of England. The horse had obviously been beautifully schooled by someone in the past and the owners were swift to point out that he had competed at Prix St George and Intermediare. They had bought him as a dressage schoolmaster and were determined to have him demoted in points so that they could compete on him at Novice level. I looked forward to helping them, hoping I could persuade them to aim a little higher as the horse was clearly no novice. They resisted this forcefully, even becoming angry with the horse because his outline was 'too advanced'. 'He must learn to do what we want!' was the attitude.

When I rode the horse I realised just how fine a creature he was. Every button I pressed he understood; every nuance of the seat he responded to. It was like riding my own horse and I immediately felt a great empathy with him, realising that to change his way of working, alter his balance and destroy all that hard-earned self-carriage would be nothing short of cruelty. I discovered that he had been in the hands of Alan Doxey, a superb rider and one whom my late husband and I had always respected – no wonder he responded so well. I explained to the couple, as tactfully as possible, that to try to change this horse back into a novice would be rather like sending a professor back to kindergarten. What they must do was learn to come up to the horse's level, and for this they would need help. It might take some years but, with patience and dedication, the opportunity was theirs for the taking.

Everyone attending the clinic was rooting for the horse; they could all see my words made sense and half of them would have given their eye teeth to own such a horse. To the great sadness of all of us, the owners were unmoved. 'We are not ready for this,' said the wife firmly. 'My husband and I wish to compete this season and the horse must learn to comply with us.' Over the next few days I worked with them as best I could but as they found more and more fault with him, the horse became unhappy and began to resist as they ignored my advice for sublety and tried to turn the clock back. Subsequently I learned that they punished him one night by removing his feed against all better advice in the hope that with less rations he would lose his pride and submit in the way they wanted.

Instead of praise for his beauty and ability, there was nothing but resentment. I tried again with them on the last day; I even wrote from home offering support and suggestions as to who might help them further but I never heard from them again. It was clear their minds were closed.

The arrogance of people who refuse to see the truth, have no real desire to be helped, knows no bounds. There is, of course, another side to the coin and more common by far are those who want too much too early. These are the dreamers who love the look of a floating *passage* on reins of silk and think this can be obtained by missing out on the basics. Their horse has been trained to 'do *passage*', so why bother with more mundane work? I well remember the disapproval of one lady in our breed society who, as I was working in before a show went off complaining loudly: 'She's one of those people who only believe in walk, trot and canter!' She was right, that is what we always do before any form of gymnastic work, we establish the basics. And that is why, at the age of 23, the same horse whose work she chose to despise can still, when asked nicely, offer a worthy *passage, piaffe* and *levade* in addition to his walk, trot and canter!

It is those who disregard the ABC of riding who deny the horse the very feel and thoughtful approach he needs if he is to aspire to the higher airs. Feel is something which should be encouraged; positive thinking and looking for beauty are also important but we still need to establish fundamental procedures and exercises through discipline and study. Those who disregard this and allow themselves to fall for the easy option are not doing their horse a service. They are gullible and become easy prey for the charletan or false prophet. With the best intentions in the world, they may abuse the honesty of the horse they purport to revere and what starts in sentimentality may end in brutality. Often this is not recognised until it is too late.

I remember as though it was yesterday when I was teaching in California. A young woman enters the arena on a huge, high-stepping Spanish stallion. The horse is magnificent – he snorts, twirls around, stares at everything, deftly sidesteps. He is as elastic as indiarubber, as powerful as a Ferrari. The woman smiles; she thinks she looks wonderful on her prancing horse. I wait for the horse to settle, thinking this is her way of accustoming him to the arena. I wait in vain; the horse continues to huff, puff, stop, start, sidestep. The woman, with loose reins and a loose body, allows him to do just exactly what he wants. When he goes too far she is angry, spurs him and snatches at the rein. He ignores her and becomes obstreperous. She does not have the knowledge to channel his energy so he continues fitfully round the school, in the wrong bend, looking for objects to spook at. It is time to intervene.

The rider seems amazed when I bring her on to a circle, ask for a contact and insist that the horse goes forward in a correct bend. She is clearly not used to this form of simple discipline. 'I came on this clinic to work on my *piaffe*,' she protests. Instead, we spend the whole lesson on teaching her horse to go forward from the leg, but I want her to learn where and how to apply those legs so that her horse understands her. As there is clearly little communication between them, it is firmly back to the most simple work. She seems to find it hard to believe this is classical riding. What had she expected, that we would allow the horse to become even more uncontrolled and dangerous in the hope that at some point he might produce a High School movement? I am constantly amazed at people's egos and the popular conception of classical dressage.

In another lesson in Wales, we find a man on a hunter. The horse is on his forehand, gangling and lacklustre; the rider believes he is being very kind and that the horse is moving nice and freely when he is actually rapidly trying to get away from his rider. Quite unconsciously, the rider has allowed his horse to become a beast of burden by his lack of understanding about his conformation and his natural balance and by his refusal to learn the proper procedures. He believes that to bring the horse together so that he may carry himself from behind is unkind as the horse himself has not offered it. The horse cannot offer it. He does not choose to move in this running, sprawling way; he has little option. As a result of the man's imbalance, the horse feels threatened and topheavy.

To make life better for the horse, I explain to the man how he must become disciplined himself. Initially, this will be difficult for him and his horse but, in the end, it will make life easier for them both. Classical dressage demands as much, if not more, physical and mental discipline from the rider as any of the more dangerous aspects of equestrianism.

The requirement for an uncompromising, disciplined and academic approach is well understood in all the other recognised arts – sculpture, drawing, architecture, landscape gardening, poetry, music, etc.

Unfortunately, riding is not yet accepted by all as an art in itself so one can see just how easy it is for some to delude themselves that the art of equitation is only about a state of mind and has no roots in applied science. Reiner Klimke made a very strong point at a press conference for the Association of British Riding Schools when he came to Britain to teach in 1994. 'Without discipline, your horse can never be a partner. A rider who thinks he can ride without having to study will fail. As for a rider who doesn't read books – he will never be a serious threat in the competition arena.'

Anybody who has experience of the *beaux-arts* will know that every subject has its laid-down principles; all demand a varying degree of scholarship as well as practical application. One cannot paint a masterpiece by fooling around with a brush; even natural geniuses like Leonardo had to apprentice themselves for many years to masters who might not have enjoyed the same ability as their pupils but who could teach them technique. Only after years of practice and study did those pupils branch out to become masters in their own right.

Without discipline there can be no ordered creation. Imagine a piece of music without octaves and semibreves; a story without grammar; a plan of a city without perspective; a house without foundations! Imagine riding a dressage test without an understanding of the classical principles – yet many do! As someone once said, poetry is precision in motion. The same should be said about dressage.

In each and every sphere, therefore, it is the ignorant who are enslaved and the educated who become liberated. Freedom to develop an art to its fullest flowering and create beauty has to come from certainty, an assurance of the fundamental principles. Having arrived at this point, the honest student will be content with nothing unless it can be achieved in a humane and civilised manner at all times. It has to be said that submitting to discipline ensures our humility but will empower us for life.

I was showing this chapter in draft form to a friend and pupil, Monique Taylor, who lives in Colorado and who has worked with horses all her life. She underlined the parts she liked and put question marks against certain paragraphs. I soon detected that the question marks were against any sentence which used the word discipline. At the end of the chapter she wrote: 'You discuss opening ourselves up to enlightened ideas – perhaps now is the time for the word "discipline" to go out of the window. It's time to think up a new word.' I think she is probably very right.

CHAPTER 4

In the beginning – the power of positive thinking

Ido not believe it is possible fully to appreciate the logic of academic study and the relevance of the classical principles of riding if one has not first been well tested in the field. A good rider is not necessarily the one with the best trained horse; often that may be the work of other people. The real test comes when the rider can improve any horse, from the untalented or recalcitrant to the hypersensitive.

Tact and talent generally emanate from a strict, often uncomfortable, apprenticeship which involves much asking of questions in addition to addressing and finally solving them. The most empathetic riders tend to be those who have ridden all types of different horses, including the young and the difficult, and who have, at some stage and over a considerable period of time, met all the difficulties and challenges that practical outdoor riding brings. Long before we can begin to appreciate the intricacies of the *manège*, or the skills of the showring, it will help if we have been tested in all kinds of country and conditions, hardened to reality and exposed to disappointment as well as to triumph.

My own riding life began in a very humble way and, having at one time misprized the lack of glamour, I see now that I would probably never have appreciated what was to come later had it not been for those early days.

Like so many children, I had wanted a pony for most of my life but, before that, I remember having a passion for rocking horses. There was something about the rocking horse, so noble, so firm, so carved, with its qualities of solidity and balance that it reassured.

Whenever we visited other people's houses I believe it must have been a source of embarrassment to my parents when the first question I asked was: 'Is there a rocking horse?' If there was, that was the last anyone saw of me until it was time to go home. I remember the disappointment of moving house when I discovered the rocking horse we had seen in the nursery was no longer there. I had thought it went with the house! What did go with Hill House, an eighteenth-century three-storeyed Scottish farmhouse contoured

Two faithful farmyard friends, Dick and Minnie, were working Clydesdales
on my father's farm and taught us how gentle horses can be.

into the craggy hillside of a small Midlothian village, with a direct view to
the east to Arthur's Seat in Edinburgh and to the south the Pentlands, were
two real live, 17 h.h. work horses. Wonderful solid creatures, Minnie and
Dick, a pair of bay Clydesdales, worked the land before the plough and
brought in huge cartloads of hay, potatoes and swedes which would be used
as fodder for the sheep and dairy herd. Perhaps the horses were
symptomatic of the refusal of my father's grieve, as a foreman is known in
Scotland, to move ahead with the times. A kindly, but clearly inefficient,
man, he ambled about the farm and little got done while my father worked
in Edinburgh all day. His motto, that 'a live coward is better than a dead
hero' went down in the annals of our family's history. Consequently, it used
to fall to the two able dairy maids, my elder brother or my father at night or
at weekends to organise the more pressing tasks and to drive the tractor.

We all worried about Daddy tackling the dangerous Ayrshire bull which
no one else would handle. Even at the age of five, I remember my mother's
anxiety that he took so little rest as well as putting his safety at risk. After
fifteen years of business life in the tropics, where my father managed one
of the South Indian branches of the great Inchcape shipping line, recurring
malaria had caused him to be invalided home and left him forever more
vulnerable and easy to tire. The war did not help when, as a captain in
charge of the ack-ack guns at the Forth Bridge, he continued to struggle
with poor health. If farm life was supposed to help him get stronger, it only
seemed to debilitate him further. The problem was that he was an incurable

workaholic and just never stopped. There was always some new scheme into which he poured his heart, energy and soul but there were only so many hours in the day.

We left that elegant, grey stone house after just three years. If it broke my father's heart at the time, he never allowed us to know and perhaps it was a relief, but the younger of my elder brothers was devastated and, although very young, I also felt sad. There was no option, however, farming was in the doldrums and political decisions made at Westminster did little to help sheep and dairy farmers in Scotland during the decade after peace was declared. With a doctorate of arts and an MA which he had hoped never to have to use, my father took up full-time teaching at a well-known boys' public school in Edinburgh. He loved his art but his heart was not in teaching it to a crowd of rumbustious, rowdy schoolboys.

I believe it was at this time that the seeds of ambition were sown that one day I would make things right for my father; that one day I would live again in a stone-built house in the hills and that, whatever I did in life, it would involve animals. In that empathetic way of children, I recognised that under the sunny, boyish exterior there was an ache inside for the things that might have been and, despite his enthusiasm and his accomplishments, he was not very strong.

He was most relaxed when water-colour painting around the Berwickshire coast or the sealochs and mountains of the West Highlands. Browsing through an article in a recent copy of *The Field*, Lady Noble's remark: 'You don't need a therapist if you've got the hills,' struck a deep chord in me. We were always surrounded by hills and frequently painted them. As a family we would all sit perched on canvas stools and when the boys got bored my father took them off to fish. He and my mother always entered into everything with us and made us feel involved in all they enjoyed.

As portrait painting took up more of his time over the next several years, part of my childhood was spent visiting some of the grandest houses in the land as well as in playing quietly in the hushed corridors of the Edinburgh National Portrait Gallery. Here, Daddy would be installed with easel and palette, undertaking the commission of copying and reducing someone's massive family portrait, which had gone to the nation, into a more practical and manageable size. It was here, I believe, that I awoke to the classical disciplines of balance and proportion as well as falling in love with the baroque horses of Van Dyck, Rubens and Velasquez. The latter was my father's favourite artist and my elation when he turned up later in my A Levels owed everything to the inspiration my father had quietly instilled.

My early longing for a rocking horse was never fulfilled but my father did find someone to teach me riding when I was seven. She was the teenage daughter of a friend and her pride and joy was Privet a 14.2 h.h. pony, black and solid, with a proud, arched neck as firm as any rocking horse. He was a kind pony to a little podgy girl who had only sat perched with a parent's steadying hand on a very large carthorse. My first lesson was a walk out on Privet, his owner close beside us, with a light hand on his rein. No one was very safety conscious in those days and only professionals owned lunge lines or other suitable teaching equipment; even lead ropes were a luxury.

By the end of an hour, I remember passing a frozen pond but was too warm inside to notice the weather. My instructress had taken the hand away and we walked home unaided.

The second lesson was on trot; she ran valiantly beside me and encouraged 'Up, down! Up, down!' with her voice and I can still remember the teeth-chattering jolting and bumping to start with and the hard, frosty ground. On reflection, Privet was a very high-stepping pony and had been used in harness, which seemed to knock all our new-found unity for six. Then, suddenly, on the way home again, it came – the miracle of the rising trot. I can remember the exact spot on the long private drive in Kirknewton House policies to this day. Icicles sparkled in the yew hedges, my nose was numb but deep inside was a thrilling warm glow.

In the spring, we ventured out of Privet's home territory to a grassy lane, hemmed in by the Edinburgh to Glasgow railwayline on one side and a fence on the other. It was a clever place to choose for our first canter as this was to be undertaken solo – even my agile teacher had decided she would not be able to keep up with that! She closed off the entry to the lane by planting herself firmly across its path, then I was bade to ride to the stile at the bottom, turn for home, then kick on. All this was done with such conviction and trust, I in her, her in me and both of us in Privet, that everything went beautifully and without mishap. That first canter, as it must be for every child, was the most heavenly sensation ever. Privet was as steady as any rocking horse, his great dear neck stayed up in front of me, there was no snaking away or dropping of the shoulders and we were all elated when we arrived safely at the end of the short distance. All five furlongs had been sheer magic and I will not forget it to my dying day.

Sadly, those six or seven odd lessons were the only ones I was to have on Privet. My newfound friend went away to university and Privet was sent to a new home. Nevertheless, it had been a wonderful and easy introduction to 'riding' and, of course, I was now desperate for more. Late that summer, when my father found a small stable on the edge of the Earl of Morton's estate, only half an hour's bike ride from home, my destiny seemed fixed.

Alvin Nichols was a retired ballet dancer. Small and neat, with elf-like ears, his lightness on his feet belied a powerful sense of ego and all his pupils had to perform every task exactly as he said without argument or question. I was extremely nervous of him but not of his ponies. Thunder was his prized New Forest dapple grey 13.2 h.h. gelding, there were two yellow dun garrons and I was to ride Pixie, an 11 h.h. reddish dun who was the old stager. After Privet's generous proportions, I was a little disappointed, but not for long.

Riding out together in company gave one enormous scope after the obvious limitations of one person on a horse and the other on the ground. Without more ado we were attached to a leading rein and set off for our first 'lesson' on a two-hour hack by way of the woods which bordered the lodge where Alvin Nichols ran his small yard. 'Heels down, knees in, hands together, now, duck your head to the side, otherwise you'll get a bloody nose,' were my first instructions as we threaded our way between birch, rowan and beech which grew in profuse confusion on either side of the rabbit path we were following. Past the curling lake, though the deer park and on towards the big house – 'Like a canter?' – and that was how I learned to ride.

Thank God for the Pixies and the Privets of this world. I often think children like us, brought up in the days when hard hats were not the *sine qua non*, where few possessed safe, sand arenas, and the main object of riding was to become proficient enough to hunt over hill and dale, were wonderfully blessed. Somewhere a guardian angel was clearly hovering.

By the age of nine I had begun to dream of hunting. As the L&S[1] passed through the woods almost every week and I had learned to skim along on the patient Pixie in the wake of Mr Nichols and Thunder over the lovely natural jumps that the Hunt maintained, it was just a matter of time as to when I would be allowed to go to the meet. These things were simply expected, taken in one's stride and the countryside, with its clean, open spaces and biting, east-coast cold air, beckoned deliciously.

The Morton estate was full of variety. Grassy tracks bordered the golf course and farm lanes wound up the quarried hill of Kaimes, where our next house, a derelict cottage which my father would later buy and do up, nestled at the bottom. Dalmahoy Hill, with its smooth turf, and moors swept away to the south, and we rode on the tracks leading up to the base of the Pentland Range near Bavelaw Castle, through Currie and Balerno and down the back of the farmland which now houses the Herriot Watt Agricultural College. It was wonderful riding and hunting country, only

---

[1] The Linlithgow & Stirlingshire Hunt whose country stretched westward past the Forth Bridge from the environs of Edinburgh towards Stirlingshire,

farm traffic on the back roads and, if one rode west towards Kirknewton, two beautiful private estates stretched like mini Badmintons through which to canter, gallop and jump to one's heart's content. There were no antis in those days and no one who lived in the country ever questioned the morality of hunting. In the way of children, I took it all for granted. My only worry was would I ever be good enough to hunt? And would I ever have a pony of my own on which to do it?

I had been riding with Mr Nichols for about two years when my father took the plunge and bought the ruined lodge. It was incredibly romantic and if my mother's heart sank at the prospect of such isolation (we would be three miles from the nearest village and 600 feet above sea-level with weeks of being cut off by snow in the winter), she never complained. I was thrilled. A singularly superb 25-acre field went with the cottage through which ran a lively burn. The land was undulating, with wooded parts on the tops of the corries while a lovely flat plateau of good grazing lay immediately behind the house. To the the west side, surrounded by ancient Roman fortifications which gave a curious amphitheatre effect, was a self-draining, smoothed-out area of velvety grass of about 40 metres in diameter. It was the ideal natural school and little did I know then that I was destined to spend many years teaching in that arena until I finally left home soon after my twenty-first birthday.

The house had been boarded up for years but it was dry inside and I think what attracted my father and me as much as anything else was the beautiful dark-panelled drawing room. On the sunny, west side of the house was the carved stone coat of arms of the Welwood family and there were those pleasing little turreted steps on the gables that the Scots have always enjoyed and incorporated into their humbler dwellings as well as into their grander castles. The walled garden was all poppies and thistles but there remained a gnarled plum tree. Two ancient yews stood sentinel to the fortifications and the house was approached by a magnificent, if overgrown, drive of tall, mature lime trees where bees hummed all summer. This was the southern entrance to the Kirknewton House estate and to a child of ten it was idyllic.

We lived in a caravan for the first five months. Finally, the builders moved out and we moved into Kaimes Cottage. I suppose you could say this was the irrevocable step which led to my life with horses.

The first pony arrived not on his own but accompanied by two others. My father, always kind and somewhat susceptible to sob stories, had, in purchasing Tommy, a grey destined for me, ended up paying triple the price because Tommy's owner was going broke and was going to shoot himself

How proud I was the first time I sat on Tommy – my very own pony at last.

and his horses if he couldn't pay his debts. It had broken his heart to part with Tommy; now misfortune had struck and he could not cope with the others. Somewhere Mr Nichols had a part to play in all this and when we moved into Kaimes and a float arrived from his yard with three animals instead of the expected one, my mother, usually mild and rather vague, suggested firmly that all ties were severed. My father rather sheepishly agreed and Alvin Nichols the ballet dancer was seldom mentioned again in our house. I was not really sad as he was a sharp-tongued man, but he was a good disciplinarian, had got me going and, under his watchful eye, I had learned never to question or to baulk at anything I was asked to do on horseback or round the stables.

It was probably for this reason that when he first produced Tommy from his 'friend in the trade', it did not occur to me to tell my father that the pretty grey that everyone had admired so much was an inveterate bolter. Only now do I admit that he was probably the most unsuitable pony in the world on which to mount a ten-year-old girl. In company he pulled my arms out, but worse by far was the way he would suddenly turn and gallop for home every time we were alone together. This always happened at the same spot, the furthest and thickest point of the woods. I soon learned that there was nothing to do but to crouch to one side of the naughty grey neck (I never forgot the lesson of the bloody nose, or for that matter of King Rufus), to wedge one's feet deeper into the stirrups, turn the knees in and hope and pray that a branch above would not sweep one off, or a root below turn us spinning upside down in that mile-long, headlong flight for home. Thank God for those guardian angels.

So now I was on my own. Mr Nichols's maxims of toes up, hands down, look up, chin down and, most important, heart up would stay with me forever and he had certainly taught me how to look after ponies with his strict ways and quick eye, always ready to spot a fault. The lively Tommy, although fond of his triumphal gallop at my expense, was an otherwise impeccable pony. Once home, he was mannerly to handle and noble and obliging in the stable. He always whinnied for his food, blew down his nostrils politely at the right people, stood like a rock to shoe, clip and groom and would never have dreamt of kicking or nipping. As I became a more competent rider, he gave me many hours of pleasure and both my parents, who gave me tremendous support and help in those days, grew to love him as much as I did.

It was around this time that I suddenly became very allergic to horses and had to be whisked into the Edinburgh Sick Children's hospital when, after an anti-tetanus jab at school, I came out in scarlet hives, couldn't breathe and was quite seriously ill. No one seemed very sure why the injection had caused such a reaction but it was suggested that I had been given an overdose. The next time I went near a horse everything started to burn – eyes, nose, ears and throat – and life became very difficult. In those days, horse serum was used as a preventive against tetanus, instead of today's chemical inoculation, so any contact with horses created a huge reaction. All the doctors wanted me to give up riding but my father backed my determination to tough it out, although it was my gentle, patient mother who had to deal with a child who lived on pills, was regularly absent from school and who streamed and wheezed continuously. At sixteen, pleurisy almost finished me off in hospital again.

My argument that it was not the horses' fault wore a little thin years later in the Algarve when, blue-faced, I was whisked off by ambulance and attached to an oxygen cylinder with seconds to spare. Left unattended in Loulé hospital, there was a nasty moment when a wandering incumbent from the asylum next door decided to visit and fiddle with my tubes. However, again those guardian angels came to my rescue and, having survived this and the asthma attack itself, it was decided I would give up ever trying to groom or muck out horses again. I did not miss the latter but was actually very sad about the former, particularly with my own horses.

Today life is very much easier, with all the desensitising drugs at one's disposal. Of course, I now have a good excuse to employ a groom, but the allergy has been a setback and must prove something about one's dedication to an animal which, through no fault of anyone, has the ability literally to drown one in one's own pulmonary fluid.

If sneezing and wheezing kept me off school, they did not put me off turning out at four on a frosty morning to spruce up and plait for the first meet of my life. It was the greatest thrill ever to go hunting on my own pony. No one in our neighbourhood owned a box or trailer at that time so hacking great distances was normal. My father deemed the Children's Boxing Day Meet at Ingliston, close to the Scottish Showground, to be the most suitable for a complete novice. This involved a two-hour hack first, but one thought nothing of this, despite the searing east wind and the hint of snow so often in the air. Here, I discovered one might as well hunt with the adults as, unwittingly, Tommy and I soon left all the children and their careful parents behind and were out at the front of the field, up with the hunt servants. Tommy was very fast and very fit but I worried myself sick that he might do the unforgivable and pass the Master. My gloved hands were blistered raw trying to persuade him otherwise and it was the one preoccupation which spoiled those happy, carefree days. On the one occasion it did happen, I was growled at by the huntsman, but the Master, a charming man called Colonel Usher, let us off with a wry smile, and: 'You'll have to school him a little more, Miss Cameron.'

Until that time, the word 'school' in relation to horses meant very little indeed. As for 'dressage', such a word would have been considered pretentious in one so young. Certainly, I knew that something would have to be done about the other two ponies we had acquired. One, a grey Highland mare, Beauty, of indeterminate age was the sweetest, most placid animal to handle but she had an outrageous buck which invariably landed me and all who rode her on the floor. The other, a dark bay 14 h.h. gelding, Trojan, fresh off the boat from Ireland and probably unbroken, was pretty impossible all round. He bit, kicked, hated being handled, hated all of us. Somehow, however, with a combination of ignorance-is-bliss and kindness, he came round and, of all the three, I probably got the closest to proper schooling when I worked with him.

Despite my own lack of knowledge, I nevertheless recognised in him a sensitivity with which I hoped I could do something. In some ways, I felt more able to school the wild Trojan than Tommy who was far too set in his ways and pleased about himself to want to change anything. Trojan made me think. He was mean and moody and reminded me of a book which had moved me terribly, called *The Wild Black Stallion*. Occasionally I would don my brother's Scout hat, put on jeans instead of jodhpurs and pretend Trojan was the stallion in the book and I was a sort of Wild West girl.

By the time I was twelve we had acquired two more equines. Word gets round when someone has a generous field and a generous heart. Friends of

Day dreaming on Trojan about being a Wild West girl was not exactly
helped by a typical English hunting saddle! Me at the age of eleven, struggling
to sit centrally on a very naughty pony.

my father were moving south and needed a good home for an ancient
hunter, Drummer, and a small, fat, outgrown Shetland pony. They did not
want to separate them and, to help them out of a dilemma, my father agreed
to take the pair in a moment of weakness. Looking after a thin-skinned
blood horse is very different to caring for tough ponies. The field shelter
Daddy had built when we first moved to Kaimes was inadequate in those
harsh Scottish winters and when my brother came back on leave from the
navy, he and my father embarked on an ambitious programme of
converting an old stone barn into a series of looseboxes and stalls.

It was laborious work but, despite working hard all day at his teaching
job as well as portrait painting at his studio in Edinburgh's West End and
restoring old masters, by the end of four years my father had completed a
byre for our Jersey cow, a workshop, greenhouse and, my pride and joy, a
row of freestanding looseboxes which is still there today. Those sensitive

hands, which could paint a miniature on ivory, had dug out stone from the hillside and built a homestead.

By the age of fourteen we had so many equines that I had started to teach. One of the reasons I never boarded at my public school in Edinburgh, unlike so many others who lived outside the city as we did, was because of the horse commitments. My parents had been wonderful but I knew they were struggling to meet the ever-increasing feed and hay bills, and the time had come to make the stronger incumbents support themselves. It started with a small ad on the girls' general noticeboard at school: 'Kaimes Riding School is now open for business. Private lessons and wonderful hacking in unspoilt country. Apply below'. They trickled in, one by one, mostly younger girls and sometimes a parent or two and, gradually, word got round.

From then on, every weekend, every half-term and school holidays were filled with teaching commitments. There were complete beginners, others who could ride but had heard about our wonderful hacks through the policies, past the lake, through the ornamental gardens of Kirknewton House, past an American airdrome and across disused landing strips to the further reaches of farmland which, in those days, seemed to boast plenty of headland and grassy tracks stretching towards the Pentlands and the reservoirs. Up the back of Kaimes and Dalmahoy Hills we rode, round the quarries, through the gorse, heather and woods and then back alongside the railway track, always finding new paths, new streams, new fallen trees to jump and new ways home. It was a child's paradise.

By this time, the horses had settled well and come into a sense of orderly behaviour. Drummer, at 17 h.h., was ridden by me or the odd mum who joined us, the smaller ponies being used by the very small and Tommy for the very experienced. He had not bolted for years, although he did have one more ignoble try one day with my unsuspecting mother who had not ridden since she was a child but who, thankfully and miraculously, stayed on. Beauty had been subdued by good feeding, a well-fitting saddle and my father riding her regularly. As strong as an ox she had, nevertheless, decided against the wisdom of bucking off a 12-stone man.

There were new acquisitions, most of whom had found us, although by the time I was sixteen I had bought in another two suitable school ponies as business really took off. I had started summer camps. The idea had come from Pony Club which I kept up regularly to increase my own knowledge and whose ethos and discipline I worshipped. The general enthusiasm of the many children whose parents made the long journey out to us from Edinburgh each weekend seemed to spread and we welcomed children from as far away as Durham and Newcastle-upon-Tyne. I took eight on the

With kind but firm handling, Trojan was to turn into a butter-wouldn't-melt
pony. In those days we weren't so safety-conscious!

summer camps. This number was dictated by the fact that a big bell tent
(which we hired from the same firm in Leith year after year) sleeps eight,
head to canvas, feet to pole. I think at the time we had about twelve ponies
and horses, for one always needed extras and substitutes and it seemed the
optimum number.

Each child was allotted a pony for the week. The paperwork for these
exercises was generally done in a prep lesson at school and the results
typed out at home on an old typewriter. I started a horse magazine, written
and illustrated by some of my older pupils and myself. This came out every
month over a couple of years and each pony had its own page of news to
recall. Horses were always people to us which is not such a bad philosophy
to carry from childhood to adulthood and one which, thankfully, many of
the world's most empathetic riders still have. It is the ones who don't think
like this that one tends to worry about.

Despite the wonderful hacking, I began to enjoy teaching in the Roman
amphitheatre more than any other aspect of my horsy life. I had come to
understand the importance of bend and suppling achieved through circle
work and serpentines but I had no understanding of how to bring the
horse's weight further back, how seriously to lighten the forehand and how
collection was achieved. As a keen jumper, I had taught some of our ponies

to achieve a flying change through a change of direction but this was done largely on the forehand and they changed more out of self-preservation and not because one had asked correctly.

My own lessons at Pony Club rallies, which I tried strictly to emulate at my own camps, never included anything which could perhaps have led to a heightened awareness of balance or collection, although the basics were well addressed. To me, the word 'balance' simply meant the horse going easily forward from the leg. As I had never felt a horse come deep under me with his hocks, round his back or raise the forehand (other than in jumping), it did not even occur to me that such a thing was possible. In other words, my limited experience gave me the temerity to teach because, quite simply, I believed that that was more or less all there was to it.

Few people talked about dressage and, when they did, it was assumed to be more a form of obedience testing than a work of art or craftsmanship. As long as the horse was able to walk, trot, canter and turn at various spots, everyone was happy. There was little talk of outline in those days and people generally rode with quiet hands as we were yelled at if we were ever seen to interfere in front. Some of those who hunted rode with double bridles and the necessity to handle two reins required a sensitivity with the fingers that is too often lacking today. We were taught to turn the horse from the leg and as per the Pony Club's book of golden rules, the *Manual*, 'light hands' were prescribed at all times. The rider must 'know when and how they should "ask" and when they should be "soft". The hands should remain at the same level and be steady'.

It is odd how this sound advice, which formed part of the education of every Pony Club child, is no longer to be found in today's *Manual of Horsemanship*. Instead, it has been replaced with advice such as, 'It is vitally important for you to be able to move your hands independently of your body', which, to my mind, is somewhat confusing. I would have preferred to see: 'It is vitally important that your hands remain quiet, irrespective of what your body is doing', and perhaps it is advice such as this which has led to the busy hands which many regard as the curse of modern riding. In those days, we may have been ignorant about the finer points of the seat but at least we were taught respect for the horses' mouths.

As I improved, I remember being placed in the odd dressage test at small horse trials but rated these small victories of no more importance than winning the bending race in which my new hot 14.2 h.h. pony, Trigger, excelled. There was only one prestigious event which stuck in my mind as it took place away from L&S country, with the East Lothian branch of the Pony Club at Haddington, a hitherto unknown venue. No one was more surprised than I when I won the cup at a one-day event all on the 'strength'

Trigger probably taught me more about feel and balance than any dressage horse at that time. I believe this indirectly helped my schooling of young horses later in life, despite the difference in the disciplines.

of my dressage. I was fairly sure there had been a mistake as the gelding I had taken had none of the pzazz of Trigger and for me everything had seemed rather flat although he was obedient enough. However, there was no mistake; for the first time I had eights running all the way through my test sheet and, not for the first time, as I collected my rosette, I thought how queer life was. When you think you've done well, you get nowhere, and when you do not really do anything special you suddenly find yourself first!

That irony had been brought home to me with bitter force a few years before when I had failed my Pony Club C Test. This was considered fairly elementary then as now, and I had understood from the District Commissioner that I would sail through. Nevertheless, it was not to be. In those days, people were less worried about children's self-esteem than they are today, thus, when I received the news of my failure, there was no kindly hand on the shoulder, no words of explanation or sympathy.

I was mortified, particularly as I knew that I had passed every section of the stable management and the jumping had gone well. It must have been my general riding that was at fault. Sure enough, I was baldly told it was my seat. When I enquired politely what was wrong with it, no one seemed able to tell me. In fact, there was a distinct feeling that I should not have asked.

Failing that early test was a wretched blow to self-esteem but, looking back, it was probably the best thing that could have happened to me at the time. It made me think. I began to study the other two girls in my ride who had passed with flying colours. Senga Aglen always rode very quietly and competently. Another stood out in an indefinable way which I know had something to do with her seat. She and her pony just looked so much part of each other. Lucy Cullen was small and neat and her 14.2 h.h. Sonny was a dark bay Thoroughbred-type who always looked as though he was up on his points, so light, springy and collected was he, so obviously full of breeding.

The point about Sonny was that Lucy could make him do things without apparently moving. She sat so still and proud, without a blonde hair out of place; there was an inner confidence about her which I longed to emulate. I believe that was my first awakening to the importance of sitting still and being part of the horse. I knew as yet this had not happened for me, but if it could happen for Lucy and others, and I could study them long enough, perhaps it could happen for me. After that, whenever I rode, I would try in my mind to bring back a picture of those two girls moving effortlessly through their dressage tests. Still, erect and absolutely central in the saddle, it was a powerful image which may have rubbed off a little as, in the pursuit of further exams, no one ever said again what a terrible seat I had.

In 1963 John and Sheila Douglas, later to become Earl and Countess of Morton, took me with their children to Badminton. The sophistication of the event when compared to our relatively rustic hunter trials in Scotland was screamingly noticeable even to a rather countrified teenager. In those days serious eventing was still largely dominated by the army and I was thrilled to be introduced to the handsome Captain Dudgeon, a relative of the Mortons from Ireland, who looked wonderful in his uniform as he swept round the course making everything, even the lake, look easy. We did not see much of the dressage, having come only towards the end of the first day but few people were interested and only a handful of spectators surrounded the arena – so different from today. Thus whatever half-passes, shoulders-in or counter-canters that might have been going on were wasted on me. I doubt if I would even have recognised a half-pass if you had showed me one.

What Badminton did for me was to inspire me to jump better and to be bolder across country. The problem was that I had outgrown my really good coloured jumping pony, Trigger, and the time had come for a serious horse. There was one particular grey I had drooled over when seen out with our Master for most of the past season. She was a flighty six year old called Mercury and, to my amazement, she turned up for sale at our local dealers, Alan and Margaret Beck. Apparently the Master had not enjoyed being tanked off with and as he was a slightly built man and of a certain age, he

Eight enthusiastic horsy youngsters enjoy life under canvas at Kaimes Cottage.

had decided on a quieter, mellower mount on which to finish his last season. It was Spicer the huntsman who tipped me the wink when I enquired where Mercury had gone and I shall never forget that kind, sensible man who cared for his hounds like children and whose quiet ways and big gentle hands made horses as soft as dough under him.

At Gogarburn Stables, on the east side of Edinburgh, there was always something new in a box, generally just 'off the boat', which meant Ireland, or via Kelso or Hawick Sales in the Borders. Alan Beck was always to be seen at the ringside, joined as though by mystical link to the hand of the auctioneer. When his hand went up, Beck's head went up, when the hand went down with the hammer, Beck's chin followed. 'Knocked down to Mr Beck for forty guineas,' was a familiar cry at these auctions.

How I enjoyed going to these occasions, first with my father and later as part of the horsy crowd and trusted out alone. Without realising it at the time, watching horse after horse go through the ring and ticking them off in my catalogue I think I began to develop an eye for a horse. I'll never forget making my first purchase without anyone there to guide me and when I went out to admire the lovely black pony mare I had spotted and ridden earlier, and who was now mine, I was over the moon when a local farmer came up and offered me more. It was a sweet feeling to refuse. Little did I know it then but Pollyanna, who had cost me 30 guineas, would remain at home long after I had grown up, gone to work abroad and married. Cared for by my parents, she finally died at the age of 34.

Beck was a dark, swarthy man said to be of Romany origin. Whether this was true or not mattered little, the fact was that he was a dealer and people

From the very beginning, I found teaching children, with their natural seats and balance, extremely rewarding. Cassidy came to us from Ireland and, between us, we taught his new family to ride.

were wary. Nevertheless, neither he nor his sweet-faced wife had ever crossed me and, indeed, I rather liked them – they were so very different. I sat on Mercury in their muddy ring and it was love at first sight or, rather, feel. I knew I had to buy this beautiful, elegant Thoroughbred mare, all 16.1 h.h. light-limbed, fleabitten grey of her and to hell with not being able to stop. I had faced that problem before with Tommy! *Plus sa change . . .*

As hunting became more thrilling, cross-country jumping all the more daring and riding in general more challenging, realisation slowly began to dawn. With the acquisition of Mercury, a true hotblood of sensitivity and quality, I gradually learned to face up to the fact that there was very much more to riding than I had ever realised before and that it wasn't enough to whistle down the wind or to pray. As I began to ask more questions of myself and the horse under me, it irked me that the answers were no longer so readily available. Trial and error were no longer enough; I craved to know more.

The only problem was the more that I wanted to know, the fewer people there were who seemed able to help. I had spent the past decade immersed in ponies and horses and had learned a great deal, but now I needed to go further. Mercury had made this patently clear. The dilemma was where in Scotland could I find someone who could not only answer the questions, but also show me the way? Most of the top riders had moved south to compete and I needed more than my faithful *Manual* if I was to progress.

Although I did not know it then, I would have to go very much further

For the first time in my life I broke from horses
to travel overseas. This is me in 1967 on the S.S. *Reina del Mar*,
sailing out of Southampton bound for Lisbon.

afield to find some of the answers. Some years later I arrived, quite by chance, in Portugal. There was something about the Portuguese which made me feel instantly at home and reminded me of the people I had left behind when I broke temporarily from horses at the age of 21 in order to pursue a secretarial and editorial career in London. Their Celtic reserve, understatement and gentleness made stepping through the cobbled streets of Lisbon like returning to old Edinburgh. The guttural speech, with its 'shs' and 'chs', was not unlike the language of the Gaelic-speaking people where we used to spend our summer holidays. It was like coming home. Little did I know that moving to Portugal would change my ideas forever, both about horses and about life itself.

CHAPTER 5
First lessons in lightness and feel – a humbling experience

Have you ever felt an explosion happen in your brain? Have you ever looked at something which is so right, so perfect and so much what you were looking for all along but which you could never quite put into thoughts or words, that you realise all your preconceived ideas were totally, utterly wrong?

All this happened to me in one blinding flash of light at my first Portuguese *corrida*. I had gone with doubt in my heart; I had gone half-grudging the loss of my only afternoon off work in the week, when I could have been lying on a sandy beach soaking up the sun. I had gone totally unprepared, as no one had told me about it, but I had thought to myself: 'When in Rome' and had joined the long line of people queuing on a Sunday afternoon outside the Cascais *praça de touros*, determined to lap up some Iberian culture.

I will never forget my first sight of those horses and riders as they *passaged* into that small, circular, intimate arena as though carved in ebony – only these carvings, magnificently caparisoned in scarlet, magenta, black and gold, lived, rippled and breathed. The poise, the elevation of each trot step, held in the air, was so supremely collected that there was a surreal quality about it. Heavily beribboned, silk threads of red, silver and blue intertwined through luxuriant manes, the sheen on the dark bay coats, the glow of a dun trapped the sunshine out of the very sky only to bounce it back off bits, spurs and buckles glistening among ornate cruppers and breast plates. All was held in suspension as four stallions paraded together in front of the President's box and silently gathered themselves into a perfectly matched, highly animated *piaffe* while the trumpeter blew his opening volley.

It was the grace and lightness of it all which riveted the eye. One-handed control, a picture of shimmering ease as vibrant hocks flexed and bent under a mass of rippling muscle, and arched necks and proud forehands rose up from the withers. It was as though a great heroic canvas had come

I had never seen horses move with such grace and ease in full, effortless collection. It was as
if two baroque statues had come to life.

(Photo: courtesy Arsenio Raposo Cordeiro)

to life, the horsemen were gods surfacing out of the sea, hands on the
lightest of reins, the upright posture, the careless gaze mocking the
difficulty of the task ahead. I saw the image of the centaur – man and horse
come together – trusting, prepared for whatever lay ahead, and I thought,
'Can this be dressage? Is this the culmination of all that schooling and
working round and round in circles, which I never really understood? Is
this how it can look?'

It was then that I determined I had somehow missed something. I knew
then that those competitions I had entered half-heartedly or gone to watch
at some prestigious event were also missing something. Where was this

The one-handed riding of the bullfighter necessitates a highly obedient and submissive horse. Nevertheless, it is the pride of the horse which ensures the safety of the partnership. This proud stallion, Giro, was to be the father of my own horse, Palomo Linares, and is ridden here by his breeder.

(Photo: courtesy Joao Bareto Freixo)

feeling of lightness, pride and poise that these horses and riders displayed? Where was the message from Xenophon who, rejecting force and domination, counselled that we should allow the horse sufficient freedom so that he may glory and delight in his work: 'so when he is induced by a man to assume all the airs and graces which he puts on of himself when he is showing off voluntarily, the result is a horse that likes to be ridden, that presents a magnificent sight, that looks alert'.

Why it was here! The figures from the Parthenon frieze had come to life before my very eyes and, surprisingly, it was here in Portugal.

It was this easy partnership which was to stay in my mind forever, only to be reinforced again at odd intervals in my life. You do not have to be a rider to appreciate it – anyone who has a feeling for beauty, a sympathy for the arts, knows instinctively when a partnership is balanced and right. Torvill and Dean did it on ice, Pele with a football, Markova with her

Every step we take in dressage should merely be an echo of how the horse would move
naturally in the wild.
(Photo: Kit Houghton)

Siegfried in *Swan Lake*, Colin Cowdray with a cricket bat. It is a wonderful
thing when a rider and his horse can also become a living masterpiece.

Much has been written concerning the fact that all we are trying to achieve
in dressage is to restore the horse to the natural balance with which nature
endowed him. Every movement required in Grand Prix dressage is merely
an amplification of those natural manoeuvres, bendings, sidesteps and
turns with which our horses express themselves in freedom. For the
purpose of understanding, these have been separated, named and defined,
but it is only when the component parts are brought together in a living
display of controlled energy which ebbs and flows under the rider in the
most natural and apparently effortless way possible that it can be regarded
as dressage. The whole picture is what matters, and too much
preoccupation with movement by movement can be stultifying and turn
something which should be joyful and liberated into something which is
rigidly mechanical.

It is important to remind ourselves that each individual movement is merely an echo of how the horse would behave in the wild, an expression of his animation, his instinctive and emotional response to an external influence at that moment in time. In dressage we school the horse to engender these natural movements and this often requires a sustainment longer than might be normal. Little wonder, therefore, that these movements will be hard to reproduce on demand when the horse's attitude and mood may be very different.

Let us look again, however, at how these movements develop. By stripping away the mystique, perhaps we can take a more understanding view in our training methods. The pirouette is displayed even in the horse's early months, when the young foal shies away or spins coquettishly in front of his mother or another playmate. The *levade*, too, can be an act of mischief or of more serious supremacy, when the adult male draws his weight back, thrusts his hind legs deep under his bodymass in a display of power and lifts his forehand with magnificent purpose to mount his mare. The floating, effortless half-passes and sidesteps show a horse moving away laterally, as though carried by a glancing wind but, in fact, succumbing, without losing impulsion, to natural caution in order to take a second look before a return, full frontal into a sudden stop to face the object of his attention. The impatient, urgent motions of the *piaffe*, where the horse gathers himself to beat time on the spot in anticipation of something new, some excitement ahead which has captured his attention and may require his presence, is also natural. When this gives way to the altogether more elevated, passionate trot where the arousal of the senses creates a yearning to display and desport himself in front of his peers or his prize, the horse becomes lightfooted, ethereal and floating.

All of these movements, therefore, have sprung from a sense of play, appraisal, display, readiness to act or supremacy. Observing the horse in this light should show riders that, far from insisting that the horse should be our slave, it is imperative, if we are to reproduce these manoeuvres at will, that we must encourage the horse to *want* to display or show himself off. As Xenophon urged, to endow him with a certain sense of freedom, so that he is able to feel he is choosing to make these movements himself, is vital.

I will never forget that first feeling of balance when a horse I had schooled myself offered me collection – real collection. And it came from the horse! She was feeling good and at that moment in time I must have felt good on her back so she offered it. Two years had elapsed since my first *corrida*, and I was still in Portugal, this time seriously back with horses in my life, engaged to and learning from a man who was a brilliant horseman in his own right but who had come to this land of horses and horsemen to learn more himself.

I was on the way to the blacksmith on a little brown mare called Andorinha. For days, weeks, months I had been working in the school in circles, voltes and serpentines, suppling, bending and trying to understand the hard lessons of balancing a horse. This had led to the rudiments of lateral work and beginning to appreciate the difference in feel between a horse whose inside leg was engaging and carrying more weight because he was laterally bent and a horse who had left his legs out behind and was throwing his weight on to the shoulders because he was stiff through the back. All this was very new to me, so totally different from anything I had learned in the hunting field, in the jumping lanes or at Pony Club.

I had been given this wonderful young Lusitano mare to school and, despite having become much more aware of what it should feel like on a number of schoolmasters, I was still not fully prepared for the amazing sensation this young, generous mare was to give me, totally out of the blue.

Although over 25 years ago, I can picture it now. Like the first canter, you never forget important moments in your life. I still see the actual spot in the road where the eucalyptus trees leaned their stringy-barked trunks over the highway, the sun glistening on distant red rooftops, the grass sparkling with dew by the river. We were on our way to the forge in the old fishing town of Portimão, now a big bustling port and tourist centre, and the man who was teaching me, later to be my husband, jogged along on a high-stepping dun stallion.

Suddenly the mare lifted her back, rounded her loins, dug her heels deep underneath herself, pushed upward and, without warning, we were moving along as if on air in a marvellous, sedate, springy, measured and rhythmic trot. It was highly collected, highly impulsive, extremely slow and I felt as though I had all the power of the horse at my disposal coming up at me through my own body. So different was this from the power of my hunters, always thrusting somewhere out in front of me, that it was all the more surprising. This was altogether different, something I would never forget – it was like flying only, instead of being flown, I was in the cockpit, flying by the seat of my pants.

Once you have experienced something that feels like magic, you are terrified to lose it. I was so afraid she would come down to earth again, I scarcely dared to breathe. I sat, perched in my Portuguese saddle like a statue, willing myself to be light on her back to receive this gift and not to reject it. Somehow, I found the control to push my tummy forward as I had been told so that I could match my centre of gravity to hers and not push against her. For a few more precious seconds, it seemed as though we were joined in space. Light, effortless, floating and for a few strides the trot became *passage*. It was wonderful and it took a very long time for the smile to leave my face.

Discovering feel, recognising true balance was not something that had been arrived at lightly. That occasion was only the beginning of a lifetime of sensations. None the less, I had been riding Lusitanos for many months in Portugal before I met Henry Loch but he was the first person prepared actually to teach me. I had discovered that the Portuguese experts I had encountered were much too polite to tell you how to ride, preferring instead to demonstrate in silence or to provide horses they hoped you were receptive enough to learn from. Nevertheless, at this stage in my ignorance, I often found myself casting around in the dark wondering whether it was me or the horse when a schoolmaster offered 'special things'.

Special things had not exactly been in store for me one embarrassing morning shortly after my arrival from England. I wished then that someone had prepared me for the first time I would sit upon a fully trained High School horse. Now, on reflection, I believe it was highly providential. I had gone to lunch with a charming Portuguese couple I had met in Lisbon on business, who had invited me to drive out to their *quinta* along the coast near Colares and who were particularly keen to let me taste their home-produced red wine.

When we arrived, the first thing I saw was a man schooling a magnificent grey stallion. He sat as still as a rock and, fascinated, I watched a complete re-enactment of all the movements I had once seen when the Spanish Riding School came to Wembley. No matter that here the arena was just a dirt ring, little more than 25 metres in diameter, the atmosphere was very relaxed. Under the midday sun, horse and rider were clearly enjoying themselves and every move, every feint, every twist and turn made by the horse seemed effortless and spontaneous. It was impossible to see if the rider had in fact aided the horse as the two moved as one and there was no visible sign of instruction.

Dressed in trousers and having rather naïvely exclaimed that I too loved horses and could ride, there was no excuse to refuse the invitation when the stallion was *passaged* up to me and brought to a dramatic standstill. Not that I wanted one; I could not wait to sit on such a beautiful noble creature and feel for myself the obvious power and control that I had just witnessed.

I will never forget the next few moments. I felt comfortable despite the unfamiliar fighting saddle which seemed to put my body in a completely different position from anything I had experienced before with my forward-cut jumping saddles at home. The horse stood like a gentleman and I believed his rider when he said in broken English: 'He is very kind,

The horsemanship of the Iberian Peninsula somehow seemed so quiet,
so contained, so understated and yet so proud, that I could only assume
that it mirrored the people themselves.

(Photo: courtesy Promark)

do not worry.' What happened next, however, was mindbending. I say this not because we sailed forth into a wonderful display of Grand Prix movements; on the contrary, I could not ride this horse at all.

I was quite unable to achieve any form of forward movement. The prancing stallion I had so admired stood as though rooted to the spot as I applied all the normal aids known to man in order to say walk on. As I squeezed my legs again, this time a little further back, I felt my face redden as the beautiful horse moved backward. Half way round the ring we went – all backwards! It was incredibly disconcerting and I had no idea how to get out of this backward progression. Fortunately, I was swiftly rescued. 'Just sit up!' said his rider. 'Don't worry – he is sensitive, he feels your tension.'

As far as I had been aware, I had not been tense, although the embarrassment of the moment was undoubtedly having its effect. I squared my shoulders and immediately the horse answered to the leg but my next problem was all too apparent. How to keep this animal on the circular track? To my utter dismay, we kept wandering into the middle in ever-decreasing circles. Later, I found I could not even walk a straight line in order to change the rein. Everything I did seemed to result in over-kill. One moment we were moving too much to the right, then as soon as I had corrected that with a firm backward leg, we were too much to the left; it was almost impossible, I found, just to walk forward without deviation in the time-honoured way.

I could go on *ad infinitum*, but that was my first introduction to Portuguese horses and for someone who had previously been involved with the backing and making of so many different animals over the years, it was a bitter pill to swallow – I felt I really knew very little at all. It was harder still to admit that of everything which one had come to understand about the seat, my aids were at best misguided, at the worst mistaken, and that clearly one would need to go back to school. At this point, the thought crossed my mind that I could forget what had just happened to me, forget about riding in Portugal and wait until I returned to Britain to resume my riding on less highly tuned horses. However, as soon as I saw the stallion's rider back in place again and watched the continuation of their work, so much together, so much personifying the centaur, I knew then that I had, by some miracle, landed up in the right country to start my real apprenticeship in the art of riding.

That night I went back to my apartment and started to analyse what had happened. I had felt something completely different. I had felt a horse under me which clearly responded to my every movement, but the responses were not those I expected. It was obvious, therefore, that it was I who was mistaken, I who must go back to school and I who must learn to feel what was right.

This early and unique experience, which I can only call the first awakening to feel, made a huge impact on my life. It transformed my thinking. It made me open to what was outside my own body, and made me learn how to be receptive to the balance of the horse. Had it not been for that moment of humility when I could not make the horse walk forward, let alone maintain a straight line, perhaps I would not have found the later inspiration and drive to help others. To try from the outset of training to help people become aware of what they should be feeling instead of doing, that was the secret. As the wise words of Franz Mairinger, a former

It soon began to dawn on me why the name *cavaleiro* was used. Classical riding encouraged gentlemanly attitudes and deportment. It ensured that everyone could aspire to be a *cavaleiro* both on and off the horse. (Photo: courtesy Promark)

oberbereiter of the Spanish Riding School, shout out from his book[1] 'the horse knows how to be a horse, it is we who need to know how to allow him to be so'. Note, dear reader, the word is to 'allow' – not to 'make'.

After that first experience there were others, equally illuminating in their way. In the Algarve I was given an ex-bullfighting horse to ride which offered me just about everything in the book yet none of it was consciously asked for by me. To spring from *passage* into *levade*, to zoom backwards and then forwards again, only sideways and very fast and all at a moment's notice, can be disconcerting to say the very least. Yet, that is how a few people like me came to discover riding in Portugal in the pre-Revolution days.

[1] Franz Mairinger, *Horses are Made to be Horses.*

Outside the Peninsula life went on and a very different equestrian world was evolving, a world where dressage, once considered rather dull, was just beginning to catch the imagination of the riding public. Not unsurprisingly, it was the Germans who were leading the way with their strong, genetically nurtured, ex-artillery horses and their military style of riding. By the early seventies, they would dominate competitive dressage but this was an aspect which, as yet, held little attraction for the traditional Portuguese riders. Their horsemanship was for real, life and death, bound up in testing the courage and quick reactions of their horses in tauromachy – the closest derivation of hand-to-hand combat from whence all original dressage movements had sprung.

The Iberian attitude to teaching was also different. Yes, the military and the cavalry ran their illustrious and highly disciplined schools for officers, similar to those in France, Sweden and Germany. A more aesthetic and altogether more spontaneous form of equitation, however, was the preserve of the great landed families, the people who bred the Lusitanian horses which were so suited to this art. Far from running commercial establishments, their techniques, based on the work of Marialva, an eighteenth-century nobleman and Royal Master of the Horse, were jealously guarded and handed down from father to son, maestro to apprentice, behind the closed doors of the family *manège* or *picadeiro*. Passed off with an air of nonchalance, I was later to realise that the disciplines were just as exacting, if not more so, than within the military schools. It was just that those wonderful gifted riders made it look so easy. The unspoken ethos that a gentleman must never appear to labour made it all seem very much a family affair. I found it mindboggling.

As the British were regarded with real admiration for their Thoroughbreds and their boldness across country and over jumps, I soon began to realise that the Portuguese felt it was not quite the done thing to instruct the British of all people on how to do things – at least in matters equestrian. In the same way as I had done (I still blush to think of it), visitors from overseas tended to say they could ride even if they knew only how to adhere at walk, trot and canter. In Portugal, the word for rider is *cavaleiro* – literally, cavalier. This not only denotes good breeding but generally that you are versed in the art of High School. You can imagine the confusion and consternation of some Portuguese masters when first faced with British pupils who called themselves riders! With the influx of visitors nowadays, things have changed, but there were earlier occasions when I found myself whispering in a Portuguese ear that the British do not mind being corrected. No, they are not all *haute école* riders and, yes, they want to be told! This information has been gratefully received by more than one famous man.

Had I not gone to Portugal and lived through these illuminating experiences, I very much doubt I would still be teaching today. As with religion, there is nothing quite like the convert returning to the land of their birth years later to preach the gospel and spread the message. It was 1968 when I first set foot on Portuguese soil and was so inspired by what I found there. Like other children of the sixties, the Beatles, Cliff Richard, Frank Eyfield and Cat Stevens, all of whom discovered the Algarve about the same time and found inspiration under the sun for their music, I too now saw a way to find my own personal light at the end of the tunnel.

Initially, all this had to be fitted around a demanding job. I was designing and installing discothèques for Julianas of London as a very young overseas director in a very young but exciting company. We were putting sound systems into the big golf hotels which had recently opened up in the Algarve at Alvor, Vale do Lobo and Praia de Rocha. Under the old Caetano government, which followed on from the right wing Salazar dictatorship, life was extremely glamorous for those in the fast stream. I found myself being flown by private plane to and from Lisbon and down to the unspoilt southern coast where the programme was for luxury development and strict planning control over tourism. Portuguese ministers were determined that none of the concrete eyesores which had spoiled the Benidorm and Malaga coast in Spain would sully their golden Atlantic sands. In those heady, pre-Revolution days therefore, cheap package tours, beer cans and fast food simply did not enter the picture.

With the luxury hotels came the jet set. Fast cars swept along empty roads where the only other traffic was the odd mule cart or pannier-laden donkey. With the natural hospitality and generosity for which the Portuguese are renowned, came invitations to private stud farms and wonderful country estates. Here the beautiful people gathered and as beautiful horses were very much a part of their life, so were the bulls. I had begun to realise that the two were intrinsically linked in this country of ancient tradition and old empire.

In the private arenas of these elegant families, I saw horses that could pirouette on a dinner plate, and watched another hold an animated and vibrant *piaffe* for minutes rather than seconds while the rider balanced a glass of brandy on his rump and everyone clapped. I marvelled as another cantered upstairs in a palace, only to come down again backwards, with a girl riding pillion. All of this spontaneous equitation was performed one-handed, with much laughter and gaiety from guests and *cavaleiros* alike, and the horses loving the chance to show off. More horses would be brought, fleet of foot and combining all those qualities of athletic versatility to dash in and out and around the bulls on the nearby hillside, separating the steers and parading back, triumph in their eyes, to the waiting guests who lined the balcony. It did not take many of these visits to realise with shocking clarity that here was horsemanship, as old as the hills around us, being conducted on a scale of mastery which one had never dreamed possible.

To have the chance to ride these wonderful bullfighting horses was something quite unique. One bullfighter, Austrian by birth but adopted during the war by the aristocratic Infante Camera family, was particularly kind to me. Gustav Zenkyl gave one such confidence when one was invited to sit on his best horse in his indoor arena at Vale de Figueira that one just absorbed everything the horse had to offer and allowed things to flow. In this frame of mind, storing away the feelings instead of trying to make things happen, it flowed surprisingly well.

It was in this way that I came, very gradually, to find answers to the questions which had first raised themselves in my late teenage years in Scotland. During those hot Sunday afternoons in the sun I watched and learned and came to love the Lusitano horses which, in those days, no one at home had even heard of. It was this effortless horsemanship where horse and rider seemed joined together as they feinted, circled, poised, pirouetted away from and around a mock bull's horns, often in an area not much bigger than a large sitting room, that I realised how a horse can give himself to his rider and how the rider can learn to be totally at one with his horse. I began to see how the Greek and Roman concept of the centaur lived on in this country of white sunlight and purple shadows, of golden port and crimson claret, of stark contrasts, of rich and poor and of horses and bulls.

When, years later, I learned that those same stud farms I had visited deep in the heartlands of the Alentejo were built on lands where the Romans set up their early cavalry studs and built rings for horses to dance in, to parade before their women and to train for javelin practice, the past seemed to merge with the present and I realised that here in Lusitania, alive and intact, existed a form of horsemanship, a living treasure, known to Xenophon, Alexander the Great and Marcus Aurelius.

Around this time, others were coming to Portugal. An American called Phyllis Field had discovered a highly talented and respected trainer named Nuno Oliveira who ran a school of dressage horses at the family home of the Borba family just outside Lisbon and who took visiting students from overseas. Soon, Americans and Canadians were flocking to Portugal to be taught by the man they called Master, and he would fly to the east coast of

All the great Portuguese masters, including Oliveira, have been influenced by the teachings of the eighteenth-century Marquess of Marialva, Master of the Horse to King Dom Jose I, whose book is still followed in Portugal today.

America to continue the work there. At the same time, certain discerning Europeans were also discovering the talents of this exceptional trainer of wonderfully light horses. Oliveira had given some very impressive demonstrations at Wembley and in Rome with his Lusitano stallions in the days when, to many equestrians, dressage meant little more than indoor riding. What set him aside from other contenders was the absolute controlled power of his horse while he himself appeared to do nothing. To the undiscerning, it was as though he merely sat there, very still with motionless legs and reins of silk. They could not fathom it out. People still talk about the moment when Oliveira, unmoving, impregnable as a rock, made his finale and cantered backwards in front of the Royal Box at Wembley. The control was unreal.

Among the lesser satellites who made the long trail from as far away as Australia or Chile to his latter-day school in the Lisbon foothills, there emerged the occasional bright star. Deeply practical and thinking horsemen such as Egon Von Neindorff from Germany, Michel Henriquet from France, Henrique Von Schaik, a former Dutch cavalry officer who ran a yard of event horses in Vermont, and Daniel Pevsner, a young Israeli teacher newly established in England, were to be more influenced by this Portuguese man than they probably ever dreamt possible. They looked beyond the obvious and found the discipline, the hard reality of technique which he could give them.

Others, like butterflies, skimmed by, sat on his beautifully schooled stallions, felt a *piaffe,* a *passage,* a flying change and went home again, thinking they could ride. Yet what Oliveira offered was very real. Even a superficial sense of feel is better than no feel. For those who took the trouble to come back year after year, there was much to learn from his patient schoolmasters and, as the Master demanded, 'Shoulder-in! Half-pass! Pirouette! Do it!' it mattered not perhaps that the horses knew to make the movements irrespective of what their riders were doing or not doing. As far as Oliveira was concerned, the main object was achieved – once feel had been established by riding a movement again and again, the battle to reach through to the inner recesses of the rider's mind was halfway won. Those feelings could be reached for again and again, at a future time, on a future horse and in a future situation. They would never be forgotten.

Lessons in feel should never be underestimated. If the classical principles are ever to be thoroughly understood, they have first to be recognised and this can only happen through constant practice. Learning to become one with the horse requires concentrating the brain into measuring and weighing up the feel. Beautiful riding may seem unconscious, but clearly it is not. If you watch any good rider with their horse, they concentrate one hundred per cent on what the horse is doing and how he relates back to them one hundred per cent of the time. Only from this two-way exchange can good timing and judgement develop. Without feel, it is impossible to execute a smooth delivery. Even the simplest exercises require knowing when and how to address and create changes of direction, changes in gait, changes in balance. Only with constant application and practice will all this become refined.

It is of little use knowing how to apply the aids if we have no awareness of when they should be given. Pupils cannot be expected to appreciate the minute timing which is required for the correct riding of movements if they do not know precisely what the horse is doing at a particular moment in time, or how he is moving underneath them. Balance can only be attained and retained when the rider knows exactly where his horse is in space, which leg is on the ground, which leg is free to act and where the weight of the horse is concentrated – again at a particular moment.

There can be no true impulsion, rhythm or flow if the balance is even momentarily out of sync. Cadence cannot emerge if these prerequisites are not addressed fully and all the time. Indeed, without feel, there is no control. However, control on its own is not enough; it has to be effortless, which means pre-empting every movement; changing things before they happen, to *allow* them to happen the way you want. Only then will the horse appear to work without the intervention of the rider, of his own volition, as though in freedom. Only then will art emerge.

Unfortunately, sensations such as these cannot be learned from a book; neither will they be experienced on a horse firmly entrenched on his forehand. If the horse is not schooled to a certain level so that the hocks are well engaged and the weight and power of the horse are retained behind, it will be very hard for the student to feel anything. They certainly will not be able to learn how to use their own weight to complement or change the balance. A horse on the forehand is a horse out of balance and only the expert rider will have enough feel to be able to alter that.

To educate people to become experts you must therefore help them by giving them horses which are finely tuned already. The higher the degree of schooling, the more sensations and feelings will be offered by the horse. It takes time to build up a sufficient range of feelings for the rider to begin to separate and understand these, but the opportunity must be there in the first place. Sadly, too many riders are denied such an opportunity and perhaps this is why there is often so little understanding and respect for the horse in today's riding establishments.

Without feel, every aid you give your horse is meaningless. Like me on that first patient, proud stallion, aids given at the wrong place, with the wrong emphasis and without an appreciation of just what is happening under the saddle become worthless. At worst, they become counter-productive, creating tensions which block both rider and horse from the important receiving, bonding, uniting, moulding feeling which is so vital if riding your horse is to be about partnership.

Where teaching riding is concerned, there is nothing more satisfying to a conscientious instructor than to talk a rider through their position, explaining the small body adjustments required to discover feel, then to direct their attention to the vital areas which will be addressed in the horse. Over the years, I have found that the horses themselves tell me what is needed by the pupil in an extraordinary telepathic way. In Portugal we had a horse named Castiço who first made me aware of this gift – not a gift of mine, but a gift from the horse to those who care to watch and listen. He was a fiery little grey Lusitano, a stallion of great calibre who was a favourite of my husband and who was so sensitive that you could just feel through your eyes what needed to be done, and so, on that basis, one instructed the pupil.

It is particularly rewarding when the pupil, in their turn, is able to tell you they have felt something different and special and share that moment with you. I have seen the pursed lips of instructors not prepared to share their secrets. I have heard the cold arguments that novices are not ready for this feeling or that, not ready to sit upon such an advanced horse and so on. I have noticed that the people who make such remarks do so generally out of self-defence. If they are not able to offer such technique or such horses themselves, they will do anything to denigrate those who can.

Every serious, thinking rider should have the chance to sit on a fully schooled, light and willing horse under supervision. Every establishment should endeavour to provide at least one horse who can give people the ability to feel. A light horse enlightens. He is worth his weight in gold and I hope the day will yet come when we find more such horses scattered among the British Isles.

I have also heard the argument that if one did provide such a horse, he would be quickly ruined. This will certainly happen if there is no one on the ground with sufficient knowledge to retune the horse or to help and advise the rider. Provided, however, that the teacher instructs on a strictly one-to-one basis, huge progress can be made. In 25 years of teaching with fully schooled horses, I have rarely encountered a pupil who has not been humbled and supremely moved by that first hand experience of feeling a horse in full balance, a horse poised as though captured in porcelain, a horse so beautifully empowered on his hocks that the rider knows instinctively that the slightest movement, even a breath, can disturb that precarious balance and lose it for all time.

As my late husband used to say to all his students: 'First, you must build up a library of feelings. Gradually, as you remember what you did last time in a certain situation, you reach out for that feeling – as though selecting a book off the shelf – and you put it into practice. If your memory served you correctly and you were able to reproduce the same sensation as before, you will have learned to make something happen – just through feeling. Finally, everything comes together naturally; you think it, feel it and it is all there.'

CHAPTER 6

In pursuit of lightness –
the value of the schoolmaster

Not long ago I was giving a lesson on my elderly Portuguese schoolmaster Palomo when an experienced local dressage judge stopped by to watch. I knew her quite well and had invited her to stay to lunch. I had previously explained that my pupil that day would be a lady who owns her own horse, who competes in dressage, but who was experiencing great difficulty in bringing her Elementary-level horse off the forehand to achieve any degree of engagement or collection. She felt that only by riding a schoolmaster would she attain the feel of balance she required if she was ever to help her own horse acquire this at home.

This is not only a sensible but a logical approach and I welcomed her motives. To give people the sensation of the horse working more from behind, I generally start them off with some concentrated exercises in shoulder-in. Of all the movements, particularly if performed at walk when the rider has time to think, this is perhaps the simplest way to introduce the basics of collection. Once the rider can really absorb and sense the engagement of the inside hind leg as it steps more under the horse's body mass, they begin to appreciate the change in balance. Not only is a feeling of upward thrust experienced from under the saddle, but the rider will also note the lightening effect of the forehand through the fingers. All this takes place and can be felt simply because the weight of the horse is brought back by the nature of the exercise and he has to round and lower his quarters in order to step more through and under.

We were scarcely five minutes into the lesson, with the old horse obliging nicely, when my acquaintance interrupted from the sidelines and called me over to the fence. 'Sylvia,' she said, 'your horse is not even; he does not step so much under with his right hind leg as he did with his left. I can recommend an exercise to help that.'

I looked at her and have to confess I was lost for words. She was judging the lesson like a dressage test and seemed to have failed to understand what it was all about. Did I have to explain again that the stallion was over 23 years of age and, like most elderly people, could be a little stiff in the joints for the first few minutes? Did I have to say that he was not there to be 'improved' at his late stage in life but, instead, was there to help others? The fact that he adores his work, complies generously and that such exercises not only help him to stay supple and alive, but also give pupils a wonderful opportunity to work with a wise old horse who knows his work backwards had obviously passed her by.

In this case, the unevenness might well have been the fault of the rider but at that moment in time we were not working on the negative. The idea was to concentrate on the positive by allowing the rider to feel collection, experience the sensation of engagement and to be aware of the horse laterally flexed and moving forward, sideways and lightly into her receiving outside hand. How can you teach people to *feel* if you hassle and sidetrack them before they have even got started? Achieving perfect length of strides is for the expert towards the end of training, not for the novice who is learning to understand and communicate.

I shall never forget Reiner Klimke commenting on how sad it was that Colonel Nyblaeus[1], for all his knowledge, often forgot to look at the whole horse in the tests he judged. His permanent preoccupation with the length of each horse's strides, the regularity of the footfalls, caused him to miss so much. 'He was always looking for a perfect way of going; in this regard it was all too easy never to see the horse.'

I felt sad that my friend had misunderstood the purpose of my lesson; sad that there are not more horses like Palomo to allow people a sense of feel. Wise old horses of this type are without price for they raise the standard of all who ride them. With a generosity of spirit that is awesome, they can give people a chance to experience movements and sensations they may never have felt before in their lives. They can illuminate a muddled, murky picture; they can give hope when all confidence is gone.

One may read about concepts of lightness, balance and the weight of the horse being transferred to the hindquarters until the cows come home. If you have never felt it for yourself, however, such words can be meaningless. To portray something in words alone is similar to explaining the taste of champagne. If you have never sipped it, never felt that honeyed tingle on your tongue, never experienced the lift, the headiness and the sense of well-being that it brings, you have little idea.

My own apprenticeship to feel started in 1971 with Henry Loch at a place called Odelouca which lay in the foothills of Monchique near the old

---

[1] Colonel Gustaf Nyblaeus, former President of the FEI Dressage Committee and Olympic dressage judge, who died in 1988.

Roman town of Silves in the Algarve. Although by this time Henry was heavily involved with Portuguese and Spanish horses, no one could have inherited a broader equestrian background than he. His father, Douglas, later to become a highly decorated major general as Lord-in-waiting to George V, may have been a guards officer rather than a cavalryman, but he always found the time to take his eldest son hunting and to ensure he was well mounted, first with ponies and later with hunters. At home, they attended the meets of the local Newmarket and Thurlow in Suffolk. On special occasions they would box their horses up by train, as was the custom in those days, travelling them to the finest country in the Shires. At New Year, hunting took place from Uncle Bim's Northampton home, Castle Ashby, where the famous mile-long Chase provided an irresistible gallop for a horsemad youngster. On other occasions, Compton Wynyates, where Henry's mother was born, provided a good day out with the Warwickshire.

Distracted by horses all through a singularly unpromising school career, Henry eventually scraped through Sandhurst not long before war broke out. By then he had ridden High School horses in Switzerland with the Knie family, entered several point to points and ridden a couple of amateur steeplechase races. As a young cavalry officer, there was more hunting, ample polo, including a trip to California, an exchange visit to Saumur in France and a varied life of horses waiting for him in Egypt where his batallion was situated outside Alexandria just prior to the beginning of the war.

When we first met, Henry was living a hermit-like existence in a small rented farmhouse with a yard of seven horses. Twenty-nine years older than me, there was a boyish, somewhat irreverent, quality about him which endeared him to the young. He was also incredibly fit and strong and looked totally at one on any horse.

Hidden away from the tourist trail, with his school set high above the river, he was busily engaged in teaching young people to ride in a way which seemed extraordinarily advanced for their age. As he explained to me, there were no riding ponies in Portugal so, above all else, 'these kids' would have to learn to be safe. Quite simply this meant riding correctly, the classical way. All his horses were schooled to a high standard and there was no way he would ever compromise his horses through the inadequacy of someone's bad riding. Thus lessons started on the blanket at the end of a lunge, and only when the rider's seat and confidence were sufficiently developed were they allowed into the saddle and in full control of the reins. Then it was straight into serious work and woe betide anyone who pulled his lovely light horses in the mouth.

However experienced the rider, Henry always believed in first establishing a quiet, independent seat in all the gaits, working on the lunge. A *voltige* roller was used with handles for rebalancing, so that the horse's mouth was never touched.

If you are taught to ride under such conditions from the beginning, it is scarcely surprising when the usual mistakes are avoided and bypassed. Henry's main source of pupils was the Algarve's only International School at the time. Here the sons and daughters of Portuguese, Swiss, Swedish, British, American, German and Dutch business people and ex-patriots were taught in English under a British curriculum. One of the highlights for these children was their weekly trip to Henry's farm at Odelouca and, whatever their nationality or background, all learned in the same way. Respect was ingrained from day one; respect for the horse and respect for the system.

Henry recognised that the Lusitano had unique qualities of sensitivity and generosity. By offering these children the chance to ride properly trained horses which offered so much, he was confident that what they learned with him would benefit all horses in the future. It was not a case of his horses being better or more expensive than anyone else's. On the contrary, some had been rescued or given to him where others had failed, but he had a knack of choosing the right ones to act the role of professor to his pupils. With fine tuning and patience, he had brought all to good basic levels of lateral and collected work, while a couple were working at the equivalent of Grand Prix. With the Lusitanos, he saw every reason to give

Young riders could only take charge of the reins once they were upright, firm and balanced in the saddle. The horse must never be pulled in the mouth; the neck must be extended with just a soft flexion from the poll.

all his pupils a feel of lightness and balance from the very beginning.

I was very fortunate to have become part of that system. Under Henry's guidance I learned to sit still, to think before I acted and always to listen to the horse. Riding with him, up to four or five hours a day on schoolmasters which pointed out every little fault, and then having those faults quietly explained, changed my life. Whatever modest talent I had before, now had direction; I began to know what should be done, rather than guessing. For the first time in my life there was real purpose in my schooling. I learned to introduce the work progressively, understanding which exercises did this and that to the horse and how to recognise when it was correct. Had it not been for those sensitive hotblood horses, I know without a shadow of doubt I could not have learned so much. It is the combination of theory with practice and feel which is so vitally important to the learning process.

It was not too long before I was helping Henry to teach. Wisely, he gave me the adults, or the odd nervous rider who required special attention. Without saying it I think he knew I would learn more by working on particular problems with someone who could articulate their worries, their dilemmas, which would, in turn, give me greater insight. There is nothing more satisfying to a conscientious teacher than to talk a pupil through their work, correcting body posture, noting the necessity for small adjustments through the seat and legs to master balance on a sensitive horse. Schoolmaster horses not only help the rider, they help the teacher by directing attention to those vital areas which need to be corrected, particularly within the context of weight aids. Thus, as one corrects the rider's lower leg it is seen that the knee is not sufficiently deep, this in turn is seen to be caused by the hips not being level, which in turn shows up a weakness in the rider's back – one side is more braced than the other, and so on.

In this way, we learn from teaching. From looking, from analysing, from having a feel for what the horse is feeling, nowadays one can go straight to the root of the problem, but teachers have to learn too and it takes time to acquire that knowledge.

There was no doubt that Henry's talents achieved the most spectacular results with young people. Visitors to his yard were amazed to see thirteen and fourteen year olds mounted on stallions and mares, riding in disciplined formation in the large sand arena. The children were taught in cavalry tradition, orders given in short precise tones, the military influence apparent but never obscuring the sense of challenge and fun he brought to these lessons. From day one, the standards were set and they were high, but he was very approachable after each session had ended. A bevy of pupils would crowd around him, cleaning their tack and asking endless but sensible questions. They were quite clearly inspired.

After I gave up my work in the tourist industry and we returned from a short visit to England as man and wife, we began to plan a move of the stables to a more central location on the coast. We ended up buying a ruined farmhouse with 5 acres of olive groves in the foothills of Loulé, a market town only 20 miles from Faro Airport. The conversion from peasant dwelling with no running water or electricity to small equestrian centre took some considerable time, but the sand *manège* and stables were completed before we moved in and we were already used to gas refrigeration and a routine of oil lamps from Oudelouca. It would be some time before we had a generator, telephone or a proper road to our house. Nevertheless, despite the difficulties of reaching us, our small business very soon became bustling and fruitful as we continued to attract visitors and young people from all over the Algarve.

A new International School had started at Vale do Lobo and junior and senior pupils arrived by Land Rover twice weekly along the rough dirt roads which led to our hillside retreat. With the school visits and coming in their own time at weekends and in the holidays, our pupils clearly wanted the chance to prove their growing expertise. Soon we had organised rallies and the odd small show to which various dignitaries and the British Consul

Henry was often mistaken for an Iberian rider. Here he is at Quinta das Esporas, Loulé in 1975, mounted on one of our school horses, Xairel, who was blind in one eye but totally obedient in every way.
(Photo: Charles Hodge)

came. So impressed were those parents and friends who came to watch these children ride that it was not long before the adults wanted to join in too.

I will never forget one amusing occasion when a visiting instructress from England expressed surprised indignation to see some of our young teenagers riding a dressage test which involved demi-pirouettes in walk, five reinback steps to canter, and flying change required on both reins. 'Surely, they're far too young for this?' she complained. Little notice was taken as, for our pupils, clearly unfazed, this was nothing more than a pretty fair test of their day-to-day riding. They acquitted themselves well with quiet hands and firm seats and Henry swiftly pooh-poohed the idea that this might be asking rather too much. Politely he explained to her that any self-respecting cavalry horse was expected to do such basics, and he'd hardly be worth his salt as an instructor if he could not teach such manoeuvres to a group of fit and able children. 'Wait till you see them next year!' he smiled disarmingly.

Not long after one of these events took place, a letter came from Colonel Lithgow, head of the Pony Club at Stoneleigh in Great Britain, enclosing a copy of a recommendation from a number of British people in the Algarve suggesting that we should form a branch of the Pony Club in Portugal. We were very keen but, sadly, this never came to fruition as, not long afterwards, Portugal suffered huge political turmoil in the aftermath of a revolution which, at one time, threatened all landowners and owners of horses with the sequestration of their properties and animals under a short-term Communist takeover by the military.

Nevertheless, the correspondence with Bill Lithgow was a boost to our confidence and we were encouraged to believe that if we ever returned to England with our horses, we would be welcomed with open arms by the training and teaching establishment.

As word spread about the horses and about Henry's teaching, visitations by equestrian groups from as far away as Australia and America began to take place. One such, from North America, was headed by two charming and erudite horsemen, Alexander McKay Smith who edited the US *Chronicle of the Horse*, and Ivan Bezugloff who ran an inspiring magazine, *Dressage and CT*. They arrived on one of the hottest days of the year but the driver of the air-conditioned coach which brought them to the bottom of our hill simply refused to countenance driving his precious vehicle up the winding, rutted dirt road which led from Loulé into our valley. Thus the party of twenty or more illustrious writers and journalists were unceremoniously disgorged into the dusty road and made to find their own way to our small *quinta*. I will never forget them arriving in exhausted ones and twos, having struggled up at least two steep kilometres in the midday sun. It took many glasses of water and later an overflowing jar of iced sangria to revive everyone's spirits.

Since we had moved to our remote valley, it had become increasingly obvious that we needed a Land Rover. Somehow we had got by, bumping over the ruts in my old Opal and Henry's small but tough Fiat. As is the way with horses, there was never enough money left over for the niceties in life, but we lived in the hope that, one day, somehow, we might be able to afford a more suitable vehicle.

The arrival of John Scott-Lewis had to be an answer to prayer. A letter from our English agent, who arranged parties of students who attended weekly dressage courses through an advertisement we ran in *Horse and Hound*, announced that she had booked in some people who ran a chain of shops in London. The shops were Jean Machine, and the owner was a proficient rider.

We were intrigued; we knew the Jean Machine boutiques. They lined the King's Road and Kensington High Street and other 'in' places in the early seventies, and arguably boasted the best made jeans and leisure wear you could buy in the UK at that time. Everyone knew the F.U.S label. When John arrived, we were captivated by his energy, enthusiasm and charm and he and Henry got on like a house on fire.

Jay, as John liked to be called, was totally irreverent about much of life in the same way as Henry, but when it came to horses both were deadly serious. They craved perfection, they had endlessly searching minds, they read, they studied, they were never content and always wanted more. There was a restlessness about Jay which really appealed to Henry and he worked hard to give Jay everything he was looking for during that seven-day stay. They rode up to six hours a day; sometimes they started at six in the morning, sometimes at eight. At nights they talked into the early hours; out came Henry's books and photographs and the stories and the memories all came out too. Henry was elated by Jay's enthusiasm; Jay was fascinated by Henry.

We were commissioned to find a horse for Jay. He was planning to set up a stud of Lusitano horses in England and had made contact with the Portuguese breeders but he wanted a good stallion for himself to ride and to learn from. We set about looking for a schoolmaster. Through our old friend Gustav Zenkyl we chose a wonderful former bullfighting horse, a 16.2 h.h. grey called Imperador, who came to us from Santarem and who stayed at our *quinta* to be schooled by Henry, English dressage-style, for the next six months. Jay was elated and, for the next few months, regularly flew out from London to ride his beautiful new horse.

When, finally, the day came for Imperador to go to his new home, we received an enigmatic message from the Jean Machine office. Would we be at home on such and such a day to receive a small token of appreciation from Mr Scott-Lewis? I will never forget what happened next. A few days later we were in the school with some pupils when there came the beep-beep of a noisy horn at our back gate. Henry rode out into the yard to come face to face with a gleaming dark green machine. Our present was a brand new diesel-powered Land Rover, hand delivered by one of Jay's friends. As Henry said, no one had ever done such a wonderful thing for him before.

What generally captivated those who had been brought up in the British and German traditions of riding was the lightness of our horses. I have explained before that none of them were particularly well bred or expensive, but we kept them finely tuned in between lessons and courses and as they enjoyed plenty of variety in their lives they were happy and proud in their work. Under these conditions, therefore, business boomed and standards were preserved. In every lesson, all our riders, young and old, were not only receiving instruction from us, they were also being taught by the horses themselves.

We had one particular gelding who had come to us from an ex-patriot, Baron Von Nagel, who was moving back to Germany. The horse was blind in one eye but had a particularly noble disposition. Bred by the old bullfighting family of Francisco Ribeiro, Xairel was to give people a feel they would never forget. Soft through the back, incredibly engaged through the quarters, high and rounded through the wither and neck, he was the perfect schoolhorse and the list of people to be influenced by him for life grew longer and longer. Von Nagel's own protegée, Gabriella Pochammer, is now a leading German trainer and writer in her own right. Of our Portuguese pupils, one or two have gone on to ride for the Portuguese School of Equestrian Art. Of the International School pupils, Sheila Greenfield and others are now running their own teaching establishments. All remember Xairel with huge affection.

There were other special horses over the years. Occasionally, one comes across a horse that is so generous that he will put himself on the aids the moment he feels your legs around him and you pick up the reins. For me, the first had been Castico[2], and later came Palomo, but such horses are rare indeed and even rarer are those people who recognise their qualities. On such horses, you only have to think 'up and together' and, provided you can feel, they are there for you, on the bit, poised and ready to dance.

This act of total trust, particularly on the part of the older horse, may place him at some considerable risk. A horse in fine balance becomes precarious, much in the same way as a human ballet dancer becomes vulnerable when up on her points. It only takes the merest nudge one way or the other to push the horse or dancer off balance but, by the same token, they can be made to fly.

A person who has not experienced such a horse may find this idea hard to accept, even unbelievable. Having ridden a horse of this calibre,

---

[2] Castico loved my late husband so much that when he took him to a friend's yard to turn out and recuperate from a minor leg injury, the stallion jumped a 7-foot wall when he saw my husband's car drive away and he broke his shoulder. For six months he was box-rested, but the shoulder never healed. He was put to sleep a month after Henry died.

however, they inevitably accept the truth. Becoming aware of such fine balance makes you feel alternately responsible and very humble. Only a vain or uneducated mind could fail to be overawed by a horse that offers so much.

Not long ago I was rereading Philip Astley's book, *A System of Equestrian Education*. Astley, born in 1742, ran a prestigious riding school where he passed on the classical methods of riding, which he had learned abroad, to officers and civilian riders in London. He recounts how, on one occasion at the Court of Vienna, an old *manège* horse was produced for him to ride in front of the Emperor. Astley treated him with great caution, explaining to the watching assembly:

> The Horse, never having seen me before, may shew some signs of his sagacity; and that I always made it a point, till the animal was convinced of my disposition towards him, to act with precaution, that I conceived there was more merit in preventing an accident than curing one.

After his display, he wrote,

> I stopped the Horse, dismounted and wiped his face with my handkerchief . . . and gave the Horse a couple of apples to eat, which being observed by His Majesty, he asked me which of the two were best for Horses, carrots or apples? I informed his Majesty that carrots were excellent, but I conceived that an apple greatly assisted in refreshing the mouth and that it was one of the rewards I made use of to gain their affections. His Majesty smiled and requested me to walk into the palace.

The old masters teach us that there is nothing new in these ideas of respect, consideration and the giving of reward. Today's schoolmaster is no different from the type of horse which at one time carried all our forefathers safely in and out of battle. In sword play, the rider at the greatest advantage was the rider who could trust his horse to poise when, where and exactly how he wanted him in all situations. Nowadays, it is all too easy to forget the origins of dressage and we are all guilty of taking too much for granted, forgetting that one element which often places the horse higher than ourselves – his generosity.

Equitation is unique in this respect, for where in the world can we find another discipline where the participant actually receives instruction from their medium or tool? Skis may seem to have a life of their own, and the mountains challenge you, but they do not exactly speak back to you and point out where you are going wrong; a golf club or tennis racquet may send the ball in a different direction to what you expected, but will not communicate. Sailing a boat on the open sea is perhaps closest to riding, for you have to judge and feel for the elements all around you. However, the sea is a cruel master and, however brilliant a sailor you may be, its power cannot always be harnessed according to your talent.

I have heard people say that riders should not be allowed to make too many discoveries too early in their riding career. That they must root around and find out for themselves and that it may take years – decades – before they should be allowed to learn on a fully trained horse. This is cynical thinking. Do we withhold the palette from the art student? Tell them they may only use certain colours when they pick up the brush and deny them the full spectrum of the rainbow?

Even if they wanted it, learning the hard way is no longer possible for everyone. Years ago, when life was slower, riders had all the time in the world to experiment, to learn from different types of horses and to be disciplined by an eagle-eyed master horseman who was not going to give much away. Those times are going. Riders no longer have the time, the opportunity or the money to spend years in the same riding hall struggling towards the unknown in the vague hope that this art will open up for them, perhaps even one day pervade their souls and their psyche. If we are to keep the art of horsemanship alive, we who teach must do everything in our power to enable the keen and the dedicated to catch a glimpse of the sublime in the shortest time possible, so that potential talent can be spotted and nurtured before it is diverted elsewhere.

This is not to say that a student's passage of exploration towards learning, towards study, towards application and commitment to that art will be any the less arduous or time consuming than for those who were brought up in former times. It is only the early approach which differs. My argument is based on the need to draw riders into the net and to capture their imagination from the beginning. Surely this is more important now than it has ever been in the past? It would be crass folly to allow potential artists to miss that moment of enlightenment which could change their perception of riding forever.

How, therefore, may we ensure the continuation of classical riding? Again, I believe it behoves teachers to seize an opportunity to provide riders with horses which can offer them all those colours of the rainbow. Obviously, this must be done under strict guidance. We should first make it possible for them to develop their seat on a good lunge horse. Second, we should instil in them the classical precepts and a basic understanding of the reasons behind the accepted aids. Third, we should provide experienced but sensitive schoolmasters on which to feel. Even though they may only be at the threshold of their riding, this can do no harm. On the contrary, it can only open the eyes.

Of course, horses of such sensitivity and generous disposition are not easily found in a world where mediocrity is nowadays the norm. The average school horse will have a far greater sense of self-preservation than the type of horse described hitherto and his attitude to work may have been soured. Unfortunately, many riding school horses, inured by years of indifferent or bad riders, will subscribe to a mode influenced by the lowest common denominator. This means that they adopt a defensive attitude when ridden and it takes a real expert to entice them out of it.

A horse has two ways of protecting himself and making himself less vulnerable to a poor rider. The first mode of defence is to become tortoiselike, to harden his back, to resist with the mouth and withdraw or contract the neck, thus becoming as ponderous and rooted to the ground as possible. This way of using energy and weight against the rider is similar to the way in which people can set themselves against each other in a tug of war. You pull and they do not move, you pull again and they set themselves more, firmly planted. This, curiously, can be accomplished by the horse in such a way that even while forward progression is present, and he goes through the rituals of walk, trot and canter, he is actually not using himself as nature intended, which should be light and airborne.

Then there is the other type of horse whose reactions may result in his early demise. Often with a potential for great sensitivity, his only defence against discomfort and imbalance is flight. Thus he is permanently seeking to remove himself from the source of irritation. Taking off in this way is similar to an aeroplane out of control which results in a nosediving spiral of events. Once the balance goes, whatever the pilot or the rider does to the controls will have little result. A horse which is allowed to get into this situation becomes increasingly fearful and, in the most severe cases, quite unwilling to relinquish his flight potential. Such horses are often condemned as dangerous through no fault of their own.

In addition, there are the basically obedient but somewhat dull schoolhorses – one could say the average riding school horse. These have an important part to play in allowing novice riders to gain confidence and get mileage on the clock, but they are not ideal for pursuing technique and allowing pupils to grow in experience and knowledge as, unless they are regularly reschooled, they tend to pick up each rider's bad habits. Conversely, people brought up to ride on indifferent animals will develop an indifferent style of riding if allowed to remain in this mode for too long.

The main reason why our modest school had made a name for itself was because we offered sensitive, schooled horses. As our home became more habitable and finally we had electricity by generator, there was a waiting list of residential guests. Our dressage courses became increasingly specialised and we welcomed some competent and interesting international visitors to the *quinta*. Whatever the nationality, all said the same thing:

there is nowhere at home where schoolmaster horses like these are available to ordinary riders. It was this fact which preyed on our minds and led to the conviction that perhaps we owed it to the riding world in general to take our horses to England.

Henry was less keen to go than I. He adored the sun, the countryside and the easy camaraderie of the Iberian horseworld. We had received so much kindness and support from every quarter. There was the invitation to visit the Domecqs and the Gonzalez Byass family in Andalucia, both great sherry families who bred stunning horses and whose hospitality was equally gracious.

At that time the Royal Andalusian School of Equestrian Art was still in the making and I was filled with admiration and some little envy as we watched the school's first woman rider, Mercedes Gonzalez Cort, ride under the chandeliers in the huge blue and white draped marquée on her beautiful stallion Leiria. The school was then under the guidance of the old father, a brilliant *rejoneo* rider called Alvaro Domecq whose son Alvarito would finally take the entire enterprise to its newly built quarters at Avenida Duques de Abrantes in Jerez a few years later. Alvaro Senior was a small neat figure who exuded presence; I don't think I have ever seen a rider with a straighter back in my life.

In addition, there was still time to make regular visits to the country homes of the Portuguese friends we had come to know and grow deeply fond of. There were Julio Bastos's wonderful houseparties at his palace at Estremoz where the olives were still pressed by hand and the grapes trodden underfoot. The proud bullfighter and master horseman David Telles invited us to stay at Coruche and made us feel part of his family as did Veca, acknowledged High School virtuoso at the great Portuguese fairs. Virtually the only British at that time to participate in these events, we were offered stallions to ride both at Golegã and Santarem and always in the private *picadeiros* of breeders up and down the lush Tagus valley.

Looking for horses for pupils often involved wonderful forays into deep virgin forest to watch herds of horses meandering in the care of a lone horseman. The trips revealed a host of wildlife, occasionally a wild boar, a lynx-type spotted cat or kestrels and once a golden eagle soaring above. At home, between the gymnastic work of breaking and schooling young horses, there was the unspoilt hinterland of the Algarve to explore. Riding through the umbrella pine woods, over oregano- and thyme-clad hills, deep into peach and vine orchards, or paddling down lazy rivers where we could swim the horses in deep dark pools, provided blissful and memorable experiences. Life was good and we both knew it was going to be hard to leave all this behind. Indeed, it would have been all too easy to stay on were

It was a real honour to be offered a beautiful horse to ride at the great Portuguese horse fairs. This is me, the year before the Revolution (1973), riding Imperador, the bullfighting horse of Gustav Zenkyl. Unfortunately, his stirrups were a little shorter than mine!

it not for the incessant drip, drip, drip of persuasive words echoed by so many pupils as they returned to us, year after year. 'When are you going to take these horses to England?'

When the lorries finally came to transport our precious cargo to the railway station south of Loulé, it was just five years after the Portuguese Revolution. The dream had begun when we first introduced residential courses for pupils from England but the spur which finally drove us to give up our idyllic hillside home in the Algarve was the feeling of uncertainty that grew day by day after the Portuguese Government fell before the red flag of socialism on 25 April 1974. Hard as it may seem to understand now, with a democratic Portugal and Spain firmly entrenched in the EU, the future in Portugal for ex-patriots like ourselves looked increasingly uncertain.

While the rest of Europe was enjoying equestrian sport more than ever before and we were well aware that the German system of dressage riding was influencing competition in the United Kingdom to a surprisingly strong degree, Portuguese riders were facing difficult times. The unique traditions that the Portuguese had kept alive, mainly through their work with the bulls, were in grave danger of being fragmented, even lost, through political and social change. The *gineta*[3] way of riding, dating back almost unbroken from the time of the Greek and Roman civilisations in the Peninsula, and reinforced during years of warring with the Moors, had survived through the Napoleonic Wars to the present day. Now, ironically, in the twentieth century, there was the real danger that the very people who promoted this wonderful horsemanship would be driven from their own lands.

Perhaps, as outsiders, Henry and I could appreciate the significance of such a loss more than the people themselves, for they were too close to it all. The whole country that we had grown to love and feel part of now seemed in danger of losing the one thing which made it stand head and shoulders above the rest of Europe in terms of specialised equestrian understanding and heritage as well as, of course, the horses themselves. Ugly rumours reached us through our Portuguese friends in Lisbon. There had been the wholesale slaughter of some much admired and famous High School stallions at more than one private farm. Many of the great *cavaleiros* had fled to Mexico or South America. One of the greatest riders of all, a man called João Nuncio, who saw his best stallion shot by the Communists, had died of a heart attack. Some of the country's most regarded lawyers, bankers and diplomats had been imprisoned. Among those Portuguese families who had had their lands and stud farms sequestered by the Communists were some of the most revered breeders in the land and the loss of their stock would cripple the horse industry.

In Portugal, we had discovered a way of riding which linked back directly to the courtly riding once pursued at the Court of St James by our own kings and queens and which had influenced all Europe during the baroque age. For this reason it seemed appropriate that these horses and this way of riding should again be brought to British shores and as swiftly as possible.

It was in this climate that the final decision was made. To send dogs and cats into quarantine, to uproot seventeen horses and then to move lock, stock and barrel across four national frontiers was an enormous undertaking. In those days we were not operating under the auspices of a free-trading European Union and, with Portugal and Spain playing no part in the then EEC, trade barriers in a political climate of uncertainty were jealously upheld. There was confusion about the import or export of foreign monies; funds could be held up for months in the mayhem of the new banking system in a country at odds with itself. In short, foreigners

---

[3] The term *gineta* from which came the Old English word jennet, is explained in *The Royal Horse of Europe*.

It was a proud moment when our Green Farm dressage yard was finally finished. By this time 22 Portuguese and Spanish horses were esconced in a quiet Suffolk village which attracted enormous interest from the local community.

(Photo: courtesy *East Anglia Daily Times*)

such as ourselves were more often regarded as a nuisance than anything else, despite the huge profits made from the punishing rates of exchange.

All around us was uncertainty. Officials came and went. Wherever possible, the largely Communist-dominated bureaucracy put up barriers to any enterprise which might suggest capitalism and there were many delays. To those grey, unimaginative minds which wielded power at minor government departmental level, what could be more exploitative than wanting to take such a large complement of Portuguese horses overseas to the United Kingdom? As there was no previous record with which to compare such a request (at that time there were only five Portuguese horses in England, one of which had been a gift from a past Portuguese president to Her Majesty the Queen) officials were at a loss to deal with our petition for permission to export.

In the end, it took over thirteen months to organise the paperwork for such an unusual undertaking. Health regulations were a nightmare but, nevertheless, after many false starts the deed was accomplished. Now, with the main difficulties behind us, there was everything to look forward to.

After the Portuguese sun, the reality of working horses in a cold indoor school was hard for my husband. He always thought the British rode to reflect their weather! Nevertheless, the horses adapted well and here we see stallions, mares and geldings working together under his eagle eye.

In July 1979 seven stallions, six mares and four geldings stepped neatly off the ramps of the two transporters which had collected them from Calais. After an eight-day train journey through the labyrinthine network of rail grids from southern Portugal through the central plains, over the mountain passes which link into and across Spain and finally up through the Pyrenees to France and all the way through to the Channel, with numerous hold ups, searches and long wasted days at hot border posts, the final phase into England was accomplished by road. With nothing more dramatic or overt than a few joyous whinnies and, remarkably, without a trace of stiffness or hesitation, seventeen horses from Lusitania entered their new stables in Suffolk. It was a moment of pure exultation, the stuff of which dreams are made.

Why is it that just as everything comes together, something else falls apart? Those first months in England were a great struggle, particularly as our house in Portugal had failed to sell and we required a massive loan to build our new stable yard and Olympic-size indoor school in Suffolk. An amazing benefactress came generously to our rescue, refusing to take interest because she believed in what we were doing, and it was kindness such as this which kept our spirits high. As friends and pupils rallied around and the courses slowly began to fill, there was only one thing missing. We needed recognition from the British Horse Society as no working pupils could be organised until we had been accepted into the training scheme. With our wonderful horses we had so much to offer young people and I felt confident we would be embraced with enthusiasm and swiftly put to use. We were all too ready and willing. Ironically, it was not to be as easy as that and our first application was refused.

In 1982, as President of the British Medical Association, Prince Charles, made this speech on the 150th anniversary of its foundation, to the delight of many and the bitter chagrin of others. At the time I thought how very appropriate it was to our own situation and how, indeed, it could have applied to the next three difficult years in Suffolk as we tried to run England's first full-sized academy of classical equitation on classical horses.

> I have often thought that one of the less attractive traits of various professional bodies and institutions is the deeply ingrained suspicion and outright hostility which can exist towards anything unorthodox or unconventional. I suppose it is inevitable that something which is different should arouse strong feelings on the part of the majority whose conventional wisdom is being challenged or, in a more social sense, whose way of life and customs are being insulted by something rather alien. I suppose too that human nature is such that we are frequently prevented from seeing that what is today's unorthodox is probably going to be tomorrow's convention. Perhaps we just have to accept that it is God's will that the unorthodox individual is doomed to years of frustration, ridicule and failure in order to act out his role in the scheme of things, until his day arrives and mankind is ready to receive his message, which he probably finds hard to explain himself, but which he knows comes from a far deeper source than conscious thought.

Sadly for my late husband, Henry Loch, there was to be no day arriving when he would find the establishment waiting to receive his message. The very year the Prince of Wales made that powerful and hugely provocative speech, my husband died of a massive and very sudden stroke. At the time I had no idea how I would carry on with his dream of bringing the classical horse and the classical ideals of riding to a somewhat entrenched British horse public, but I was glad that there had been golden interludes. Henry's efforts had seemed to be appreciated so much by certain people who really mattered that, for a time anyway, he had felt that his personal sacrifice of leaving the warm sunshine and peacefulness of Portugal behind was indeed worthwhile. He had never really wanted to leave the Algarve but, partly for me, partly for his pupils and partly for posterity, he had bowed to pressure. In his pursuit of the truth with his lovely light horses, he had touched the hearts and minds of many, among them some of the world's most promising riders and people who would influence dressage for many years to come. The dream he had nurtured deep down inside was not wasted.

Chapter 7

Finding the centre –
to sit or not to sit

It has long been recognised that to sit like glue over a jump is sound advice. Someone who certainly had this capability and used it to advantage was Lucinda Prior Palmer who had won three Badmintons in a row when we got to know her shortly before she changed her name to Green. Yet, despite her great talent and a string of international successes, she was the first person to admit she needed to reassess her position for dressage.

It was Lucinda's approbation and goodwill which restored Henry's spirits and faith in the project we had set ourselves with the move to England. He had first met her at a small dinner party given by Lord and Lady Clark at Rendlesham Park in Hampshire just prior to our return when he had flown over to supervise the building of our new yard. John and Olivia had been riding with us in Portugal and invited him down for a weekend primarily, I suspect, to meet Lucinda who had been having problems with a particularly talented but singularly difficult Thoroughbred horse she owned called Village Gossip.

Over coffee that evening, Lucinda confided to Henry that she had never felt any real love or enthusiasm for dressage and that, as far as she was concerned, she was not sure if she had ever felt or recognised true collection in any horse – too often it seemed forced and did not emanate from the horse himself. Olivia remarked that she had thought in similar vein until she sat on our Lusitano horses and for the first time discovered an engagement and lightness she had never dreamt possible. Lucinda became intrigued and, over a long chat, Henry convinced her that once she had experienced self-carriage over prolonged and repeated periods on horses capable of offering very collected gaits without resistance, it would give her a sensation she would never forget. She could then draw on this experience time and again for her future work. With her vast experience and understanding of balance across country, what she needed now was to develop a greater sense of feel to bring the horse's weight back and render him equally balanced and athletic in his flatwork. For this, she must sit on a schoolmaster horse and become more discerning through her seat.

The upshot of this chance, or not so chance, meeting was that, much to the delight of our working students who immediately adored her, Lucinda came to our new yard at Green Farm in Suffolk. Despite her numerous Badminton and Burghley successes, she was so friendly, self-deprecating and appreciative of everyone's efforts that our staff were soon eating out of her hand and nothing was too much trouble as they prepared horse after horse for her to ride. If she lifted the spirits of the students, she also lifted Henry's spirits. Every day, early in the morning and away from prying eyes, he lunged her on Xariel, a pure-bred Lusitano. Xairel was very proud and very light on the snaffle; at 16.1 h.h., with his great crested neck and strong, close-coupled conformation, he rode like a throne. He was so engaged he could lift into a *levade* at a moment's indication but the soft roundness of his back was deceptive for, as with most Lusitanos, you could feel every stride he took, so elevated and punctuated were his steps.

On the lunge, without stirrups and with just a blanket and *voltige* roller, Henry made Lucinda close her eyes so that she could concentrate and imagine Xariel's hind legs moving underneath her with such clarity that she could correctly call left, right or right, left, as the horse trotted round obediently and in perfect rhythm. Henry taught her literally to feel through the seat of her pants. As the muscles of the horse's back and loins rose and rounded to accommodate the upward thrust of the engaged hind leg, he urged: 'Feel the sideways movement as well as the forward. Feel how he lifts first your right seat bone up and forward, and then your left up and forward as he brings each hind leg under. Be careful to keep your seat open and your hips loose so you go with it! The horse will move you if you sit quiet and let it happen . . . never collapse or tilt at the waist and never try to make it happen by moving yourself. It is the horse who is doing the work, not you. Remember always to remain tall and proud in your upper body for this gives balance to the horse!' Then Lucinda's face would lighten as she reiterated time and again that she had never felt anything quite like it before.

'I feel now I can separate the hips,' she said. 'It's not just riding with the seat, it's knowing which hip is being moved and how to give and resist through the back at the critical moment so that the horse stays in balance.'

There were more sensations to think about off the lunge. After several intensive sessions of riding a variety of horses in collected trots, collected canters and the much maligned collected walk, Henry explained how riders must always be asking questions of themselves. For example: 'Can you feel how every little allowance you make changes the feeling of what the horse is doing? Where do you feel the weight and power of the horse? If it's not behind you, why isn't it? The horse can only be light on the hand and under you if your position is correct. Once you've discovered the centre of movement by centralising yourself, the horse is yours.'

When, for the first time, Lucinda experienced the floating feeling of an extravagant sustained *passage* as well as the upward thrust of the *piaffe*, both produced without force and with scarcely more than an easing of her weight she was elated. The lateral movements with which she was all too familiar took on new meaning and greater accuracy with this increased sense of feel. 'This is why I introduce the more advanced work even to the youngest working student,' explained Henry. 'If they don't feel the influence of the weight aids, how too much leg one way or sitting deeper into one seatbone may actually be indicating to the horse to move more sideways than forwards, their forward work will lack impulsion and their horse will never be straight. By an appreciation of the various movements, therefore, the basics are improved.'

Delighted and promising to be back, Lucinda left us to return to her busy world of eventing and writing with, as she described it, 'hundreds of new feelings under her belt'. Typically, she left a generous legacy; not only had she restored faith to my husband and me, whose application to have our yard recognised as an approved establishment had recently been turned down by the British Horse Society, creating shock waves among our students, but she wrote two glowing articles for *Riding Magazine* which changed our lives. Her approbation of our horses and our way of riding and training, particularly addressing the whole issue of feel and listening to the horse underneath, brought in a flood of bookings. For Lucinda this way of riding was obviously a breakthrough.

It still hurt, but mattered less now that we had been rejected by Stoneleigh for reasons which were never quite made clear. From then on the telephone never stopped ringing and, almost overnight, our diary was full to the end of the year. Moreover, the Association of British Riding Schools had welcomed us into their fold and had already booked us to host their next annual Open Day. Glenda Spooner and Ponies of Britain had also given their stamp of approval, ironic when we only had horses, but appreciated nevertheless. We were told by their inspectors that they had never seen such a clean, organised yard or such well-kept, fit or happy schoolhorses. Now able to start paying off our debts, thanks to people who believed in us, the dream was being kept alive. Lucinda had played a major part at a most critical time.

Why was it that in those days in Britain the relevance of the rider's seat was almost never mentioned in the average riding lesson? We had learned the hard way that any student going forth to sit their Assistant Instructor's examination must never mention the seat or they risked being failed. We understood, too, that it was partly because of placing so much importance on teaching the position and use of the seat, as well as the rudiments of collected work, to our training students that the British Horse Society Examinations Committee had taken exception to our establishment.

This may seem difficult to understand now, but one of the reasons why I wrote my book on the classical seat was because this was simply a taboo subject. Later, when a number of influential people alerted Dorian Williams, at that time Chairman of the British Horse Society, to our plight, approval of our school was finally granted with some embarrassment. Nevertheless, there was still the unspoken feeling within the educational body that we were considered alarmingly revolutionary. We taught 'the seat', our students rode movements, and we used stallions. Until now only fully fledged instructors were supposed to be acquainted with such matters.

We puzzled endlessly about these topics. If young Assistant Instructors were not expected to refer to or to discuss the rider's seat, how could they improve a pupil's position when taking a basic lesson? Here there seemed a definite contradiction in philosophy, for the verb 'to sit' was allowed! Remarks such as: 'It's just a question of learning to sit in the saddle!' or 'Sit down and push him on!' were commonplace in the most august establishments. Yet, to my mind, the verb 'to sit' could be far more misleading than the noun, what we sit upon.

This beggared other questions. Is the concept of sitting actually the correct one? And, in teaching, should we actually be encouraging riders to follow the movement like passengers? As for real novice riders, would it not be infinitely more helpful if instructors took the time and trouble to explain that the balance required on a horse has less to do with sitting and rather more to do with standing? Surely this is where the great deception of all time begins, promoted and perpetrated by almost every instructor across the land? The idea of 'sitting down' on a horse has to be one that is fundamentally ambiguous.

Again, it was the Ancient Greeks who were the first to recognise this. Xenophon wrote, 'I do not approve of a seat which is as though the man were on a chair.' Instead, he required that the rider be as balanced on horseback as if he were on the ground 'rather as though he were upright with his legs apart'. Sixteenth-, seventeenth- and eighteenth-century classical riding masters all over Europe tackled the same theme. The Duke of Newcastle was emphatic that the rider must not be tempted 'to sit upon

The classical masters placed much importance on the idea of advancing the rider's loins and consequently the stomach or waist towards the hands. This made it possible to retain the prescribed 'one hand's breadth' between the cantle and the seat.
(Engraving from *École de Cavalerie*)

the buttocks, though most people think that they are made by nature to do so'. The great French La Guérinière went on to define the act of sitting as 'centering yourself in the saddle with the waist and buttocks slightly advanced in order not to ride seated on the cantle'.

Having come to understand these matters through a fog of distracting and often incorrect advice over many years, it occurs to me that if recent generations had paid greater heed to past masters, we should by now perhaps have thought to change our riding terminology. While the noun 'the seat' may be acceptable, the verb 'to sit' is misleading and should long ago have been replaced with the verb 'to balance', 'to straddle' or simply 'to ride'. After all, we ride the train, we ride the underground, we ride the fairground roller coasters, dippers and shakers; in Switzerland, they ride the Cresta – the word 'ride' indicates immediately that a degree of proactive balance is required.

For too many, the idea of sitting indicates quite the reverse. Largely due to the modern lifestyle, to sit down may be interpreted as letting go, an abnegation of being responsible for one's own weight, no longer having actively to participate. Such an attitude can make life miserable for horses.

Historically, there is a vast difference between the type of chair used by people in active service and those designed for pure luxury. For example, the military or kitchen chair was very upright so a soldier or servant could spring easily to their feet. Conversely, some drawing room chairs seemed more like beds; from the word 'lounge' comes lounger, a chair in which to lounge. Some of these are impossible to get out of – the deck chair being a notable example. To this day, most 'easy' chairs are of the type designed to take weight off the feet so that one can collapse downward into a semi-recumbent posture. Even car and aeroplane seats verge towards this state, although in more recent times the damage wrought on people's backs by prolonged sitting in this way has been recognised and many manufacturers have tried to remedy the situation by creating more upright, correctly contoured chairs.

Nevertheless, to most people the very act of sitting still suggests a certain leaning back, taking it easy and a sense of repose. Why, of all the sports, is this allowed, even encouraged in riding? Does not riding require exacting muscle control, tone and application as much as in any other sporting pursuit? The fact that one is on a live, unpredictable and moving animal, with centrifugal force involved, should indicate to any thinking person that perhaps one might need more balance rather than less!

Imagine what would happen if we indicated to a skater, gymnast, skier or ballet dancer that they should relax and let go. Yet this is how so many teachers start their pupils off in the riding school. 'Just sit there and relax!' This is almost as irresponsible as saying, 'Throw away any idea of self-preservation and give yourself over to doing nothing!' Unfortunately, too many novice pupils are lured into doing exactly that. Only through trial and error do people quickly learn that to stay on board it is necessary actively to project forward to support the body upward but, sadly for the horse, old habits die hard. Once encouraged to be a sedentary passenger, generally at the back of the saddle and behind the movement, excessive movement with bottom or legs is generally futile and causes untold discomfort to the horse.

The initial concept must therefore be to teach the novice rider to balance on their horse so that they are master of their position in the most economic and efficient way possible. In the early lessons, the rider should be encouraged to concentrate on the feeling of the horse moving beneath the saddle and how best they may remain over that movement. A good instructor will walk side by side with their pupil around the arena perimeter, talking to them and making them aware of what is happening underneath them step by step. All riders respond to the soothing call of which hind leg is stepping underneath and exactly when. The instructor asks the rider to feel the right hind as it moves forward and under and momentarily pushes the horse's back upwards on the same side as it engages from the ground. Then, a second later, the opposite hind leg flexes forward to engage in the same sequence of events on the opposite side. Being talked calmly through these feelings focuses riders' attention away from themselves and into the horse; gradually, they will actually learn to anticipate each action and this will lead to greater confidence.

Once they understand what the horse is doing, riders are encouraged to become aware of their own seatbones; how, indeed, they are moved by the horse, projected forward in sympathy almost as though it was the rider who was walking or running. Indeed, the rider should feel that the horse's hind legs are mere extensions of their own legs, but the real truth is that their legs have very little to do except stretch down to meet the legs of the horse. At a later stage, the rider may learn to go more with the horse or to resist him, depending upon what they require at the time. This allowing or taking with the seat initiates the rider into thinking always about riding from back to front, with clear independence of the reins.

From day one it should be clearly pointed out that the horse relies upon us for his balance just as much as we rely on him. Too many riders do not understand that it is impossible for the horse to carry out even the most simple manoeuvres easily if we are seated in the wrong place. Once the rider can be made aware of certain truths – such as the fact that, in canter for example, the entire weight of horse and rider rests on only one delicate leg and, at times, the whole structure is in the air so that the minutest change of weight on our part can put the horse at risk – their whole attitude to position will change and they will start to think of the horse as well as of themselves. This is the fundamental issue which is so rarely addressed in the average riding lesson.

A secondary factor is also crucial. Everyone is aware that the seat is the foundation of good riding. What people seem to forget is that no rider can hope to control their horse effectively and easily unless that foundation is established in the optimum place for the horse. It is only when the rider has sufficient suppleness and balance to drop their weight down over the horse's centre of motion, which happens also to be the horse's strongest point, around the fourteenth vertebra, that the rider can hope to achieve that magical state when they unite their balance with that of the horse. As with a seesaw controlled by one person, the key is to find the centre. Only then is the rider over the source of movement and empowered to make those small changes which can affect the entire mechanism beneath them.

In riding, this can lead to remarkable improvements which will have a

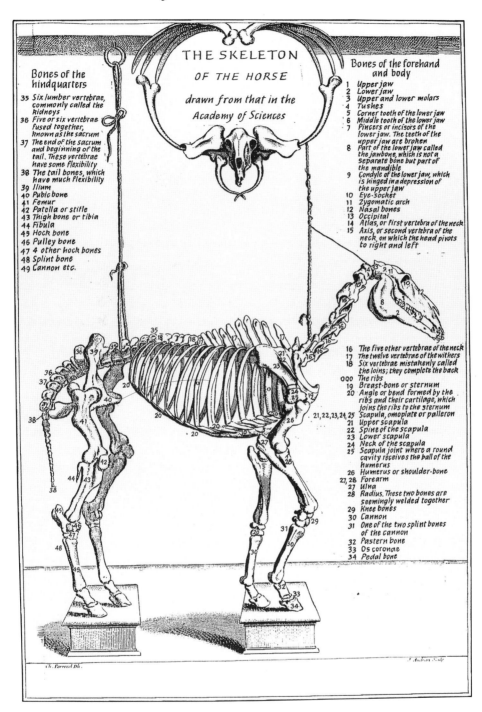

THE SKELETON
OF THE HORSE
drawn from that in the
Academy of Sciences

Bones of the hindquarters

35 *Six lumber vertebrae, commonly called the kidneys*
36 *Five or six vertebrae fused together, known as the sacrum*
37 *The end of the sacrum and beginning of the tail. These vertebrae have some flexibility*
38 *The tail bones, which have much flexibility*
39 *Ilium*
40 *Pubic bone*
41 *Femur*
42 *Patella or stifle*
43 *Thigh bone or tibia*
44 *Fibula*
45 *Hock bone*
46 *Pulley bone*
47 *4 other hock bones*
48 *Splint bone*
49 *Cannon etc.*

Bones of the forehand and body

1 *Upper jaw*
2 *Lower jaw*
3 *Upper and lower molars*
4 *Tushes*
5 *Corner tooth of the lower jaw*
6 *Middle tooth of the lower jaw*
7 *Pincers or incisors of the lower jaw. The teeth of the upper jaw are broken*
8 *Part of the lower jaw called the jawbone, which is not a separate bone but part of the mandible*
9 *Condyle of the lower jaw, which is hinged in a depression of the upper jaw*
10 *Eye-socket*
11 *Zygomatic arch*
12 *Nasal bones*
13 *Occipital*
14 *Atlas, or first vertebra of the neck*
15 *Axis, or second vertebra of the neck, on which the head pivots to right and left*
16 *The five other vertebrae of the neck*
17 *The twelve vertebrae of the withers*
18 *Six vertebrae mistakenly called the loins; they complete the back*
ooo *The ribs*
19 *Breast-bone or sternum*
20 *Angle or bend formed by the ribs and their cartilage, which joins the ribs to the sternum*
21,22,23,24, 25 *Scapula, omoplate or palleron*
21 *Upper scapula*
22 *Spine of the scapula*
23 *Lower scapula*
24 *Neck of the scapula*
25 *Scapula joint where a round cavity receives the ball of the humerus*
26 *Humerus or shoulder-bone*
27, 28 *Forearm*
27 *Ulna*
28 *Radius. These two bones are seemingly welded together*
29 *Knee bones*
30 *Cannon*
31 *One of the two splint bones of the cannon*
32 *Pastern bone*
33 *Os coronae*
34 *Pedal bone*

Academic and scientific horsemanship implied understanding the whole horse. It was therefore inconceivable to sit anywhere other than over the strongest point of the horse, i.e. where the ribs were at their longest and most supportive. How many of today's riding students are acquainted with the equine skeleton, as in this eighteenth-century engraving?

Another engraving from La Guérinière's book shows how these horsemen adapt to the horse's movement through a supple lower back. Bringing the shoulders back did not allow the seat to slip back to overburden the horse's loins, as is too often seen today. Riders had to maintain forward projection through the waist in all movements.

marked effect on the horse's continued soundness and happiness. Raising the wither and the shoulders or lightening the forehand involves bringing the weight a little back so that the horse bends the hocks underneath him and deepens the quarters. This action relieves the forelegs and helps the horse to move more athletically. This is never achieved through the hands, but, again, as with the seesaw, by weight changes effected through the rider's upper body which, in turn, affect the seat. That happy state where the horse is light in the front and engaged behind is the prize of the rider who knows how to direct from the centre at all times. Master of balance, by centring their own body, they become master of the horse without force and all with the utmost subtlety.

In the old days, therefore, the High School or combat seat was cultivated by remaining very upright with the shoulders moving slightly behind the vertical to retain the horse on his hocks for all the collected manoeuvres required in the *manège*. When times changed and the forward seat was adopted for hunting and racing and cross-country military exercise, the opposite was achieved. Leaning forward with the upper body allowed the horse to adopt a more horizontal outline on his forehand, thus giving him greater freedom to gallop, extend and stretch. Provided the rider's hips remained as close to the centre of the horse and over his strongest point at all times, whether above or into the saddle, these changes of balance for different effects worked efficiently and still do today and the horse's back was not damaged.

Where dressage and the dressage seat have become bastardised in recent times is when riders are pushing their horses on to the forehand and, in the same breath, asking them to attempt exercises which require collection. By sitting on the wrong part of the back, such riders actually prevent the horse from coming into balance, thus making these requests impossible to carry out with any degree of ease and accuracy. While anyone with a knowledge of anatomy or physics should see that demands made with the rider off-centre are doomed to failure, such is the ignorance concerning the rider's seat that invariably it is the horse which is blamed and punished when things are not as they should be.

Moreover, when riders are unaware of the importance of keeping the pelvis well forward in the saddle in order to remain as close as possible to the fourteenth vertebra – the crucial point of balance – it is virtually impossible to transfer the weight to the quarters. Driving with the seat while sitting too far back merely hollows the horse and strings him out. On any horse, dressage or otherwise, once the seat is allowed to drift towards the rear of the saddle, the horse will stiffen his loins and any attempt towards collection will be fraught with difficulty. 'Weight back' on the horse certainly does not imply sitting with the seat back – quite the reverse. Bringing the horse's weight back involves the rider's hips coming forward and the rider sitting in the centre of the saddle and collecting the horse's energy through refined aids of the legs, seat and hands. Only from the centre can the rider use the upper body to redirect the balance.

Whether in the gallop, canter, trot, walk, rein-back, piaffe or passage, therefore, the secret of manoeuvring any horse correctly is to sit as close as possible to the pommel where the horse is at his strongest but most tractile, and from whence, generally, the stirrups are slung. This was the seat recommended by the old and more recent masters[1] to ensure that the rider remained well clear of the cantle. This has always been one of the most important tenets of riding, yet it is too often neglected in the teaching of dressage today. From a correct central position, the intensity of the weight aids required to adjust the balance of the horse may, by consequence, become much more subtle and fine.

With the youngster who is not yet sufficiently muscled through the back to begin the process of engaging his hocks or transferring weight to the

---

[1] Newcastle, La Guérinère, Pembroke, Bourgelat, Marialva, Steinbrecht, Podhajsky, Handler, Seunig, Descarpentry, Wynmalen, etc. to name but a few.

Keeping the rider's weight central and over the horse's strongest point is recognised by all good jockeys, jumpers and event riders. The underlying principles of balance and weight are the same for classical dressage.

quarters, the rider should adopt a more forward seat by bringing their shoulders a little in front of the vertical. This will lighten the weight in the buttocks and concentrate or deepen it more over the centre of motion and into the thighs and knees, thus ensuring non-interference with the delicate dorsal muscles which, at this stage, should work in freedom. No horse can learn to round and swing through if his back is not sufficiently made up, and this simply cannot happen if the rider has not respected those tender parts under the saddle in the early stages of schooling. This will be discussed further in Chapter 9.

In the mature dressage horse, whose muscles and ligaments have been carefully strengthened by step-by-step athletic development through gymnastic exercise, the rider may later bring their shoulders a little behind the vertical in order to encourage more weight into the quarters and hocks by deepening the seatbones. Lightening the forehand in this way is something which requires thorough understanding, the key to its success being totally dependent upon the rider's ability to remain centred with the seat at all times.

Unfortunately, while the average rider can be taught to achieve the forward seat without too much difficulty, particularly by taking more weight into the stirrups, there are fewer by far who have sufficient gymnastic control of their own bodies to maintain the deep-seated dressage seat. For the rider to bring the shoulders *behind the vertical* without dragging the pelvis back with them requires flexion and *bending from the*

All too many riders impair the movement of the horse by leaning back from an untoned body and forcing the movement against the weakest part of the horse's back.

lower back muscles[2] if the hip joint is to remain forward, vertical and over the horse's strongest point. Too often riders drive with the seatbones by using the cantle as a launch pad for their own flawed exertions. Not only is this bad for their own backs, it is grossly unpleasant even for a mature horse.

Out of respect for the horse's back, therefore, institutions such as the Spanish Riding School of Vienna may allot up to two years' intensive training on the lunge to develop a rider's pliability through the back so that they may not only master the sitting trot but also remain central and upright in the canter and the higher airs without bruising the vulnerable equine loins. One of the greatest exponents of 'bringing the horse's weight back' is Arthur Kottas, the youngest-ever head rider at Vienna, who has addressed this subject at several lecture demonstrations given for the Training the Teachers of Tomorrow Trust of Great Britain. No one could sit more still or more central than he. Unfortunately, civilian riders rarely have the opportunity to work their own bodies in the ways of the ex-cavalry schools and there are remarkably few riding schools in the world where sufficient time and care are spent on the lunge to prepare pupils to understand and develop a good but discerning seat.

In equestrian circles, the term 'seat' is generally understood to encompass the whole position in the saddle; specifically used, it indicates that part of

---

[2] See also Chapter 8.

Improving the rider's tone and feel for the correct position is an essential part of the first two years' training at the Spanish Riding School, Vienna.
(Photo: courtesy Anglo-Austrian Society, London)

the pelvis which makes contact when we sit down. Depending upon what we are sitting on and how our legs and upper body are positioned, the feeling of contact we receive through the seat will vary enormously. For example, when we sit in the driving seat of a car with our legs stretched out in front of us, we will only be aware of the back of the seatbones. If we get on a horse bareback, however, we may find ourselves sitting only on the crotch which can be very uncomfortable unless we pull our legs up and ease our pelvis backward. In a comfortable dressage or Western saddle which positions the pelvis into a fairly neutral position of uprightness, with the legs hanging more or less directly underneath, we discover all the seatbones, front and back. The sensation is that we are sitting on what feels like the whole pelvic floor.

To bring about a change in balance, it is then just a matter of easing the weight either a little forward or a little back at will, depending upon what we require of our horse. Thus, by being centred, there is a sensation of much greater control. The most important factor about this way of riding is that the rider can remain upright as though standing on the ground. They support their own weight by remaining over their feet, and they are plumb with gravity. Thus contained, the horse finds it very much easier to carry the rider.

When the pelvis is upright, as in standing or walking, the whole upper body can be supported vertically above it without strain or stress. The head and neck can become balanced and the rider is obviously in a more commanding position. From the horse's point of view this has to be the kindest position, short of getting off his back. The logic is simple to anyone who has ever balanced a pole on their hand or watched strong men toss a mighty caber at the Highland Games. Whether carrying a light or heavy object, there is only one way to carry it easily – it has to be balanced vertically – end of argument!

Despite all this, there are still many teachers who encourage the chair seat. With the rider's pelvis behind the vertical, it is virtually impossible to influence the horse through subtle weight changes, and he will be deterred from ever working through the back. Because the upright position has a more military, purposeful bearing, it is often wrongly described by unknowledgeable people as 'stiff'. Sloppiness and looseness may be the fashion in speech and clothes nowadays but it does not help the horse. If you asked him, he would beg for discipline and good posture at all times.

Even if we depart from anatomical arguments, the whole basis of engineering is worked around similar principles to those of the classical posture. Think of the Leaning Tower of Pisa. Any misalignment in structure not only creates stresses but, ultimately, threatens breakdown by bringing pressure to bear at the weakest point. Sadly for the horse, he too often has to bear the rider's weight at his weakest point but, unlike the Florentine architects, no one seems to notice until it is too late.

One of the mottoes from the Spanish Riding School is: 'Down the weight; upright the body!' An old book that makes the same point is Colonel J. G. Peters's *Treatise on Equitation*. Even in 1835 classical trainers complained about the lack of clear instruction in England: 'There is scarcely a nation existing in which, for the high *manège*, the education of both young horsemen and young horses has been less attended to, thought of, or studied.' Concerning the preparation of the rider for active service, this revered instructor is unequivocal that it is a waste of time expecting anything from the recruit until he can:

> ride his horse with firmness, kindly and steadily, and that he should try to obtain a good, free and firm seat on horseback; that the balance of his body should rest in the very centre of the saddle; neither hanging over upon his fork or twist, nor to sit back on his breech or seat, but rest on these three points at once, in the centre of the saddle. And whenever he has lost that point of seat, he must regain it, before he attempts to do anything else.

Unfortunately, due to tension or, as already discussed, the association of ideas that surround the act of sitting, in particular that of collapsing the

Colonel Podhajsky, former director of the Spanish Riding School of Vienna, displays the classic, all-embracing seat, illustrating the idea of 'down the weight, upright the body'!

upper body, many riders end up balancing almost on the back of the sacrum or tail which throws the entire upper body off balance and out of sync. Apart from placing the rider behind the movement of the horse, it can also create unnatural stiffening in the rider's back, caused by a loss of tone. Generally, such an imbalance results in the head and neck being poked forward, the axis axle joints bearing much of the shock and strain. While the resultant nodding chin is still a familiar sight in some dressage arenas, far more worrying than this unaesthetic appearance is the fact that the rider's spine will be greatly stressed, leading to possible damage in years to come.

Another factor which is detrimental to both the human and equine back is a seat which continuously wriggles, pushes and shoves at the horse in every stride. Such action merely upsets the horse's balance and may cause great damage in due course. All the great masters, past and present, agree it is the firm, quiet, central seat which helps the horse to come into perfect balance. La Guérinère, the father of classical dressage, wrote that there were two mobile parts of the body and one which should remain still and immobile. 'The mobile parts are the body from head to waist, and the legs from the knees to the feet, *the immobile part extends from the waist to the knees*' (my italics) – indicating the seat.

Of course, a good seat must know when and where to ease and alter its emphasis to achieve a particular change, but it should not consciously move in every stride, only on the odd occasions when it is required really to push – used only as a chiding aid when the horse is reluctant to go forward at a jump or past a spooking point; this should be short-lived. Used all the time a thrusting, pushing seat will not only stiffen the horse's back but cause him to switch off, the horse's only defence against pain. Those instructors who teach their pupils to push, push and push again are not only going against nature, but will encourage the very opposite result of forward locomotion. Try pushing to and fro with your pelvis when you walk or run and discover how unnatural, uncomfortable and futile it is.

We have talked at some length about the necessity to observe the horse in nature in order to understand how he moves unencumbered and liberated. Something which is all too often overlooked is the fact that riders also need to assess and observe human locomotion before they try to achieve something in the saddle. Thus what is natural for us on the ground when we move forwards, backwards, turn to the right and so on, should also be natural on horseback. The same forces that enable us to maintain forward impulsion in our own movement should govern us in the saddle too. If it is our legs which actually carry out the action of forward movement, we should remember that our source of energy is centred somewhere around our midriff, so, as the thought enters our brain, motion is instigated from this point. It is important, therefore, to be in harmony with our bodies by projecting and pointing that part of the body in the required direction and allowing the driving force to come through. This has nothing to do with pushing and shoving, and there must be no pulling back; instead, there should be just a continuous forward projection as though being drawn forward by a string from the waist.

To know how to halt a horse should, again, be as instinctive as though on the ground. If we set our centre against ourselves – as though being pulled up short – we automatically block the continuous flow of energy so the impulsion is cut off. The feeling is no different from what we do unconsciously when we suddenly pull up, say, to cross a road. We block! We stop! Motion is arrested. If riders were made to walk every movement – think forward, think halt, think sideways, think back – before they asked the same of their horses, a much improved way of riding would emerge.

What originally so inspired me about the Iberian riders of Portugal and Spain was their superb posture. How composed, contained and quiet they seemed in the saddle. I had never seen riders more elegant and erect, yet, of course, when one analysed it, one swiftly recognised that they also

Riding, like dance, should be about projecting the inner you. (Painting by Johann Heinrich Tischbein)

maintained exactly the same posture on the ground and that the two aspects went hand in hand. If they rode with their shoulders open and back, of course, they walked with their shoulders open and back and so, in both cases, their spines were properly aligned. If they rode with a supple lower back, it was obvious that they danced in the same way; this allowed them to be flexible in the hips yet supported and proud in the upper body – particularly noticeable in flamenco dancing. If they opened their chests and lifted their diaphragms in equitation, this was also noticeable when they paraded in the plazas and streets in similar style with their wives or children on high days and holidays. In short, everything they did on horseback was because they did it on the ground naturally – they were, indeed, a proud people.

The same principle works in reverse. Unfortunately, there is little hope for riders to gain a good position in the saddle if they have consistently bad posture on the ground. British and American youth is notorious for slouching, and this has to be addressed at source if it is to be corrected in the saddle. In classical riding what is needed above all to help bring horse and rider into balance is the requirement to let go with the legs and to tone up, stretch, sit tall and expand the upper body. Charles de Kunffy tells his students to make their collarbones horizontal, Nuno Oliveira always spoke of 'an inflated torso', I demand that my riders keep their fronts in *front* of them and imagery such as this not only encourages better posture for horse and rider, but promotes better breathing and better concentration. Remember, too, that the ribcage is designed to expand and absorb movement, a good dressage rider will show plenty of breathing action through the front of the body, particularly in the sitting trot, which is correct. The part which is not designed to take the stress of all this movement is the shoulders and neck, yet think of all those nodding skulls one sees in the dressage arenas of the world!

Even for those who have ridden all their lives and who naturally carry themselves properly and erect, I would, ideally, want to give them at least two unmounted lessons or workshops prior to allowing any one of them to ride my horses. These lessons could be reinforced and enlarged at, say, quarterly intervals as the rider progresses in knowledge and experience. The first session would require that the rider actually thinks about the principles of gravity and how their weight affects the balance of whatever they straddle, whether a living creature or even an inanimate object. A seesaw straddled at the centre is not a bad training aid and, of course, there is far less unsettling movement at the centre than anywhere else which is the same as on horseback. The horse's anatomy would then be studied so that it can be fully appreciated where the ribs are at their longest and where the horse is best conformed to carry weight.

Comparisons should be drawn between the riding position and the standing position, the student always aiming to be balanced over their feet in both cases. Hands-on help will be required to show pupils how to position their pelvis vertically while the knees bend and, even as they lower their centre of gravity, to think tall. Because of imbalances in the way people move on the ground, such as collapsing a shoulder or one side of the waist very slightly, they may not be symmetrical. By touching keypoints in the small of the back, the hands-on teacher can demonstrate how each hip bone can be supported and directed further forward by proactively supporting the loin muscle on that particular side. It can also be shown how rounding the back causes the hip bones to slide back, causing crookedness in the whole pelvic region.

The second lesson would focus on the idea of centring the body in all movement and making it strong through passive resistance. For example, on the ground the student can be shown how to maintain a firm position by stretching tall but at the same time advancing their stomach forward and allowing their weight to drop down through the front of the thigh so that they feel very set over their own two feet. Using the joints of the arms and legs correctly, they can learn how to make themself so contained in this position that virtually no outside interference can dislodge them. Similar to the techniques used for blocking attacks in karate, this is a particularly valuable exercise for showing riders how a centred position allows them to deal with a pulling horse. On the trained horse, it allows them to ride with a lighter contact, particularly during half-halts, downward transitions and general collection. It is virtually impossible for a horse to pull against the rider who has mastered their own balance in this way.

By helping riders to become more acutely aware of the horse's skeleton and muscle system and how a basic knowledge of physics and locomotion empowers them, they will have learned the most important lesson of all before they ever mount the horse. Posture becomes everything once the rider understands that every component part of the body has a part to play in developing the whole. Once we understand how everything is connected to everything else, we become more aware of the circuit of energy within our body as well as that of the horse. We hear a great deal these days about a connected horse, but there can be no completeness, no merging of horse and rider, if we ourselves are not connected. The discipline must start with us.

CHAPTER 8

Cresting the wave – and when hollow means straight

For most people, the thought of life without movement would be inconceivable. We are built to move! Nevertheless, too many riders experience back pain not because they have fallen off, but because they have not learned to cope with movement.

Contrary to common belief, problems with the spine are more often caused by lack of movement rather than excess movement, although certain sports are known to be back-unfriendly, such as rugby and parachute jumping. Nevertheless, more problems are caused by too much sitting than from too much exercise. Riding is excellent provided we do it properly and do not turn it into yet another sedentary pastime.

Classical riding, where the posture complements the upright skeleton of the standing, walking, skipping, jogging figure, has, logically, to be more conducive to the maintenance of a strong, healthy back than a form of riding which scrunches the vertebrae together. Whenever we ride, we should aim to utilise nature's way of diffusing shock; this means absorbing movement through the ankle, knee, hip, elbow, and shoulder joints to name but a few. For these to operate from a balanced body, it is important to ride in such a way that we stretch and open the spine rather than compress it. Apart from improving breath control, this also allows the internal organs to be kept mobile and to operate more naturally.

It has long been recognised that the brain is energised through movement. Movement stimulates the flow of blood and oxygen to the head and, indeed, to every other part of the body and there is less risk of stagnation and even some dehydration which may take place if we spend too long in sedentary mode. Even the more aesthetic aspects of our lives depend on, and involve, movement. Music, which reflects motion and makes us want to dance, poetry with rhythm, art which swirls with movement, and photography which captures it, all mentally stimulate the senses.

A confident child sitting bareback probably shows the most natural seat possible. Here, without prompting, my daughter's weight is over the strongest part of the horse, while her back assumes its normal posture and the legs hang loose.

It has often amazed me how, when riding, one's mental faculties became so involved with the subject in hand, which requires focusing into movement, that all else is cast aside from the mind and one's worries are left far behind. In dressage, one is listening to and feeling for the movement of the horse to such a degree that one knows exactly at which moment the inside hind hoof, for example, touches the ground. This awareness of movement in one's partner leads to an appreciation of body rhythms, the marrying of balance of two moving partners, uniting motion so that the two may ebb and flow as one. In dressage to music this has the added dimension of sound harmonising and blending the whole spectrum.

There is much to compare in dancing and riding. Both involve balance, precision and the ability to project movement forward, sideways, around, backward, turning and moving upward at will. As a ballet teacher said at the end of a BBC2 theatre workshop: 'Dance is about projecting the inner you. It has to come from within. No one can make you dance, you have to open yourself, reach down deep inside and find the power and the desire from within.'

128

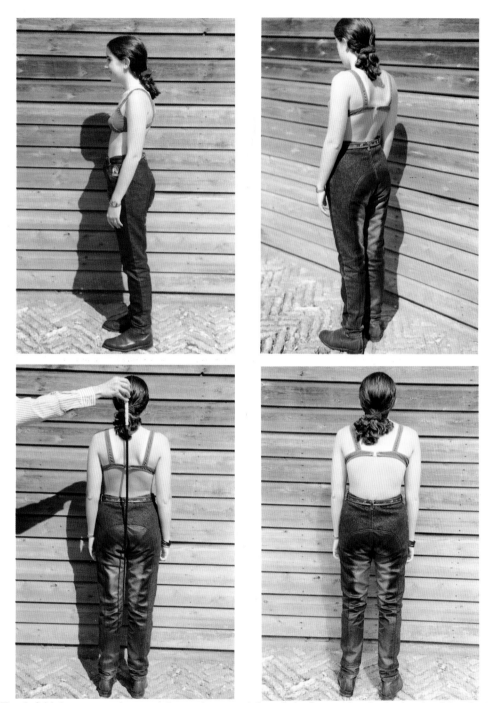

Top left/right: a natural stance demands an upright pelvis, feet under the body, shoulders back but not stiff, waist supported forward and spine showing correct contours. Bottom left: a stick shows the different planes of the back where the spine naturally departs from the vertical. Bottom right: rounded shoulders and a collapsed waist results in an artifically 'straightened' lumbar line.

When we are young, many of us tend to take movement for granted, forgetting our own fragility and not always appreciating the beautiful engineering of our bodies on which we place so many demands. It is only as we grow older, perhaps, that the odd tweak here or there reminds us to treat our spine with greater respect.

In riding, we are always hearing the words 'straighten the spine' but to do this correctly the back must maintain its natural contours. Indeed, stretching up and sitting tall increases the definition of our shape, so that the lower back may look slightly hollowed, the bottom more emphasised. There is nothing wrong in this and everything good when the front of the body is open and expansive, giving support to the whole.

In her excellent book, *Back in Action*[1], Sarah Key explains the mainstay of the human back. She likens the spine to a ship's mast which requires support from stays which 'are the balanced strength of the tummy muscles at the sides and front and the back muscles behind. Laxity in one of the stays will result in the mast either bowing forwards in the case of a slack front (weak tummy muscles) and an over-tight back stay (back muscles), or the mast bowing backwards if the front stay is too tight and the back stay is too long. The same happens if the back (stay) muscles are too weak.'

It is the important support of the abdominal muscles which is so often neglected in the teaching of riding and, yet, strengthening these will be the first thing the back sufferer will be told to work on by their medical practitioner. As with any other muscles, if the abdominals are not toned and made use of, they will become flabby and weak. In addition to making life uncomfortable for the horse, floppiness through the waist allows stresses to take place in the spinal column, which will ultimately damage the ligaments, facet joints or discs. As the latter could be described as tiny cushions lying between the vertebrae and protecting us in all movement, loss of fluidity and elasticity in the discs can be very damaging and painful. In riding we need rather more support than in standing or walking as, in addition to balancing over forward thrust, our back also has to absorb upward thrust.

This makes it even more important for us to think of stretching up when we ride as the very act of sitting tends to compress the upright stacking arrangement of the human spine and makes it hard for the discs to do their job. Sitting and pushing with the hips at the same time is even more detrimental as it tends to flatten the lumbar spine by curling it under, thus depriving the back of those natural contours which allow it to absorb movement.

[1] Published by Century, London, 1991.

130

When I start new riders off in my school, however experienced they may be, I generally have to teach them to sit more quietly in order that they may stretch up through the abdomen and give the necessary support and stability to their backs. This changes the whole appearance from one of laxity and a rag doll look, to that of a positive, assertive but allowing seat. Most riders who are new to this way of riding benefit from being talked through such a posture: 'Sit still, sit tall, and ask the horse to go forward from your leg while allowing that energy to be carried under and through you. Now amplify that movement by projecting your centre of balance. Don't push, don't pull against it, just remain supported over it and let it happen!'

Often, at this stage, it requires a hand on the rider's lower back to encourage them to understand what is meant. Riders are so used to collapsing the waist, flattening the spine and rocking on the tail to stay in balance, that they find the hardest thing of all is to do so little! 'Let your legs do the asking,' I say. 'Keep your upper body above the movement.' Generally, I then have to add, 'Imagine my hand is keeping you over the crest of the wave, matching your centre of energy to that of the horse. What you must never do is allow yourself to drop behind it. Riding is a continuous process where you become proactive with the movement. Don't follow the movement, stay *over it* – as it peaks.'

Initially, if I take my hand away, I see the rider's back and tummy muscles slacken again, while the back and shoulders begin to round. Everything starts to move and in no time at all the rider is behind the movement again, although they may think they are going 'with' it. The moment I place my hand in the small of the back again, however, and say 'Project!' the rider feels the difference, takes heart and discovers a far greater balance by sitting still.

It is a simple lesson but one which few riders will forget if they are humble enough to throw away all the old, preconceived ideas of pushing at the horse with the seat. Staying with the movement does not require more movement, but rather less. In addition, the horse is much more able to concentrate on the forward aids of the leg once the seat is quiet.

One of the difficulties of staying upright in the saddle in motion is not to allow ourselves to be thrown off-centre, generally outwards on a circle by centrifugal force or backwards by acceleration. It is all very well telling pupils not to grip but once the horse is in motion the temptation can be strong. It is the action of the calves and knees gripping upward which throws the hips back so the upper body moves out of kilter. Once the 'mast' loses its verticality, true balance is lost.

Only by developing a *full* contact of the seat can the rider hope to remain

A proud erect carriage with the breast bone advanced not only helps the horse to retain
balance but gives the rider the feeling of being at one with his mount.
(Engraving from *École de Cavalerie*)

over the horse's strongest point at speed. However, before this concept can be appreciated, it is important to point out that no amount of good intentions will help unless the rider has learned to counter balance centrifugal force by projecting their own centre of gravity forward, commensurate with the horse's forward impulsion. This is what Oliveira meant by 'taking the horse by the waist'. Indeed this centring action is required in any sport which requires a marrying of balance and movement.

To go with the movement without losing uprightness, the rider must learn to 'bend' or give in the loins. La Guérinière wrote: 'having thus laid the foundation for his seat . . . he [the rider] must obtain and try to continue the balance, carrying his body erect, upwards and square to the front – bend the small of the back a little forward, the shoulders equally square and back; the breast forward'.

This bending inwards or yielding through the back was what other authors of the time described as maintaining a 'little hollow' at the loins (namely, Berenger, Marialva, Pembroke, Peters, etc.) but the impression of concavity in the spine itself is actually somewhat of an illusion. While the lumbar muscles certainly deepen into the body line, the result of this pushing forward to support the upper body should reduce a tendency in some riders to misalign the spine. Indeed, the backbone will be 'smoothed out' at its innermost point. Thus what gives the appearance of hollowing merely shows the correct decontraction of a supported lower back placed further forward and stretched upward by the relevant loin muscles.

Stiff or slack loins have always been the enemy of good riding which is why it is helpful for many riders to be lunged with a stick between the elbows to teach them to bend and support the back inwards in this way. On the other hand, contracted loin muscles, where the back is rigidly over-arched (as in a baby throwing a tantrum) can lead to locked loins.

Indeed, it is this support of the lower back which gives all great balancers that look of pure concentrated control, whether it is a ballerina stretching up on her points in a whirling pirouette, a gymnast moving on the bar, or an acrobat turning cartwheels. Dressage riders, too, if they are to remain centrally balanced, must develop the same stretch and control in motion if they are to resist the forces which threaten to fling them off-course.

Backs which have slackened or flattened in the lower lumbar regions are generally caused by stiff unyielding loin muscles. Due to a lack of tone, these backs may appear straighter but there is all the difference in the world between an athletic, contoured back and what Sarah Key describes in her

The rider who has adapted to the movement of the horse should look quiet, poised and tall, as though the horse pivots around him, never the other way round. The only visible sign of movement will be that of the horse. The rider, supremely centred, is light to carry but as still as a statue.

(Photo: courtesy Dr Borba and Arsenio Raposo Cordeiro)

book as 'the too straight back'. This will be as problematic in its way as the overhollowed back.

Only through a controlled but flexible lower back can we fully absorb thrust to remain over that illusive cresting wave. As the spine is supported forward, it takes the rider's solar plexus forward with it, and the rider will never again feel left behind the movement. The articulations of the lower back and the strong padding of muscles which line either side of the spine give us the means to go with or resist the forces which the moving horses throws back at us.

Nevertheless, the lower back will find it hard to yield or to resist if the pelvis is not fully supported from underneath. Saddles which fix the rider behind the vertical and on to the back of the seatbones flatten out those very areas which are designed by nature to diffuse stress. Only by sitting tall with the seat supported under the fork as well as by the buttocks will the spine come into its natural alignment of 'three gently curving arches'. As Sarah Key points out these are 'perfectly designed to disperse the body weight in a balanced and effortless way'.

This idea of the whole seat in contact continues to create controversy, despite the fact that the term 'three-point seat' has been around for at least two centuries. I do know, however, that unless you have felt it, it cannot be imagined. Important as it is, let me divert the reader's attention for a moment to another scenario far removed from riding. No one taught me a full seat contact, neither had I read any books on the subject but, happily, I found it for myself. It may surprise readers to learn that I came to my conclusions and this discovery through dance. In addition to riding, it is also quite impossible to dance well unless we develop suppleness in the loins.

I had always enjoyed dancing. It started with Scottish country dancing as a child and wild Highland reels at teenage parties and hunt balls before I left home at 21. Later, like all young people, I began to enjoy disco dancing, especially when working with Juliana's of London in England and Portugal. The more I tried to improve the more I noticed that the people who danced best kept their upper bodies very supported and surprisingly still and erect, particularly in the shoulder area, but this firmness seemed to make them even looser in the hips. This led to tremendous scope with the legs which then seemed capable of endless movement. Gradually, over the years, it dawned on me that the secret of rhythmical but controlled movement was a flexible but supported lower back.

The same suppleness was required for gymnastics and one of the exercises I still enjoy doing, even after all these years, is handstands. The balance is much the same as in riding – dead upright, stretching through the ribcage, with a supported tummy and, above all, the ability to bend in the loins. You simply can't get up into the vertical on your hands, let alone stay there, unless you can bend and fix that back!

This suggested to me that to remain vertical, centred and in perfect balance over a horse, the principles were the same. So why had no one ever told me that during a riding lesson and was this something new and revolutionary?

Other bells began to ring. In my sixth form at school in Edinburgh, while swotting for A Levels, a small group of us had taken up fencing. I remember we all fell half in love with the superbly athletic and romantic-looking fencing master, Mr Feathers. It wasn't so much that he was handsome, but he had tremendous poise and inner confidence and I can still see him encouraging us to arch our backs inwards as we lined up in a long row to practise our parries. Although years younger than he, not one of us could equal him for suppleness and, as he struck an attitude of defence, I can picture him now, light on his feet, in command, totally prepared for the attack. The image of my birthsign flashed through my mind – the archer! It was all to do with a powerful centred stance from a strong, arched back.

The next time I was struck by someone in such elegant yet powerful control of their body was years later in a video my daughter was watching. By this time I was teaching the use of the back and of the seat with the confidence of knowing that none of this was revolutionary even if it was not always understood. Nevertheless, it is always fascinating to find the same principles being put into effect in a totally different context. Initially rather put off by the film title, *Dirty Dancing* – there is actually nothing smutty about it – I watched fascinated as a love story unfolded between a young girl and her handsome dancing coach at a holiday camp. Although the subject was disco dancing, the teacher, played by Patrick Swayze, was as disciplined in his approach as a good ballet teacher. His snakelike ability to move his hips, turn the body and defy gravity with his fantastic and outrageous movements all came from an absolute solidity and control from within which reminded me of teaching people the classical seat.

However, the film went further by far than just showing this athletic cool young man throwing his legs about; it was about real control, as he strictly made clear to his young pupil. What struck me first was the shoulder, elbow and arm position, all contained in the body line – again, classical seat! Any sign of floppiness in these areas or in the head and neck was quickly pointed out as a weakness. The message was clear. To dance well, you must initially set yourself as in concrete, only from a supported fixed position can co-ordination flow.

The words 'you've got to make a frame' struck such a chord with me that, later, I played and replayed that part of the video time and again. Next, I showed it to my riding pupils and once they too began to see the similarities – the foundation and solidity of the upright pelvis, the centring of the navel, the squared shoulders, the projection forward of the lower back, the *powerhouse* of movement and, finally, the arm and head position – I told them to get the video and watch it again. Every movement, every gesture, every position drew absolute parallels with classical riding – only from a deep understanding of posture could balance be achieved and maintained.

What was more remarkable was that, long after writing the first draft of this book, I learned that Patrick Swayze is a rider as well as a dancer and that he is also fascinated by the arts of combat. No wonder he looked so graceful. Everything has a connection.

Staying centred over movement from a projected solar plexus in this way is therefore a concept which has been handed down over many centuries from pugilism and the martial arts. The strength of the body comes from being able to diffuse shock, movement or a blow, by deflecting it from a centred stance. The body takes up a position where every joint of the human frame is at its most flexible – this involves all the relevant joints coming into perfect alignment. The fighting stance is astonishingly akin to the classical riding position. With legs apart and bent, and the body semi-fixed from toned dorsal muscles and a lowered solar plexus, the joints absorb any sudden onslaught to balance. The opposite effect to this position of strength is collapsing in on oneself, a reaction of submission, the proverbial foetal crouch.

Four or five years ago, when Paul Belasik came to stay, we had several long discussions on the subject. I had just read his book *Riding Towards the Light* and found in him someone else who had travelled a long way to find the truth. Paul is fascinated by the writings of Jung as well as a number of oriental religious authors. Some of these cultures are intertwined with ancient traditions of philosophy which lead on to meditation and an inner awareness of human capabilities both in the physical and metaphysical sense. As a committed Christian, the mystical aspects of Eastern religions do not inspire me, but the exercises for posture, breathing and inner awareness are wonderful. I too believe that all things are possible if we deeply believe in them and our motives are right. Prayer will not work if we are selfish about our demands; it has to be for the common good. Working with the Creator's laws has led to my being much more aware of the wonders of life that are all around us.

This has led me to become an unashamed observer and I am fascinated by all movement, particularly in dance. Whether this is classical ballet, gymnastics, tribal dance, flamenco, jive, ballroom dancing or the latest craze to hit stage or screen, the *Riverdance* from Ireland, matters not. There is a correlation in all and I love to watch it, drawing many parallels with riding dressage.

Watching the way children move when running a race or playing on the beach is very interesting. Closer to nature, one swiftly appreciates that a child's uncluttered mind allows an unconscious use of the body which complements both the martial arts and riding. I note how the young ones in particular always carry their tummies in front of them with their shoulders set easily back and their arms unconstricted and bent at their sides, yet no

A beautiful position is displayed by this teenage rider, Jodie Crisp, showing the correct contours of the back, soft, adhesive legs and quiet hands which allow the horse to move impulsively under her and come into balance. (Photo: T. Burlace)

one ever taught them to do this. Most seem to display a pronounced lordosis of the lower back, far greater than that of the average adult, and as their centre of balance is closer to the ground, they take to activities such as judo, skiing, skating and gymnastics with the greatest of ease.

It is also significant that when one places a young child on a stationary horse for the first time and says nothing about taking up stirrups or reins or what they should or should not be doing, nine times out of ten they will adopt perfect posture, about as close to the best classical seat as one can hope to see with the legs stretching away to drape the horse. I find all this unremarkable because nature is no fool and it is only we older ones who tend to abuse our bodies as we become lazier and less fit. There should never really be an excuse for not maintaining good posture at any age.

To prove my point that there is nothing unnatural about the classical seat and that our God-given posture should complement it, I illustrated a magazine article I had written with a photograph of a very normal child of eight years old to model the perfect standing position – shoulders back, open chest and tummy, bottom neither tucked in nor pushed out – in short, everything vertical. To my mind this showed a perfect alignment of the child's back. In semi-silhouette, the contours were clearly shown and a direct line could be drawn vertically downward from the highest point of her head, through her ear, point of shoulder and hip to ankle, signifying that

When asked to flatten the back, the same rider is surprised to find that her pelvis
slips to the back of the saddle and she no longer feels over her horse's centre
of movement. Unfortunately, this position is too often taught as being the 'correct' one.
Correct for whom? Not the horse, by the looks of him!

(Photo: T. Burlace)

the flow of gravity was running absolutely plumb through the middle.

This was followed by a picture of the same child riding, and others with her two elder sisters. I started both of the latter off in the classical seat by working one to one with them every week over a period of two years. On occasion, I instructed them on one of my advanced Lusitano schoolmasters. One is now in the Junior British Dressage[2] squad, while the youngest sister is now in the British Pony Club team. The emphasis in all the pictures used was on the requirement for the rider to maintain the same line of gravity through the body whether sitting on a horse or standing on the ground.

In response to what I perceived as a non-controversial article, I received an extraordinary tirade of condemnation from a reader insisting that to show such pictures was irresponsible. Indeed, it implied that the youngest, standing child was in some way deformed! I might add that the proud parent would not have been amused had I shown her the letter, particularly as her daughter was pretty, petite and beautifully straight both on and off her pony.

The main objection from the writer of the letter was that, in his opinion,

---

[2] Nikki Crisp was a pupil of mine with her pony Grindles Baronet; later I found her a second string horse, Chiddock Wordsworth.

the spine should have no gentle curves, and that anyone who rode in the way illustrated would end up in a wheelchair. It worried me that my correspondent had recently become a student of the Alexander Technique which I have always recommended to my pupils. It seemed he had confused the straightening of the spine with flattening the back.

Over the years I have been dismayed at just how ignorant people can be about their own bodies. Many have no conception of what a healthy spine should look like. Some believe it to be similar in shape to a walking stick and are surprised when I show them pictures of the skeleton. All this goes to show how dangerous a little knowledge can be and how, in the teaching of riding especially, ignorance can lead to distorted ideas.

It came to me then that, to the uneducated eye, a supported flexible lower back may look more hollow or concave because the rest of the body is contoured in reverse, i.e. the shoulders, upper back and hips are all sculpted outwards in various degrees of convexity. These natural contours are obvious in any tailor's dummy. It must further be recognised that the spine enters the waist or the lower lumbar region on an entirely different vertical plane from where it outlines the shoulders or hips. At its innermost point, therefore, the spine can only be 'straightened' and correctly supported when the shoulders are squared, the ribcage is open, the abdomen is stretched upward and the lower back itself appears to have a slight hollow or lordosis.

Disheartened by stories from pupils who told me their previous instructors had tried to flatten their backs, I discussed all this with a well-known consultant surgeon, Michael McBrien, working in East Anglia. He confirmed that I was perfectly correct to insist that riders allow the natural hollowing at the waist to take place and that, far from being detrimental to the rider's back, such a posture was perfectly correct. He then surprised me by explaining that when a surgeon operates on the kidneys (which we all know to be in the loin area), the incision is actually made at the front of the body to avoid the spine which projects so far forward at this point, around the first lumbar vertebrae, that great care has to be taken.

The spine's obvious departure into the body line behind the kidneys will show as a greater concavity in a very fit, toned rider. Weak backs tend to look flat; strong backs are more obviously contoured due to muscling. There is also the weak pot-bellied figure where the back is over-concave! It can all be quite confusing, especially when few realise that the spine is not *completely* straight anywhere! For the uneducated eye it is obviously better to measure straightness or uprightness in the rider through the *centre* of the body and not by the undulations of the silhouette.

Those instructors who have irresponsibly 'straightened' their pupils' backs by insisting that riders tuck their bottoms under them more merely succeed in rounding the spine and overloading the sacrum. This places unnecessary stresses on the discs and leaves the rider behind the movement of the horse so that they have to rock to keep up. This reminds me of the story of a fellow instructor who, for fun and without saying she was herself a teacher, went to join a group of fairly novice riders while on holiday with her daughter at a large hotel where riding under a qualified person was on offer.

During the lesson, with her usual quiet aids, sense of feel and good seat, she was able to produce quite a tune out of her riding school mount, opening up the gaits and achieving real rhythm down the long sides of the school where they were all going round and round. After a particularly lovely expressive trot, the young lady in the centre called, 'You're sitting like a statue!'

'Ah,' my friend thought, 'a compliment at least!'

A second later: 'You're not going with the movement – start moving yourself with the horse!

Sports physiotherapist Anne Gerard from Cheshire, who worked with the British athletic Olympic team, has this to say on the subject of back and pelvic posture. 'The upright pelvis allows for correct curvature of the spine which, working with the discs, smooths out and harmonises the effects of bodyweight, muscle pull and thrust due to the impact of the feet whether in walking, running, jumping or riding. This balance, which co-ordinates correct locomotion, is vital for any athlete whether on or off the horse.'

Taking a little time out to study the wise words of the old masters might be useful. Long before the motor car ruined for most of us our natural way of moving, riding instructors were under no false illusions as to the mechanics of both the human body and that of the horse. In 1754 Berenger, Master of the Horse to King George II, wrote *A New System of Horsemanship* which was moulded on the work of a distinguished Frenchman, Claude Bourgelat. Unequivocally, Berenger states: 'The horseman should present or advance his breast; by this his whole figure opens and displays itself; he should have a small hollow in his loins and should push his waist forward to the pommel of the saddle, because this position corresponds and unites him to all the motions of the horse.'

For pictorial evidence, the position of the riders shown in the superb copperplate engravings of *École de Cavalerie*, now available in English as *School of Horsemanship*, published by J. A. Allen, exemplify this meticulously. De la Guérinière's great book went through seven editions in his own lifetime and many more after his death to become the equestrian bible at Vienna and throughout Europe. In every plate, particularly where collection was required, the rider shows a definitive concave bending or placing forward of the lower back accentuated by shoulders squared a little behind the vertical. Where more forward work is demonstrated, the rider is more upright but remains proud but pliant so that the whole appearance is one of easy control over the horse. What is particularly noteworthy about all the prints from the classical period is the requirement that the stomach or waist be well advanced, in the way of small children on the beach.

To be fair to my critic concerning the magazine article, it has to be recognised that one of the most damaging things an unfit person can do is to over-accentuate the natural lordosis of the spine by collapsing the waist and allowing the tummy to sag forwards and down. Obviously, lack of abdominal support places a great deal of strain on the lower back whether walking about or riding. Projecting the centre of gravity towards the wither is, however, a very different feeling from either tensing the tummy or letting it flop. Correctly done, the horse is also projected forward from a positive influence of the rider's weight. In the latter, the horse is dropped downward on the forehand like a stone.

Most people who suffer backpain from riding do so because they have never been taught to support upwards correctly. Riding slackly over many years puts enormous stresses on the back which can result in damaged or 'slipped' discs. Riders need to learn to respect their bodies if they are to sustain the shock of movement, particularly in the sitting trot.

Even the jumping seat requires some idea of bracing the lower back forward. When modern instructors nowadays say, 'flatten your back' over jumps, they actually mean 'support the loins' which all goes to show just how misleading equestrian terminology can be. Captain Vladimir Littauer, who followed Caprilli, the prime instigator of the Italian showjumping seat, wrote of 'hollow loins', as did Henry Wynmalen and Dr Vozzoli, an American instructor who instructed the United Nations Riding Club. His advice, to keep 'the small of the back slightly braced inward' for the forward seat is really no different from what Guérinière and others of the time were promoting for the *manège* or classical seat.

The word 'brace' is actually a difficult one as it can mean two completely opposing concepts to two different people. In medical terms, a braced back is one that is supported naturally inwards to maintain a 'hollow' at the waist as already discussed. Unfortunately, to some it implies sucking the stomach back and leaning against the cantle. Such a posture actually works against gravity but has been employed by certain lady riders who have difficulty controlling their very large horses. This action causes the seatbones to dig down quite sharply into the most sensitive part of the horse's back. With the command to drive coming from one end, and the command to stop from the other, riding in this way is rather like revving a car's engine with the handbrake on at the same time – a lot of power is produced and sometimes breaks out! For the sake of clarity, I therefore tend to omit the word 'brace' from my vocabulary whenever possible.

Because of all these misunderstandings, it is often safer to improve riders by concentrating on their fronts. Once they can think of opening upwards from the waist and, in particular, keeping the navel and sternum projected, the spine will take its own correct alignment. Erik Herbemann writes of allowing the 'upper body to grow taller' while Oliveira asks us to 'expand the torso'.

The worst advice an instructor can give his pupil is to 'relax the upper body'. Even on the ground we can only stand erect by firming up our muscles. A pupil's teenage daughter recently failed an important equestrian examination for sitting too upright! Why do certain people in authority confuse straightness with stiffness? In the words of Udo Burger: 'Riders must have firm, elastic muscles, constantly under conscious control, quick to contract and to relax to a precise degree. Soft bodies who do not carry themselves properly in the course of the ordinary occupations of life, who have weak backs and lifeless hands, will never be able to control a horse.'

Some final thoughts on the use of the back, how to bend it in the right place and how to ride and become part of movement, were concluded at Disneyland. One Easter, a short time ago, I had been teaching a group of dressage riders up in the sierra of the beautiful San Fernando Valley near Los Angeles. As the trip took place when my twelve-year-old daughter Allegra would be home from boarding school, part of the deal was that she should come too and there would be VIP tickets to Disneyland at the end of the clinic. I cannot pretend I was really looking forward to this. I hate crowds and would have preferred instead to relax for two days' sunshine at the beautiful ranch where we had received such wonderful hospitality.

After a day of walking for endless miles over concrete and losing one's stomach in a variety of mindblowing rides, we joined the buzz of people lining the route to watch the much talked about *Lion King* Parade, due to emerge into the main plaza. Along with thousands of other parents, I was expecting a childish fantasy which I was prepared to enjoy superficially; what I had not expected was first to be deeply moved by the music and, second, to find absolute correlation between the dancers, the singers and the mimers, all dressed as creatures of the jungle. Somehow, they perfectly summed up my perception of balanced riding. I can hear the reader ask: 'What on earth has the *Lion King* to do with dressage?' I shall try to explain.

The music was deeply powerful. It came as no surprise when Elton John and Tim Rice won their Oscar for 'Circle of Life' for there is something quite classical pulsing behind the more popular up-beat. Not only is it incredibly tuneful, it pulls at the heart and the gut and has a haunting rhythm that emanates from the heart of Africa, and more than that – from the heartbeat of life itself. The music and the swaying figures were not just about the jungle either, they, too, somehow represented something more – they echoed the force, the vitality of movement, energy, impulsion – something that is within us all.

As the music came quietly at first, then reverberated louder around the plaza and the first dancers came sparkling into sight, I marvelled at how all the people around, young and old, fat and thin, began to sway and tap their feet. Energy, beat, rhythm, movement – there was not one person there who could resist it. Whatever our worries, our lack of communication with nature, the old primeval instincts are still there, buried deep inside – movement moves us, we feel good when we move, it is part of our common love of life.

As the spectacle began to unfold around us, I thought how much we can learn from the pure movements made by animals and people who, like animals, are in touch with their bodies, people who know how to balance their bodies, economically, practically, yet with poise and majesty. You never see a shuffling tiger or a floppy lion. The elephant may be slow but he is purposeful. All is toned, poised, erect and balanced – ready for action. So it was with these dancers and acrobats with their animal costumes, verve and psyche. They danced as though their bodies were weightless and they could move through space. They leapt and skipped, turned cartwheels and somersaults, yet all the time there was a control in them which made it possible for their energy to be released and harnessed into dramatic feats of balance, movements which made statements about energy and impulsion, gestures which seemed to encircle and amplify the throb of life itself.

Swaying this way and that with their fantastic plumage, their carved animal masks, their gleaming skins, their painted faces and firm legs, their loose hips and their powerful backs, they moved on, out of sight. We heard the music, felt the discipline long after they had gone. The rhythm had pulled them this way and that, but always it was they who were masters of the dance, who pulled the energy toward them with outstretched fingers and gathering arms. I remembered one man who did a handstand in front of us, perfectly balanced, perfectly arched, centred. I knew in that moment that everything we do in riding is linked to something else, something far far greater, to the dynamics of movement and the principles that govern life itself.

CHAPTER 9
Throughness – of light seats and heavy seats

I am the first to admit that, for all too many years, it never occurred to me to consider just how sensitive a horse's back can be. I was so busy thinking about myself and the whole idea of cultivating the perfect seat, perfect gaits, lightness and rhythm that I confess I gave scant consideration to what the horse might have been feeling underneath me. It took a particularly difficult and capricious young stallion to show me the way. Like so many horses, I suspect, he was extravagant-moving, tough and powerful when at liberty; it was only when a saddle was placed on his back, with a rider in the middle, that cohesion was lost and the work became fragmented and choppy. For once I was not prepared to accept the easy answer that it was all just a matter of further training and discipline; for the first time in my life I began to look further.

Gradually, I began to see that his reluctance to work consistently for me under saddle had more to do with the lack of proper muscling on either side of his spine and the fact that his loins were tight instead of soft and round, than with his somewhat impulsive temperament and lack of experience. Indeed, as the days went by and his attitude began to change, I realised that his hotheadedness and occasional bursts of meanness stemmed from the fact that he had been asked to do too much too early and all before he was physically ready and able to comply. It became obvious that his clear potential contrasted starkly with reality – a severe lack of muscle development where he had obviously 'blocked off' at some stage in the past. As muscles carry a memory of pain, this would account for his resistances. Clearly, if he was ever to carry a rider in the same way as he showed us when moving in freedom, he would have to be helped to achieve the necessary muscular support and dorsal tone.

I had bought this horse as an impressive-looking three year old and had paid for him to be professionally backed in Portugal at a time when African horse sickness was raging in the south of Spain. Just as he was due to leave Lisbon's Atlantic shores for England, the export ban was extended to the whole Iberian Peninsula and I lost the slot to get him out of the country in time. I was compelled, therefore, to leave the horse where he was for another whole year and, sadly, the person I had originally chosen to back him was no longer able to continue the work. What went wrong during that important formative time I know not. I only know that his personality changed drastically and when, finally, he was shipped to England I was warned of a complex cynical personality and a horse that might be dangerous.

By this time he was rising five and it was disconcerting when, the first time I mounted my fiery new horse, he took off round the school before I had even got my second foot in the stirrup – this despite careful lungeing and work in hand during his first week home to accustom him to his new surroundings. Later he learned to be quieter but for several weeks it was like riding a horse that had never before had anyone on his back. If I sat down, however carefully, he simply bucked and whizzed off and it was only by adopting the forward, jumping position that he would tolerate any real weight in the saddle at all. His back and saddle were checked but the answer was all too obvious. There was no unsoundness; he was well developed in the neck and shoulders but there was a serious lack of muscling from the base of the wither backwards. I put this down to him never having been properly ridden forward and 'through' after his initial backing. In short, he had to be rebacked and started again from scratch.

As his gaits were free and expressive on the lunge, I soon learned that if I wanted to preserve that freedom under saddle I would have to build up the dorsal muscles by getting off that sensitive back as much as possible to enable him to work under me from behind without restriction. I am convinced that it was the mistakes which had been made in the first year of his education that caused him to feel so insecure and freeze up if he felt any pressure here at all. The journey from Portugal had obviously created other tensions and while some horses sail through such upheavals, it is always the intelligent and sensitive which suffer the most. Since that time, I have seen a similar situation with many other young, finely tuned animals and, often, bucking and balking are the only outlet for their trapped energy.

When, finally, with a softly-softly approach I did achieve a mentally relaxed, fit and physically developed horse, I only introduced the sitting trot in short bursts as I instinctively knew he associated pressure on the back with other pressures. Thus, very gradually, I built up the sitting trot with a light seat rather than forcing myself strongly against him. The wait, however, was well worthwhile and, eventually, we were working happily in collection by the time the horse was seven. To some this may be considered late, but taking time to lay solid foundations reaps it own rewards. *Piaffe*

146

A good rider will automatically feel his horse's back and know when to take weight off it through the rising trot. Many young horses who look robust may have deceptively delicate backs which need to be nurtured and gradually developed through careful early training. Rising must always be off the knees and the stirrups, never off the back of the saddle.

(Photo: courtesy Dr Borba and Arsenio Raposo Cordeira)

and real rounding and elevation began to happen naturally just before his eighth birthday and changes were the easiest thing in the world. Strong, flexible and healthy, we had come through the storm, but it was clear that this horse would require tact for the rest of his life.

Lusitanos and Andalusians are not the only horses to have sensitive backs. English Thoroughbreds, Trakehners, Selle Français, Arabs – all horses with a modicum of hot blood – require an equal degree of careful consideration. Too many dressage riders forget that the young horse simply cannot be ridden in the same way as a mature schoolmaster, even although the principles of balance are the same. I well remember Robert Hall returning to Britain from Vienna and finding that the large majority of British horses which came into his hands at that time simply could not take the same amount of seat he had been used to applying with the Vienna School Lipizzaners. Having been spoiled for choice in a similar way with a constant stream of Portuguese schoolmasters, I confess I ridiculed these sentiments at the time. Now I know better and feel sorry in retrospect for my ignorant assertions. Now I empathise and admire him greatly for having had the courage to speak out – particularly at a time when it was the fashion to drive hard into the horse with the seat and back.

In this context, I cannot stress too much how it takes time and infinite patience to strengthen and encourage the equine back to round and lift. Too many riders push the young horse away from them long before he has learned to come up to meet the seat, and the problems which arise from this lack of awareness have prevented many a sensitive but potentially talented horse from ever being able truly to work through or to collect correctly.

This awareness of the weaknesses or strengths of the equine back brings us to the whole question of heavy seats and light seats. I have heard it said that there is no such thing as a light seat but this is about as shortsighted as saying there is no such thing as a light dancer. Sometimes those who are lightest on their feet may be plump and heavy on the scales, but perhaps it is their very sensitivity to weight which allows them to use it to their advantage, to project their centre of gravity and to balance their bodies accordingly.

Lightness in all the disciplines comes not from less avoirdupois but from how weight is distributed. Indeed, some light-seated riders may actually weigh several kilos more than others but because they know how to direct their weight over the strongest part of the horse, the horse carries them in a better posture with the hocks under him more. Others, weighing less on the scales, may encumber the horse with so much deadweight through a stiff unyielding body that he has to struggle to carry them and the hind legs are left behind.

Confusion about balancing weight has made a mockery of much of the practical advice coming out of the old cavalry schools such as Saumur in France, Fort Riley in America and Weedon in England, where both the forward, jumping seat and a full seat were taught to complement each other. I well remember one well-known British dressage trainer loftily saying, 'Of course, the so-called classical seat is quite different from today's dressage seat since in the former, the rider's weight remains in his stirrups and in the latter we take our weight into our seats – the only way to

Like human dancing partners, a heavily built horse can still be light on his feet.
(Photo: courtesy Joao Trigueros)

ride competitive dressage.' By issuing such a statement this trainer showed a complete ignorance of nature's laws concerning spring and the absorption of movement. As Littauer[1] points out, a figure suspended from a ceiling can display no impetus, spring or thrust in its body. It is only its connection to the ground which allows proactive forces to take place. Thus, 'in the saddle, the stirrups take the place of the ground'. Littauer continues: . . . 'evidently, the worst position the rider could have . . . [from the horse's point of view] . . . would be leaning back with the body, and carrying the lower legs forward with the toes turned down'. What made the modern trainer's point of view all the more sad was his absolute disregard for weighting the stirrups while expecting insistence upon *schwung* in his

[1] Captain V.S. Littauer, *The Forward Seat.*

149

own and his pupils' horses' backs. No wonder, therefore, that on a demonstration video which showed a very heavy, grinding seat, every one of his horses looked remarkably tense and unhappy. Had he ever stopped to ask himself why, one wondered.

As for those armchair experts who insist that you cannot alleviate the horse's back by taking more weight into the knees and stirrups as the horse still has to carry the same number of kilos, they, too, have entirely missed the point. The traditional viewpoint, as General Decarpentry points out in *Academic Equitation*, acknowledges that inclining the seat and shoulders a little forward allows, 'the weight of his [the rider's] body to be borne by that part of the [horse's] back that is situated below the stirrup bars, towards the front third of the saddle . . . The lighter seat frees the loins and facilitates the flexions of the spine. It considerably assists horses that have difficulty in reining back and, at the beginning of the *piaffe*, facilitates the moments of suspension between the beats.'

In the US Cavalry *Manual of Horsemanship and Horsemastership*, readers are warned about heavy seats and that 'inclining the upper body to the rear, or convexing the loin to the rear, places the center of gravity of the upper body in rear of the center of its base of support and causes the rider to sit on the fleshy parts of his buttocks. This faulty position tends to raise the thighs and knees, weakens the seat, concentrates the weight toward the cantle and is unmilitary in appearance. It is fatiguing to the horse and often injurious to his back. The rider is "behind his horse" '.

What too many dressage riders forget in their longing to ride in the so-called 'dressage seat', nonchalantly leaning back a little in order to look more elegant, is that adaptability is the name of the game. Unless they start the young or inexperienced horse off with a light seat which can adapt to motion and circumstance by taking the weight forward and off the delicate back of the horse and down into the body's natural shock absorbers of knees and ankles in the way mentioned above, the horse will never have the chance to free up in the back. Thus he will never be able to develop the very muscles of the neck, back and loins that are so necessary for him to cope with further gymnastic demands, particularly when he will be expected to support the rider for long periods of time in a full-seated position.

To illustrate further how weight can be used or misused, I believe it is vital for all riders to understand that the responsibility for how their weight is carried by the horse is theirs and theirs alone. For any parent, elder sister or brother who has ever carried a child on their back, it should not be difficult to understand this concept. If the child is asked to sit up, sit tall and still on the carrier's back, it is generally possible to shift them into a

From the horse's point of view, it is harder to carry the rider who leans back and no longer supports her weight over her stirrups. This requires more support from the rein, which prevents the horse from extending his topline. The result is often a little goose-stepping from the front legs – a common sight in modern dressage.

position where it is comparatively easy to carry them. If, on the other hand, the child is told deliberately to slouch, wriggle and make themselves heavy, the effect is very different. If the child then adds insult to injury by thrusting hard against the carrier with the hips, the task becomes extremely uncomfortable. Judging by the body language of some horses, it is much the same for them.

While all dressage riders strive to master the sitting trot, I am of the opinion that, even on a mature horse, people should not sit to the trot until they have learned to carry themselves in such a way that their weight remains vertical over the strongest part of the horse. This means being able to ease the weight off the horse's back and keep their balance in a semi-standing position in all gaits. If a rider is unable to do this, and I am constantly amazed how many experienced riders cannot, it is clear that the person has failed to use gravity to align and support themselves and their sitting trot will be flawed.

An instructor who cares for their horse would be unwise to allow such a rider to sit to the trot until it is more balanced. Again, General Decarpentry shows his concern for the horse when he warns against the rider who brings . . . 'the whole of his weight to bear on his seat bones and consequently on that part of the back that is situated under approximately the rear third of the saddle'.

The jumping position is an ideal one for teaching potential dressage riders to maintain the direct line of gravity from the hip into the heel which prevents this abuse of the horse's back. It teaches riders to keep their knees and thighs under them and in good contact with the horse so that they can ease or allow with their weight as required. The absorption of movement by flexed joints, particularly soft ankles, should never be underestimated. The rising trot must also be tackled in this way.

Once in the sitting trot, riders should never lose their ability to ease the weight. When they sit, they should think of lowering a vertical pelvis into the saddle without losing the balance they felt in the rising trot from bent knees. Again, this can only be achieved if the rider's feet remain firmly under the hips with the stirrups weighted. This is hard for beginners whose hips tend to slide back the moment they bring the lower leg to the girth. They should, however, study pictures of those top riders whose horses always look round and free through the back because their riders have mastered the balance of riding with the leg on the girth and with the hips remaining forward at least the obligatory 'hand's breadth from the cantle'. This position can only be maintained with a three-point contact, flexed and supple knees and ankles and the feeling that the coccyx is being pushed towards the wither (although never in contact with the saddle).

Easing with the weight has everything to do with quietness and absolutely nothing to do with an ostentatious rocking of the shoulders or pelvis. The only time I ever want to see my students' seats visibly move is during the free walk on a long rein when they are not requiring the horse to round up to them but, rather, stretching it away, long and low. The expression 'moving with the horse' was never intended to mean the busy to-ing and fro-ing we see from countless pelvises these days. The idea behind the cliché was to keep the rider's centre of balance forward through a supple back, which is what everyone does when standing upright in a moving train or bus. Horses can move quite happily without a permanent thrusting from the rider's seat which, although it may be used sparingly to encourage longer strides from time to time, certainly does not create either more impulsion or engagement.

For the work proper, the aids of the seat should always be minute and virtually invisible to the eye of an onlooker. The yielding, fixing and supporting of the lumbar muscles are a secret between horse and rider. Driving with the back of the seat pressed against the cantle has, logically, got to be counter-productive. The front legs may push out impressively but, over a long period of time, such action will stiffen the horse's back and leave the hocks trailing behind.

The action of this famous dressage horse, Olympic Bonfire, would look rather more natural if he were allowed more freedom and softness in the neck. The action seems somewhat staccato, although the horse is very athletic and the rider very competent.

(Photo: Kit Houghton)

One of the more interesting dressage books ever to come on to the British and American market from Germany just after the war was Wilhelm Müseler's *Riding Logic*. There is a great deal to like in this book and certainly much common sense for cross-country riding. While some of the advice in the dressage section is steeped in tradition, some is highly contentious, illustrating, perhaps, that Müseler's background was not as strictly academic as that of many of his contemporaries. Henry Wynmalen was a Dutchman who settled in England and wrote two empirical books on dressage which have become classics in their own right. Wynmalen, brought up in the French and Dutch classical schools of riding, felt that the advice given by Müseler, on bracing the back, according to a certain German school of thought at the time, verged on the ludicrous. Not only did it not look supple, it looked stiff! Indeed, as Wynmalen writes: 'It is quite possible that such stiffness is more apparent than real, although it is

153

difficult to deny that the apparent stiffness of the seat is almost invariably accompanied by an equally apparent stiffness in the rein-control. We do not seem to see that grace and lightness so much beloved, and in my opinion rightly so, by the French School.'

In fact, Müseler's and other trainers' methods of bracing the back – *das kreuz anziehen* – were never universally accepted in Germany among the upper echelon of riders. Such action seemed to have been condemned by the classical Gustave Steinbrecht, in his *Das Gymnasium des Pferdes*, published in 1886[2]. Leafing through Fritz Stecken's 1977 training book recently, I was heartened by this leading German trainer's captions to photographs of some of the top dressage riders from the pre- and post-war period. It soon became clear that this author heartily approved of those who rode in the traditional vertical classical position, while those who drove too remorselessly with their seats while leaning severely backward merely placed the horse on the forehand. Candidly truthful comments, such as, 'note high croup, insufficient bending of hock and hip joints, head and neck too low, exaggerated stretching of the front legs (goose stepping)' were then proffered alongside such pictures to demonstrate the error of their ways. Oh, for a judge of such discernment and understanding in this day and age!

Stecken had been particularly influenced by the great rider and teacher Otto Löerke who displayed many horses one-handed and often with a pronounced *descente de main* so that the horse flowed fluidly and unconstricted under him. Real importance was put on the stretching forward and freeing of the horse's neck, a facet of riding which is nowadays often marred by the backward bracing of riders behind the centre of balance and consequently behind the movement, which prevents the horse from working through from behind.

While riders of the calibre of Reiner and Michael Klimke and their predecessors, Neckermann, Watjen and Staeck, never braced backward in this way (the latter three would probably have turned in their graves to hear it dubbed 'the German method'), other less harmonious riders still use it in competitive dressage today. By emulating the braced back of Müseler, it is almost impossible to ride without considerable tension on the reins as the rider is no longer in balance with themselves. As a result, the horse shortens the neck, ducks the poll down and turns his face back to meet the contact. The result is an extravagantly moving horse, Stecken's 'goose stepper', which is, nevertheless, tight in the shoulders and 'broken' in the neck, unable to bring his weight back from lowered quarters to offer the more

---

[2] Steinbrecht wrote: 'When the stirrups are in the correct position they are practically the pans of the scales for the correct distribution of the rider's weight.'

collected movements such as *piaffe* and *passage* without considerable difficulty.

While very strong warmblood breeds, correctly trained in their early years and now working at high levels, may learn to cope, the harshness of this driving seat is rarely accepted by the finer breeds of horse, particularly those with Thoroughbred blood. Portuguese and Spanish riders have often been criticised for inclining their upper bodies a little forward in the *piaffe* and *passage*, but they do this with a purpose – to lighten the seat. They are only too mindful that their horses are shorter-backed, unlike their cousins the Lipizzaners, so they ride them with great respect for the horses' loins. In Germany, now that the heavier Holsteiner type is less popular today, many Germans who previously rode with a more backward position of the pelvis have rethought their posture and reverted to a more upright balance. Today's much lighter Hanoverians and Trakehners perform very much better with a more sensitive, allowing seat.

Re-reading Müseler not long ago reminded me of a memorable occasion when Henry and I were visited at Green Farm by a famous lady from the world of international dressage competition. As luck would have it, the lady in question attracted a certain amount of publicity. Before we knew it, BBC TV had asked permission to set up cameras and record some footage of the event for the weekend news programme *Look East*. This turned out to be not such a good idea.

It was a cold and blustery day and when the cameras set up their intrusive position in the indoor school and hoardes of journalists trooped into the gallery while our students were schooling, prior to the appearance of our distinguished guest who was to ride with Henry, a slight circus-like atmosphere pervaded the air. The horses were swift to feel this, particularly when the odd click and 'giddy-up' emanated from members of the crew. I regret to say that, as cameras whirred, a few unintentional airs above the ground were offered. One could almost read the editor's mind – 'Who cares about boring dressage when these magnificent white stallions start *levading* and parading all about the place?'

Thus, when the star appeared, in immaculate breeches and highly boned boots, for her first experience of a Portuguese High School horse, the atmosphere was already electric. Henry had selected Notario, a really imposing dapple grey stallion, much bigger than the average Lusitano and measuring almost 17 h.h. He had not been schooled by us and was basically in transit from Portugal, but had come to stay for some last-minute fine-tuning prior to being flown out to Cyprus for a member of the ruling family. Perhaps Henry would have been wiser to use one of our school horses, but only the biggest and best would do after the generous proportions our guest was used to, and he felt Notario was the horse most likely to make her feel at home.

However, Notario was not a warmblood and, although a forward-going and very advanced horse, the aids by which the Olympic contender's horse performed were clearly foreign to him. Perhaps Henry should have explained that the horse was light to the leg and the seat. He had plenty of impulsion and, indeed, required little aiding, just an erect upper body and feather-light touches of the fingers and legs would have sufficed. What Notario did not need was a pushing feeling from a sharply inclined backward seat and back. No, he did not hit the ceiling; neither did he shatter the chandeliers – as yet unhung. All Notario did in response to those pelvic thrusts from the person who sat in his saddle was to become slower, heavier, more ponderous and finally crooked and wandering in his progress around the track. Not only were the seat aids too strong, the legs sent him this way and that. He simply refused to remain in a straight line.

I was pregnant and under doctor's orders not to ride at the time but half of me wanted to jump into that saddle and show just how forward and straight the horse could be. The other half wondered if it was we who were out of step. It was a highly embarrassing moment all round but the situation was vaguely saved by the onset of a sudden migraine which caused our visitor to dismount and leave for the house. She did not ride again that weekend.

It was a great lesson to me on how seats can change from country to country, horse to horse, and how what may work in one sphere may not always work in another. The transition from that particular Olympic horse to Notario was too great. A chasm stretched between the two styles of riding and it made us all think. Today, having weathered the doubts and misgivings which we all encounter along the way, and having watched other Olympic combinations which are pure magic, I know in which direction I am going and which way all horses would like to go.

A similar thing happened years later when, long after Henry's death, and after I had remarried and moved to Sudbury, an Australian rider, Kim Langley, came to stay. Kim was blonde, very tall, very gangly, fit and as thin as a rake. She rode like a boy, untidy and sprawling but wiry and strong in the saddle with legs that just seemed to wrap round the horse with no grip but plenty of adhesion. Laidback in the yard, around our home and in the saddle – 'Ride tall, Kim!' I was forever saying – she had a relaxed manner and total confidence with horses. She was very helpful with a young and difficult stallion I was backing and I could well understand how she had gained a reputation in and around Melbourne for breaking and starting off the most recalcitrant animals. I knew, also, that she had achieved some considerable success on the show jumping scene.

Nevertheless, Kim's first introduction to one of my horses was noteworthy. The horse was Bruno, a Lusitano gelding I had bought from Marion Larrigan but which had originally been backed in France. I had been working with him for no more than six months and, as Marion rightly told me, he was quite sharp. The thing about most classically started horses is that they are generally soft and malleable through the back. By sitting tall, you allow the horse to round up to you; by making the seat aids delicate, the muscles have a chance to flex under the rider and the horse learns to move forward with freedom and fluidity as well as to elevate as he grows in strength.

When Kim first sat on Bruno and applied her strong driving seat aid, learned in Australia, to push obstinate horses forward, he simply stopped. 'What's he doing?' she cried.

'You're doing too much,' I replied. 'Just close the leg, sit still and he'll go forward.'

She tried again. This time, he moved backward. I had to laugh. All the memories of my first ride in Portugal flooded back to me and here was another keen young rider getting her first dose of humiliation from a sensitive horse. 'Look, just sit up, stretch tall. Don't *do* so much.'

It took at least 30 minutes before Kim could get round the school in trot without Bruno stopping. There was a point when she became annoyed, particularly when I admonished her for moving about. She retorted that she was doing nothing; but it was all too obvious that it was too much for Bruno. Here was a horse full of energy and impulsion being stopped and blocked because every time he tried to balance under her, she was moving the goal posts. What Kim had to learn for herself was that a collected horse working from behind is like a finely balanced precision machine. If you upset the balance, nothing can tick or flow any more. In the end, red and hot, she yelled, 'God, what's wrong with this animal – I'm only following the movement!'

'Yes,' I replied, 'that's the problem – you're following it but you're not over it. He wants to be under you, not out in front with you running to catch up!'

It was a lesson, Kim told me later, that she would never forget. After two months at my yard, mastering her own balance and that of our sensitive horses, I found her a job with good friends in Portugal. The Countess of Cadaval comes from a long line of breeders of Lusitano horses and her huge stud at Salvaterra de Magos, on the rich banks of the River Tagus, is a haven for any horse lover. Back to her forte of breaking and schooling

Kim Langley riding one of the superb Cadaval Lusitano stallions in Portugal.
A picture of elegance and concentration.

young horses, Kim was able to expand her knowledge while riding trained schoolmasters in between times under the instruction of João Pedro Rodrigues a senior rider of the Portuguese School of Equestrian Art, who has provided horses for Nicole Uphoff to enjoy when she visits Portugal. At the end of two years, Kim had successfully brought twenty young stallions to Elementary dressage level, had produced two champions of show for the Cadaval family and had improved her technique with regular lessons on Grand Prix schoolmasters.

When next I saw her ride at the great horse fair of Golegã at the end of her first year in Portugal, I thought I was looking at an Iberian *senōra*. Gone was the slouchy, laidback posture and the boyish look. Here was a straightbacked, highly disciplined collected young lady who, now that she used every inch of her six-foot stature, actually looked stunning. Like themselves, the horses had taught her how to get herself back on her own hocks. It was a transformation in every way.

How sad that the use or non-use of the rider's seat has become such a contentious subject when so much inherited wisdom is available to us and when so little has changed between the human being and their horse since the days of Xenophon. My own early experiences were so disappointing in this context that my desire for enlightenment and self-improvement led me into a relentless pursuit of the truth and an almost messianic desire to help others as I would have liked to have been helped myself. Over many years I have made an academic study of the work of the great masters past and present. I have read, studied, dissected, questioned, analysed and philosophised at enormous lengths. I have consulted with veterinary surgeons, sport therapists, osteopaths, physiotherapists and orthopaedic surgeons studying the skeleton and muscle structures of the equine and the human frame. More important by far, I have also ridden and ridden and thought and thought. Hundreds of horses, of all types, ages and capabilities, have been my teachers and their message has been plain enough. With humility and, above all, feel, my conclusions have not been arrived at lightly. They are not peculiarly my own but, thankfully, are shared with some of the most wonderful riders of our time and also approved by the medical profession. Were it not for this secure knowledge that I am not alone in what I teach – although sometimes I have felt very alone – I would keep my mouth firmly shut and my pen idle!

Today, probably more so than at any former time, there are many false prophets and armchair experts who have neither needed nor wanted to school a horse from scratch. Too many teach when all the work has been done by others; only their competition results have provided the necessary CV. Those people who give up horses with increasing age sometimes change their views so that there is conflict between what they preached when they were riding every day and what they *think* they remember from those days. There is no doubt that every one of us needs constantly to reassure ourself on horseback about any form of academic theory.

At the end of the day, horses are the very best judges of the truth and will tell you when or how you are going wrong. The body language of the horse gives away many clues as to how he feels the rider on his back. Of course, some of his problems may have been there for years, but a good rider can always make a little difference to the most difficult horse. As each horse is different, no one can afford to be complacent or rigid in outlook. There are many matters which I now wish there had been room to address when I wrote my first series of articles, 'The Classical Seat', later to become a book. At the time, I was trying to help the average person on the average horse; I wish now I had written more concerning the need to lighten the seat on a young, sensitive, unmuscled horse like my difficult stallion.

Later, I was able to address these issues in my video because the horses themselves required it. Older horses demand as much care as younger horses if we are to preserve soundness, particularly remembering to ease the seat through upward and downward transitions. Sitting hard into an elderly horse through a change of gait is like forgetting to use the clutch when changing gear in a car – it simply breaks off the energy, preventing the horse from coming through and under with his hocks. It may also cause pain.

There are some instructors who pooh-pooh such an idea and insist that their pupils constantly drive more to make the horse submit his back. This may occasionally work with the coarser, heavier breeds but for how long? Generally, it provokes all manner of resistances to the point of losing trust and even damaging the horse's back. My advice to any rider whose horse tends to be hollow, rigid or resistant, for whatever reason, is to work him initially with your weight off the back and only gradually to sit deep, taking care to keep a hand's breadth forward from the cantle.

As the horse becomes stronger, developing more dorsal muscle, the rider can sit for longer and longer periods. Leaning backward behind the vertical will engage the seatbones more deeply than from the upright position and, at the beginning, must be used sparingly as an aid to extend the mature horse in the medium trot or canter. Decarpentry warns us: '. . . the movement that brings the shoulders back causes, by reaction, the seat to push forward, but the pushing effect only lasts while the shoulders are *moving backward*. If the shoulders stay back after they have completed the backward movement, they also fix the centre of gravity backwards, which is *unfavourable* to forward movement. . . .'It is therefore important always to return to the classical upright position in between these requests.

There is the argument that taking the weight a little forward and directing it downward through the knee and through the front of the thigh may overload the forehand but this is not so provided the rider still keeps their upper body tall and expanded and the stirrups remain directly below the hips. More important by far is that it *allows* the horse's back to come up in the first place. Once the equine back is up, the hind legs can step under more. This allows greater longitudinal extension for deeper engagement from the hocks so the horse can lower his haunches and bring his weight back.

This is the way in which I introduce the rudiments of *piaffe* to my horses, working in increasingly shortened steps from a collected walk. I have found that this method is one hundred per cent successful with all horses and the beauty of it is the lack of stress which is caused to the horse. He literally steps up and into the space provided by the lightened seat. Of course, none of this can be achieved without impulsion in collection and the legs must softly encourage him into the movement. I have been able to teach *piaffe* in this way with a variety of breeds without, in the early stages,

The importance of easing the weight a little forward to free the loins and allow this young mare to round and raise her back in *passage* is displayed by Bettina Drummond, long-term pupil of Nuno Oliveira. Here she works with Nevoa at home in Virginia.

(Photo: Audry L.D. Petschek, courtesy of Linda Osterman Hamid, USA)

ever having to help the horse with a stick from the ground. Only later, when one tries for more accuracy and height, may the stick be applied sparingly, but for me *piaffe* and *passage* have to start with the rounding of the horse's back, freely offered if it is to be of merit.

A further reason for lightening the seat is to obtain good deep work. Again, further encouragement is required from the rider's legs, acting in light taps at the girth to stimulate the nerve endings, support the forehand and engage the horse's hind legs. This is the ideal way in which to encourage the frame to lift and swing as the horse follows the hand into a low-set, softly inviting rein. Through his own upwardly inviting balance and projected centre of gravity, the rider encourages the horse to work off his hocks and to stretch, elevate and round his back like a curved bow. This simply will not occur by sitting full-seated too early; we should think of making more room to receive the horse's rounding back, never of squashing it as it lifts.

Once, however, the horse has become strong from firm, toned muscles spreading over the hindquarters, loins, back and neck, he should be able to carry the rider full-seated and in easy balance. There is nothing more beautiful than the full-seated classical seat of the supremely upright rider, with shoulders squared, hips forward, projected centre of gravity and spine properly flexed from supporting loin and abdominal muscles, with the seat quiet and legs which hang gracefully down, the heels drawn lower than the toes – this all subscribes to the perfect position.

This is the posture for which we all must aim but in our haste to get there we must never forget our horses. As with all things, the way forward is one of progression, meeting each demand step by step, listening to our horse and knowing when and how he will be ready for the next step, knowing and feeling when each lesson has been successfully learned but also understanding when something we have asked for is too difficult and when more time is required. We must recognise that a good classical seat is no longer a good classical seat if it is applied to a horse which is not able to receive such a seat.

The other day, a pupil was flicking through the pages of her dressage magazine and pointed out the difference in style between world champion German Nicole Uphoff Becker riding the *passage* with Rembrandt and the same movement being ridden by another German, the policeman Balkenhof on Goldstern. She wanted to know which was more correct. Nicole rode the movement with shoulders forward, slightly on her fork and thighs, taking the weight almost off the seat of the saddle and into her stirrups. Balkenhof, by contrast, sat well into his horse, the shoulders absolutely upright and all seatbones forward and in deep contact. Both horses looked as though the movement was being correctly executed, although, if anything, Rembrandt's frame was a little higher but perhaps a fraction tenser. Everyone is aware that this horse is hotly sensitive and requires very subtle riding. Nicole's position may not have been textbook but it was just right for her horse in that particular movement at that particular time.

I told my pupil that both were correct, and explained why. 'Classical does not mean unchanging, unyielding; it means the best, the right, the correct one for the horse. It works within certain laid-down guidelines, but it is always receptive, able to respond to the need of the occasion.'

I well remember the time when, at a demonstration, a Thoroughbred mare was brought to me who was stiff in the back, resistant in the mouth and whose gaits were protracted and choppy as she was unable to bring her hind legs underneath her bodymass. Working quietly with the horse in front of an audience, I explained that the first thing I would be looking to do would be to free up the back so that the horse could work through. As I asked more from the leg and lightened my seat accordingly, I became so fascinated and delighted with the responses the mare began to give me, as she began to yield through the jaw, soften into my hand, flex her poll and bend around my inside leg on big circles, that I grew silent and worked on. Soon she began to offer and lift her back and for the first time I felt the power as the hindlegs started to push through. After less than ten minutes I was able to hand back to the delighted owner a horse that was light, round and engaged. When it came to question time, however, I realised how ignorant people can be – the first question dropped like a bombshell: 'I thought this demo was about classical riding; can I ask why you couldn't keep your seat?'

How banal, how ignorant certain members of the riding public can be! However, it was a good lesson in PR. Nowadays, I risk insulting the spectators' intelligence by explaining not only what, but why, I am doing this or that. As the Americans say, rather appropriately in this context – one has to protect one's ass wherever one goes!

After experiences like this, and there have been other, similar instances, especially when one is quoted out of context, one is tempted to enact the fairy story of the emperor's new clothes. Just go out there, sit there, look pretty with a perfect seat on a horse which is freezing away from you, do a twiddly bit here and a twiddly bit there and, after a few minutes, trot up to the gallery and say loudly and full of confidence: 'Now, isn't he going better; can you see how much he's improved?' I've seen this happen with my own eyes and everyone goes 'ooh' and 'ahh' and nods approvals – except for one person – the horse. Animals are not as easily fooled as people.

If the proof of the pudding is in the eating, the proof of a good seat is the state of the horse's back. Much can be disguised with a rider aboard but, once you take the saddle off and notice the presence or non-presence of muscling on the horse's back, everything is given away. It is also a compliment to a rider when a colleague from Germany, America, Portugal, Austria, Italy, Britain or Spain rides one's horse and immediately achieves a successful partnership. When a horse which does not know a rider immediately submits with pleasure and accuracy to their requests, it confirms that the common language which exists between classical horsemen and women has been correctly taught, correctly interpreted.

As I said earlier, a few years ago, Paul Belasik, author of *Riding Towards the Light*, stayed with my family. Over a couple of relaxed days we talked endlessly and, still jetlagged and tired, he watched me work my horses. Finally, I persuaded him to sit on my mare who, broken only at seven, was a late developer. Until that time she was only ridden by me, except out on hacks, although I now use her as a schoolmistress. The moment Paul settled into the saddle, she collected herself up and they moved off into a pleasing display of quiet gymnastic work, nothing flashy, just simple basic movements. What was delightful to me was that not once did she try to push off into a floaty, hovering *passage* – one of the little evasions she and other advanced horses will often try to catch one off guard – in order to avoid the work proper. Not once did she say, 'No!', not once did she deviate from his request, not once did he push the wrong button and produce something unexpected or uncalled for.

The best thing was when he commented on the lovely soft feel she gave him through her back. 'It's so giving and round,' he commented. 'She comes right up to meet you.' This was a special compliment when Paul is one of the few trainers who talks about 'the sacred back' of the horse and really understands what a responsibility we have not to abuse it. I smiled to myself as I thought of all those years of rising trot to unstiffen her loins and bring about such malleability.

Classical riding is about communicating through our bodies in a way which allows the horse's body to act. There must be no forcing, no abuse. Neither can there be any deviation; gravity only works one way, straight down and plumb and when we learn the aids which complement nature's laws, we too learn to be plumb. Once we are plumb in our every movement, every turn, every circle, the horse has little alternative other than to offer what we require of him, provided he is sufficiently fit, supple and muscled and is offered sufficient freedom actually to act. The classical way allows the horse to carry out these requests not from compulsion but as though it was his idea in the first place.

CHAPTER 10
Off the leg and into the flow!

One of the hardest things for the newcomer to dressage to understand is that speed and running have nothing to do with impulsion. How many horses run round the dressage arena at the lower levels? Thousands! How many are actually off the leg, using themselves in the way God made them and propelling themselves from behind? Very few. Even at the higher levels, where collection and self-carriage are required, many horses are trying to run but are held back, imprisoned by the outline their rider has imposed upon them. This requires taut fingers and flexed biceps. Yet, one cannot altogether blame riders for this state of affairs. Although the FEI rules demand lightness, those judges who do not know better – often because they do not ride – may demand just the opposite by insisting that a horse is not working from behind unless there is extreme tension on the rein and the horse appears to be bursting out against the rider's hand.

There are many stories concerning how some of the world's greatest competitors have been run away with prior to, after or even during a competition. I once witnessed this first hand at an international event and could not help feeling I would never wish to compete on such a horse, however talented, if I did not feel master of its energy. As dressage is supposed to be about harmony, co-operation and empathy, being carted has to be a denial of the basic aims.

In this context, Franz Mairinger, former *oberbereiter* of the Spanish Riding School, tells a wonderful story of how, not long after his arrival in Vienna, he was given a fully schooled stallion to exercise out with others in an open field and how they had to pass under an overhead railway line just as an express train roared by. Despite his venerable age, the stallion took off and Mairinger was left hanging on. The old instructor who was in charge yelled at him for pulling. The next day they were out together again and the same horse began to play up near the same spot. It began to run round and round and there was nothing young Franz could do. Eventually, the wise old man showed him. The following description says it all:

How not to stop a horse! Severe hands will generally cause resistance through
the head and neck, often leading to hollowing as the horse tries to back away from his
rider which is altogether counter-productive and can even be dangerous.

He mounted up and you could really see that weight sink into that saddle. The
stallion was bouncing on the spot, his nostrils flaring and he looked about to
explode at any minute. To rub it in the old instructor said, 'I told you. You held him
too much.' He threw the reins away and the stallion could not do a thing. He
couldn't do a thing because he had to balance himself under that weight. It might be
hard to understand if you have not experienced it yourself, but that weight going
down anchors him to the spot; he can't go, if you don't let him go. It is important
that you let your weight down.

To understand exactly what Mairinger is saying, the rider has to appreciate
the relevance of the upper body posture and how the position and use
of the leg below determines what the horse is feeling under the saddle.
If that 'old instructor' had not allowed his weight to go down into his
stirrups with the legs deep, unconstricted and absolutely under him, the
result could have been quite different. I suspect that at that stage Franz
himself was trying to lean back against the cantle, ram his feet forward and
home in the stirrups and push his weight against the rein, which is the
wrong way to stop an agitated horse. Only by letting the weight down,

Halting or arresting energy should have little to do with hand action. It is simply a question of dropping the rider's weight straight through the centre of the horse from an upright position of knee and thigh, thus uniting the horse to the ground through gravity.

through you and through the centre of the horse can one affect the energy of the horse so that he stays under you. In this case the old instructor was able to earth his stallion to the ground, with his body weight going down like a bolt of electricity.

It is the component parts of the rider's seat and legs which are responsible for the creation, encouragement or dampening down of impulsion. To understand these functions better, we may liken them to the accelerator and gears of a car. Thus the energy produced by the engine can be harnessed to produce low gears or high, overdrive, or reverse. The effects of the seat are incredibly powerful but, as with a high-powered, synchronised car, the timing must be right and you cannot afford to crash through the gears.

While most riders are aware that their legs encourage the horse to move forward (acceleration) and that their judicious use is the key to releasing energy, fewer riders realise that the leg, together with the seat, can transform this energy (gearbox) in order to collect, redirect or, as described above, stop the horse going forward altogether. To be able to find such control, however, we have to become as close to the horse as we possibly

It is not always appreciated that the rider's seat and leg can redirect the horse's energy upwards as well as forwards. Again, this can only be achieved through a very centred position, with full contact of knee, thigh and seat.

(Photo: courtesy of Anglo-Austrian Society, London)

can, not only through the seat but also through an adhesive thigh, knee and leg. The idea of adhesion is very different from the idea of grip. Closeness is achieved by understanding how to make our own bodyweight work for us so that we feel as though we are doing nothing!

To promote this closeness, this adhesion to the saddle, the old masters placed much importance on the opening of the rider's hips so that the legs could then fall into place to embrace the horse with apparently no muscular

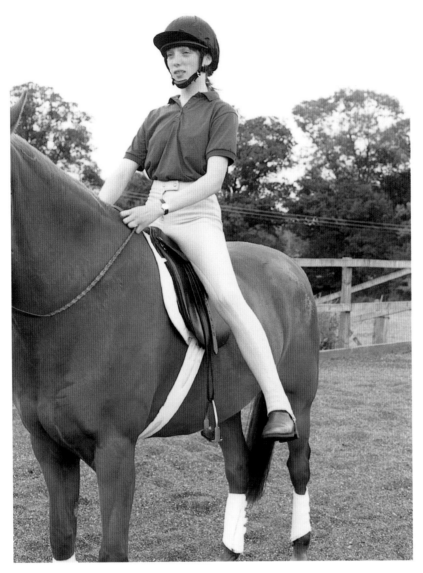

An independent seat will only be gained when the rider is sufficiently supple through the hip joints to open the thigh away from the saddle so that the leg may return to its correct position (flat against the saddle) through gravity, rather than by tightening the thigh muscles.

(Photo: T. Burlace)

effort. This first involved rotating the back of the thigh slightly outwards and away from the horse so that, on its return to the saddle, the knee would naturally turn in and the flat, inner surface of the thigh would be brought to bear. This opening, turning and closing action produces a small hollow around the hip joint. With the ensuing contact, gravity alone would keep

169

the leg in place. As Pembroke[1] wrote in 1778: 'the natural weight of the thighs has a proper and sufficient pressure of itself'.

Those few modern riding instructors who also, commendably, encourage their pupils to free their legs up with exercise on the lunge will recognise that this rotation and draped position of the leg can only take place when the rider's pelvis is vertical and the lower back supported forward, flexible and upright. Dancers at the bar also have to employ the same good posture to acquire freedom through the leg. While great care is taken in the ballet class to warm up, limber up, stretch muscles and open joints, this rarely occurs in the average riding school.

Yet it is virtually impossible to apply the vital leg aids correctly without this initial freeing up through the hip joints. While most recognise that it is the combined effects of seat and leg which are so important to the horse, insufficient mention is made of the fact that it is all too easy to send out conflicting messages all at the same time. As teachers, one of our primary tasks should be to explain to the rider the link between the leg and the pelvis and how the position of one affects the position of the other. In addition, the rider should know why they are applying a particular aid at a particular time and appreciate how each action of the leg will not only have an effect on the horse's sides but will change what he is feeling under the saddle. Thirdly, timing and synchronisation must come into the equation as no single aid is of value unless asked for at the propitious moment.

Exercises achieved on a dummy horse would imbue students with greater understanding. The instructor can demonstrate how any drastic tipping backward of the pelvis will partially lock the hip joint, resulting in stiff legs which can no longer rotate and drape around the horse. In contrast, they can show how a fork seat, with the legs too far back, can block impulsion before it reaches the forehand, thus preventing acceleration. They can show how adopting the forward seat may still allow the horse to remain forward, 'through' and in balance, provided the hip–heel perpendicular plumb line is retained, with the rider weighted over their own two feet. The instructor can demonstrate how a tight, gripping thigh and calf muscles actually push the rider's seat and leg away from the horse, and so on.

As the hip and leg position are clearly interdependent, it should become clear on a moving horse that too drastic a change in either part may affect the equilibrium of the whole structure.

Let us imagine, however, that these matters have been addressed and our horse is working forward in a nice active trot, while we, tall, upright and

---

[1] Henry Herbert, 10th Earl of Pembroke, *Military Equitation*.

roughly over the fourteenth vertebra, are sitting adhesively to the trot. In a vertical posture, everything feels fairly neutral and balanced on the equine back so the horse can flow happily beneath us. If we have a good understanding of feel, we will be able to enhance movement by slight weight changes, generally emanating from the leg but felt by our horse through our seat. These are the fine-tuning aids which have been handed down to us over many centuries to become the accepted training aids of today. Unfortunately, too many people learn these aids parrot-fashion, failing to realise that they can only work to the benefit of the horse if certain adjustments are made elsewhere in the rider's seat to counter-balance any deleterious effect on the horse's equilibrium.

When we require more impulsion, therefore, we must take care that, in applying the spur or the lower leg to the girth area, our seat does not slide back, which would hollow the horse. Instead, we must send the seat bones forward more which can be done by bringing the shoulders back but supporting the hips through the lower back with a waist-towards-the-hands feeling.

Similarly, if we wish to collect the horse and retain him under us more, the leg moving a little back, to gather the hind legs, must not encourage us to sit heavier on the crotch. Due to the mechanical effect on our pelvis when the lower leg moves behind the vertical line of hip to heel there will be more contact here but we can counteract this by stretching up more through the abdomen and thinking tall.

Provided the rider appreciates that everything is connected to everything else and that no aid can work in isolation, they will learn to think before they act. In this way, a naïve or crude-seated rider can be transformed by a sensitive, highly tuned horse. Long before the instructor has uttered a word, the horse will show how a carelessly applied forward leg aid can cause him to hollow and disengage, whereas a backward aid can make him stop. In this way, riders very soon discover sensitivity and moderation, learning to ride from a discerning seat as well as a discerning leg.

Many riders try to create impulsion by mistakenly opening the knees and contracting the calves inward to urge their horses on. This necessitates heavier and heavier aids and when such action fails, as it generally does, the rider resorts to tightening the buttocks and grinding down against the horse. Contraction tends to create contraction, so the more the rider works with seat and legs, the more the horse struggles. As that great Olympic French rider Jean Saint-Fort Paillard[2] wrote, driving can certainly 'force a

---

[2] *Understanding Equitation* by Commandant Jean Saint-Fort Paillard, Riding Master to the Cadre Noir, Saumur.

Here Dutch Courage, ridden by Jennie Loriston-Clarke, shows good forward impulsion, with the rider correctly aiding him on the girth with legs that enfold the horse rather than constrict, while the hips remain central and do not impede the movement from behind.

(Photo: courtesy of *Horse & Rider Magazine*)

horse to move forward, and eventually make it obedient to the aids but it will never give the horse impulsion, that supplementary quality of obedience composed of generosity and almost spontaneity'.

It is this misunderstanding of the way in which impulsion works, i.e. from back to front, which leads to so many horses setting themselves against their rider at every stage of their forward progression. Others, trying their hearts out, have no option but to lower the wither in order to pull themselves forward from the shoulders in the way of a draft horse, as the rider makes it impossible for them to push from behind.

Yet, far from bringing about detrimental change, the legs also have the ability to transform the horse into a gymnast by amplifying his natural power. For example, the same leg placed forward on the girth, which can cause the hips to slide towards the cantle and block the horse in the loins, can convert itself into a light, positive, asking aid when the lower back lends extra support to keep the hips in the centre of the saddle. Coupled with the upper body stretching tall and the shoulders moving back, the rider can then invite the horse to swing through more. Used appropriately in this way, the forward leg aid creates greater impulsion by tapping into the sensitive girth area while the seatbones deepen and encourage from the centre.

Insufficient riders make use of the powerful aid made by the inside calf or ankle bone closing around the girth area where the nerve endings from the intercostal nerve are at their most concentrated and sensitive. Often, this requires only a tap or a lightning touch; Oliveira spoke of 'electric shocks' in the appropriate spot to ask the horse to move impulsively forward and off the leg. Such action is far more effective and far less tiring for the rider than the usual squeeze, squeeze, squeeze backward that is so often seen and which so often deadens the horse's sides. The girth area is also the reflex point which vets use if they wish to lift the horse's abdomen and spine during an examination of the back. A light, closing leg or succinct spur applied here therefore lifts the horse as well as sending him forward.

Contrary to popular belief, therefore, effective impulsion from behind can rarely be achieved by bearing down hard and certainly not by squashing the horse. Thinking upward through the transitions and riding with open hips, which broaden the base of support, and light legs which receive the horse's back and ribcage, allow and encourage the hind legs to manoeuvre in greater freedom. It is this allowing feeling which helps the horse to propel himself forward and through in true impulsion. It is always the horse who should do the pushing, never the rider.

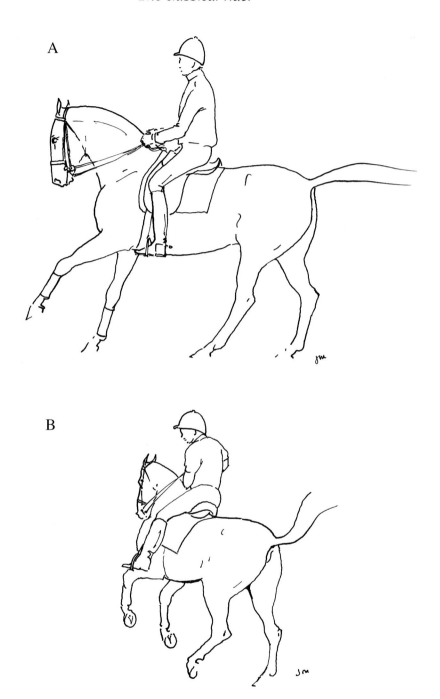

A

B

The correct use of the rider's bodyweight is imperative to teach the horse flying change. In A the rider's inside hip complements the action of the inside leg by remaining forward and supportive while the seat is quietly light. In B the inside hip has been allowed to slip crudely backwards. This has thrown the rider's seat to the outside, which will impair the horse's balance and make it very difficult for the horse to oblige.

Another function of the lower leg is to help to support and lighten the forehand through bends and particularly in figure work. In the absence of such an aid, when both legs are pulled back behind the gravity line of the rider's body, the lazy horse will want to support himself on the rider's inside hand instead, preferring to turn his corners like a ship with the quarters swinging out rather than remaining on the track. Kicking is of little avail save as an irritant leading to further contraction in the horse's thorax. The secret is light support at the girth from the inside leg, while the outside leg encourages the hocks to push and lengthen the outside of the horse's frame.

Correct flexion of the forehand comes not so much from the inside leg pushing the horse into the outside hand (although this image is helpful in the early days) but from the outside leg working the horse into and around the inside leg which acts as a pillar. A horse which really uses himself on corners will require a little softening forward of the outside rein as well as a *descent* with the inside so that his shoulders can move freely and expressively round. Although the outside rein will always provide a little more support, too many riders block the horse by retaining too strong a contact particularly in the turns and circles.

In the turn on the hocks or the demi-pirouette, it is the outside leg and outside rein which take the horse into the turn and the inside leg which supports and retains bend and impulsion. The inside leg must, again, be applied immediately after the turn, but if it fails to remain on the girth to send the horse forward, the horse cannot move off straight. So many turns about the quarters are spoiled because the rider allows the inside hip bone and lower leg to drift backwards and the horse moves off crookedly with the purpose of the exercise altogether undermined.

The outside leg, moving back behind the girth, also initiates the canter depart. Once into canter, the leg should remain in place so that if the canter requires to be freshened up or increased in amplitude, it is ready for use. If we remove it from its temporary place, bringing it level with the inside leg again, the horse should not be blamed for returning to trot. Canter is a lateral movement. The aids require to be given in a unilateral way which complements the horse's movement. As the rider's outside leg mirrors the pushing-off effect of the horse's outside hind in every phase of canter, it should remain there quietly, even if not in active use, until we indicate that our horse is to finish with canter. Only then should the leg assume its bilateral place for the diagonal gait again. Again, we need to remind ourselves that what we are doing with our legs is felt by the horse through our hips on his back and that the memory or sensation of the gait should remain in our own body until such time as we wish to make a transition.

175

In this World Cup class, we see the rider 'sucking' the horse up into *passage* by stretching taller. The picture is somewhat marred by the contact, however the demands of the Grand Prix test, particularly in the transitions, do not always encourage harmonious riding.

(Photo: Bob Langrish)

Once the horse knows this, there will be little difficulty in teaching counter-canter and still less when we come to reverse the aids for flying change. On a well-schooled horse the downward transition from canter to trot is achieved simply by bringing the outside leg out of the canter depart position. The horse feels the two hips square up again and obediently moves forward into trot. So many horses are blamed for breaking in canter when it was really the rider who broke.

On an impulsively moving, highly schooled horse, legs moving back bilaterally will have a collecting effect which contains the movement providing the rider enjoys an enveloping open seat with supple hips and relaxed thighs. Used with delicacy and support from the upper body, legs aiding well behind the girth, as though stretching down to meet the hind hooves, can help to achieve more height and cadence in the trot. By expanding the torso and drawing the rider's centre of gravity upward, as in *passage*, for example, the forehand is raised. Nevertheless, the rider has to use this weight aid with real subtlety. When the legs are moved back in this way, the front of the rider's seat deepens to act as a steadier, as though changing to a lower gear. If the position is held in balance and the legs then applied again to encourage more juice in the engine there is nowhere else for the energy to go other than upward which is exactly what we want.

The secret of a good *passage* is being able to stretch up through the abdomen and to take the horse with you. Even at Grand Prix level we see riders snatching at the reins to draw up the forehand but this is counter-productive. The leg action in *passage* requires great subtlety and discipline if the result is to be good, and riders are soon made aware that leg action alone achieves nothing if the rest of the rider's body is not in balance. Used ignorantly, such an aid on a very sensitive, uneducated or nervous horse could cause a sudden stop or even a rear.

Applied as a halting aid by closing down and dampening down impulsion, the leg moving back may also take the horse from the halt into the rein-back. Again, horse and rider must be in good balance to feel the effect of the pelvis deepening in the front of the saddle to take the horse backward and under the rider's weight.

At this point, if they have not done so already, readers should now understand what Mairinger was talking about when he said it is important to let the weight down.

On teaching clinics one of the first things I try to do with riders whose horses have a problem going forward is to reduce or lighten their leg action. This always surprises people who have become accustomed to trainers telling them to 'give him a good boot in the ribs' or to apply longer and sharper spurs. I am not against the use of the spur provided the rider has enough control and understanding of the aids to use it sparingly and appropriately. To apply it in every stride is inexcusable. To puncture a horse's sides is nothing short of abuse. Yet, once the rider learns to relax the leg muscles and lighten up through open hips and a good posture, horses will listen to a mere tickle of the leg – provided it is given in the right place and at the right time.

There is absolutely nothing new or revolutionary about all this. Past and present masters warn that true impulsion will elude the rider who rides with strong or heavy leg aids. In eighteenth-century England, Berenger wrote of 'legs which hang down easily and naturally'; Baucher wrote of 'equitation in bedroom slippers'; and his compatriot, d'Aure, of 'the breath of a boot'. General Albrecht, former Director of the Spanish Riding School of Vienna writes of 'relaxed thighs, hanging loosely from the hip joints by their weight alone'; and Nuno Oliveira of legs which 'adhere to the horse

Nuno Oliveira achieves great elevation with a deep knee and the lower leg draped gently back as though reaching down to the horse's hind feet. Note the soft contact with the bridle so that the *passage* is achieved without any degree of force.

(Photo by special permission of the late maestro)

without any muscular contraction' and 'with the utmost gentleness and the least effort'.

To understand all the aids more fully, it is helpful to use imagery to visualise the flow of impulsion which works through the horse. 'Straight, forward and calm!' was the *leitmotif* or favourite expression of Colonal Alois Podhajsky. For him, it summed up the absolute prerequisite of correct riding, knowing how to direct the horse from source without appearing to interfere in any way with the natural life-force beneath him. In this respect, the energy of the horse can best be likened to the flow of a river. As with the river, the flow of that energy, known as impulsion, must travel forward – towards the mouth. Like rivers, some horses will be swift flowing; others will be sluggish. Nevertheless, the actual direction of the flow should always be the same – from back to front. Riders should take time to appreciate this irrevocable fact before they attempt to aid the horse and channel, rechannel or stem the flow. It is all too easy to forget to apply the aids from back to front and to allow contortions and crookedness to appear on the way.

During that endless forward progression, however, it is all too easy for equine energy, like that of the river, to be diverted quite unintentionally. Often riders think they are straight and forward when they are not. Small cracks or inconsistencies may appear in the structure and this can result in the impulsive forces spilling out through crooked quarters or straying shoulders. They may also simply evaporate into thin air if the horse resists through the neck or in the mouth, thus breaking off the current. Here again the similarities between the sweep of the river and that of the horse emerge: the energy of the horse really need *not* be lost on the way.

Provided that every component part of the rider's body is indicating through and forward, the flow can be recycled. Draped legs, square hips, upright waist (both sides), square shoulders and united hands with the reins light against the neck all serve to form a channel for the river. With knowledgeable and sympathetic riding, the horse's impulsion can therefore be harnessed, contained and collected in the same way that power can be generated from water. Moreover, it can be brought back to its source and used again and again through the correct application of the rider's aids.

Only a rider who understands the full use of the seat and upper body aids, as well as those of hand and leg will discover just how to retain and make use of this energy in a way which seems effortless, harmonious and yet wonderfully controlled. The key word to all this is 'throughness', for many people know how to ride forward but all too few have a conception of how to allow the horse to move through them while still retaining his balance.

When I start teaching a new dressage pupil on a schoolmaster horse, after aligning the seat and making sure that all is correctly balanced, one of the first things to establish is that the aiding process, to allow energy to flow without unintentionally blocking, is clearly understood. The next stage is to make sure that the pupil also appreciates how they may stem, rechannel or arrest impulsion with intention. Riding is all about opening doors, closing others, half-opening some and partially closing more. As with water in a hosepipe, far greater power can be generated when we do not release everything at once.

The untutored rider often tends towards a seat which allows or opens the door so wide that the horse streams past them in every stride. Here impulsion may be offered but is wasted as it is allowed to escape. We have already discussed the weaknesses of the passenger seat and how it may damage the horse's back; another aspect is the fact that the rider is left with little or no influence over how their horse will use his natural life-force. Too often, through non-intervention, all the natural impulsion of the horse simply falls forward, outward and downward like a waterfall.

Once impulsion escapes through the horse being ridden on the forehand in this way, no amount of kicking with the legs will create more impulsion, neither will redirection be very easy. The lazy horse will become more and more ponderous, leading to stiffness; the forward-going animal may produce running and speed. This will be fine for racing but is inappropriate for any form of gymnastic work. Just think how long it takes to bring a racehorse back to a walk after he has streamed past the winning post! A horse on the forehand is totally inappropriate in a dressage or jumping arena – if we want control, it is only fair to the horse to unite or gather him.

Metaphorically speaking, the horse which runs straight under and past the rider is not only impossible to manoeuvre with any degree of nicety, he is like a river in full spate – beyond control! These are the horses for which the manufacturers create more and more gadgets, draw reins, gags, martingales, balancing reins, special nosebands, and a variety of severe bits. Unfortunately, by addressing those problems at the mouth of the horse (the mouth of the river), the designers of such products and the riders who buy them seem to have forgotten the mainstream and its source.

In Chapter 7, we addressed the subject of the opening aids, stretching up, squaring the shoulders and riding proactively forward from the waist. By the same token, the rider should become aware of the dampening down and absorbing aids. Discreetly applied, and coupled with a subtle use of hand and leg, these collecting aids can actually lead to increased impulsion, so that the horse offers power without speed, and slower, statelier gaits with greater engagement and a lighter forehand. The walk is the first gait in which the horse can learn to push more from behind. It is irritating when we hear well-meaning experts say, 'You must never interfere with the walk; you can ruin the walk by collecting it.' Clearly, their idea of collection is not the correct one. We are not talking about shortening or restricting the horse in front; rather about increasing the magnititude of the push from behind so that the flow of power comes up at us through the horse's back which will give greater scope and freedom to the shoulder. If the horse does not learn to rebalance and elevate more in the walk, what hope is there for the other gaits?

I like to think of the closing and opening aids of the seat and legs rather like little sluice gates on our river; they may allow more impulsion to flow through by opening here and there, but they may also close down, in part or even entirely, depending upon what is being required at the time. Just occasionally, particularly with a horse that pulls against us, we may even want to build the odd dam here and there.

It should be recognised that none of these openings and closings will be permanent. Like the river, the energy of the horse is a vibrant, living thing and just as weather affects the water, impulsion will be determined by his mood, his state of fitness and other more general conditions. Interacting with energy is all part of a living process which gives us the power to channel the horse in every stride, every gait and every moment. It should be so subtle that the horse will think it is his idea and the only part of the rider which should be working hard is the brain.

There are some riders who have such a good feel for tuning in to the horse's energy that they know automatically how and when to direct, collect or change its pattern without appearing to think about it. These riders may never have studied an academic theory in their lives, their reactions are intuitive and instinctive, learned in the field. In short, they are natural horsemen and women and are much to be envied. I would like to say that there are many of them but, sadly, I would be misleading the reader.

Whether just to improve our riding generally or to ensure better jumping and dressage results, the vast majority of us will need initially a pair of eyes on the ground to help us to aid the horse correctly and in a way which conforms to his anatomy. Hips, legs, waist, shoulders, head and fingers all have a part to play in the channelling process and with the sensitive horse it may only take one collapsed hip or crooked shoulder to throw the energy out sideways and away from its central course. I am constantly amazed how a well-schooled horse will show up something as small as a slack knee or misplaced thigh by starting to 'fall off' the track. The pull of gravity should never be underestimated.

It should also be explained how every aid requires a supplementary aid to redress and equalise the balance, and this includes amplification and increase of impulsion as well as its collection. All too often riders use the hands alone to counter-balance when, instead, they should be taught how to achieve this through their weight. This certainly does not mean throwing the horse in the opposite direction by leaning this way or that; a mere letting down of one seatbone, the forward flexion of one loin muscle or the increase of weight into the stirrups are all powerful aids. The latter aid is one I have been teaching for many years, but it was only after the translation of La Guérinière's *School of Horsemanship* that I found, finally, I was not alone! The following passage is oh so true.

> The aid of putting weight on to the stirrups is the subtlest of all the aids; the legs
> then serve as counterweight to straighten the haunches and to hold the horse straight

in the balance created by the rider's heel. This aid presupposes a high degree of obedience in the horse and much sensitivity, since by the mere act of putting more weight on one stirrup than the other, a horse is brought to respond to this movement.

These words of wisdom have vindicated me against those critics who have never understood the value of riding with more weight into the legs, insisting instead that everything is done through a heavy seat bearing down on the back of the horse.

Nowhere is the inadvertent use of blocking aids with the seat and legs more obvious that in the transition from the *piaffe* to the collected and then extended trot. To put a rider who has not learned the art of directing weight into the stirrups on a horse which knows the difference can be mindboggling for both. Some riders may get stuck in the *piaffe*, as I have seen with my own horses, others seem unable to get out of extension, also seen. 'What do I do to stop him?' the pupil cries in frustration after the twentieth step of bouncing on the spot or being run away with round the arena in a spanking extended trot. Fiddling with the reins is of little avail; a good horse responds to much finer body aids than that. If only people thought more about *where* the energy is coming from they would understand what to do. In the case of the *piaffe* rider, all they have to do to release is gently open an imaginery door at the centre and take more weight into the stirrups[3]. In the case of their counterpart, it is just a question of closing the door and doing the opposite. It should be simple.

It is the riders who fail to make themselves clear who get stuck in a mode. In self-defence the horse often goes into auto-pilot because this was the last true instruction he received and if a rider has not neutralised the seat, the horse feels safer continuing in that pattern.

Nevertheless, confusion in these areas is quite not as ridiculous as one might think when, for example, the aid to the horse to go forward is to close the lower leg on the girth, whereas the aid to halt or to slow down is also to close the leg, albeit slightly further back. It is the manner in which we either tone up or let the weight down in between which makes the difference to what the horse is feeling.

This is why instructors have a duty to explain how each aid feels to the horse, exactly where it should be applied and how vital it is that after every aid is given and obeyed there must be a moment of respite. This moment of release, quietly saying 'thank you' to the horse, is what the French classical school describes as the *descente de main* and the *descente des jambes*.

On a very well-trained horse, the use of this may be prolonged, the horse

---

[3] La Guérinière also wrote: 'by bearing down upon both stirrups equally we may "quicken its gait" when it holds back more than it should', *School of Horsemanship*.

ridden on parole; yet on a more modest scale it is a vital factor in the training programme for any horse. Without the *descent*, the horse will have no reference point other than a tweak in the mouth or a jab with the spur to tell him, 'Yes! – you did that correctly!' And why, logically, should he do it again if he has received only unpleasant feelings? Isn't he more likely to comply with generosity if, instead, he receives a reward? This may sound banal, but the momentary release, the second's respite, is more sensible by far and makes the horse want to perform again and again as well as keeping the mouth sweet and his body listening for more.

Similarly, the *descente des jambes* indicates the feeling that all is well, the end of a movement correctly done, a form of neutralising the aids before we go on to the next request. This release, the letting go of the leg, is never more appropriate than in a showing class when you see horses lined up in front of the judge. Almost always, there will be one or two horses which continually try to shuffle sideways or move backwards. This is irritating for the judge, the rider, spectators and, most of all, the horse. So why is he doing it? Invariably, it is the rider's legs, too far back, supposedly straightening the horse but in fact contracting against him and sending the energy awry, which causes such restlessness. One longs to say, 'Let your legs hang! Let the weight down! – then he'll stand!'

In similar vein, I have had problems with certain pupils on a particular soft-backed schoolmistress mare called Andorinha. The rider asks for halt. Obediently, she halts, but the rider is still asking with the leg, forgetting to release and say thank you. She is so off the leg that even if the hand has yielded, her response is to rein-back. 'Hey,' they cry, still with the aid on, 'I never asked for that!' But they did, not just with the leg but with the seat too.

By this time they are halfway round the arena, all backwards. 'Let go!' I cry. 'Let your leg drop, give with it and just sit up!' They feel foolish when they realise how simple it all was, but it is a lesson well worth learning.

Even the most novice horse will respond and learn far more quickly if the aid is applied and released immediately in this way. Never go on closing down or you will lose the generosity of your horse. That is why riders must always return to the correct, upright, neutral position after giving an aid. Staying in an asking position, such as the driving seat, after the horse has complied is to punish him if he has already given his all. Overkill is absolutely detrimental to horses; it destroys the learning process for they can only learn by association and the door must always open again after it has shut. 'Open the door!' was the phrase that rang around the indoor riding school of the Cadre Noir, more than any other, under General l'Hotte.

The correctly trained horse performs happily because he knows his rider

Like so many masters, Henry would focus into the back of the horse's poll in the higher airs.
Nevertheless it was his deep, centred seat which allowed his horses to be light.
(Photo: courtesy *East Anglia Daily Times*)

will let him get on and do his job painlessly and without obstruction between requests. If the aids fail, a swift tap with the stick is kinder by far than stronger and heavier aids. Superior impulsion is seen in the horse which can obey the rider's every request immediately because his weight is in his hocks and his engine is permanently engaged. This horse will be light and free in the forehand, the energy soaring upwards like that of a bird in flight.

In this way, all the aids should be mere nuances. They are developed by feel and they cannot just happen overnight. The silent language developed between horse and rider takes years to perfect. It can be much helped along the way, however, by visualisation and positive thinking. The French cavalry officer and author Beudant – so much admired by Nuno Oliveira – reminds us time and again to 'observe and reflect'.

We see many ugly sights in dressage today. We must take care only to copy the best and not to be distracted by the crude. A new fashion is the waterskiing position where the rider leans behind the vertial, the arms outstretched against the rein which acts like a pulley. Riding backward in this way is the very last sensation we should indulge in if we wish our horse to be forward thinking. Contrive instead to copy something balanced and beautiful, watch the riders of the Spanish Riding School on video and note how easily their posture relates to classical ballet or opera singing.

As I was finishing this book, I went to Wembley in London to view the much heralded Royal Horse Gala where four respected but private trainers from four different countries had gathered together with their horses to produce a spectacular dressage event staged by *Horse and Hound*. The commentator was quite clear that this would involve four types of riding – classical High School, an exposition of competition dressage, bullfight riding and circus.

While the horses used in the display varied quite considerably in shape and type, the Friesians dominating in terms of power and size over the Portuguese, Spanish and Lipizzaner breeds, it was fascinating to note scarcely any difference in the national styles of riding. All rode quietly, all rode upright, no one's hands or head seemed to move and practically all had brought their horses to a high level of obedience and accuracy in their particular field. Whether we were seeing a circus bow, a High School *capriole*, a parry before a fantasy bull or an FEI dressage half-pass, the posture of each rider was the same, the correct one. The fact that some of the acts were a little less polished than others mattered not. What riveted and enthused the audience was the fact that the horses seemed to enjoy it to the full. Most noticeable was the fact that there was no shying away from the clapping; indeed, they lapped it up. From countless lips, the comments were the same at the end. 'Didn't the horses enjoy themselves?' and 'Didn't the riding look so quiet and effortlesss?'

Lightness, therefore, is the key to forward impulsion and flow. If we think logically about that current of energy travelling through the horse from behind, along his back and sides, up his neck and into his poll, to be delivered through the mouth and back to our hands, we should begin to understand that all that marvellous energy is at our disposal if we encompass or embrace it in a light way. Any heaviness with hand, seat or leg is going to fragment that energy, block it and make it very hard for the horse to answer every request as the thought enters our head. The river flows, the power is offered, the rider accepts gratefully and offers back and the recycling process can continue. It is a never-ending circle.

CHAPTER 11

Bones of contention – the magic triangle

Not very long ago I was asked to give an after-dinner lecture on the subject of riding and good posture. When it came to question time, someone remarked, 'What you are saying about projection sounds very sexually aggressive.'

You could have heard a pin drop. The speaker was a middle-aged woman and I could not help noticing that she was round-shouldered and drooped in her chair. I felt she could have been quite attractive had she not had such a hang dog look about her. She made it clear she was a rider but as I had never seen her on a horse I could not help wondering if the horse had a hang dog look too because, like it or not, horses do generally mirror their owners.

'Look,' I responded, trying not to appear as though the question had thrown me – which of course it had – 'if looking sexually aggressive means not being ashamed of one's body, then perhaps you have a point. Perhaps we all need to make a statement about who we are; I am who I am, and I'm not ashamed to be that person. However,' I added, 'I don't think it's got anything to do with sexuality or aggression, just about you as a human being, and accepting yourself. What I can promise is, once you ride in the way I have described, and take it seriously, you soon find that you will want to move that way in your everyday life. And once you move that way, it gives you added confidence. People notice you! Statistics show that muggers back off from people who move with purpose; it's not a question of aggression but it is about moving with confidence. If you look like a victim you may be treated like a victim; if you look in control, they think twice. As for your own comfort, if you master the initial difficulties of setting aside the habits of years, life will never be quite the same again. You will never again be comfortable slouching at a dinner table, or be tempted by a saggy old armchair and, furthermore, you should never suffer from back trouble. Neither will your horse.'

At that point I noticed her next door neighbour nudge her meaningfully;

I heard later that both she and her horse had back trouble.

In life there will always be people who want to heap scorn, minimise or argue about anything which is presented theoretically. The world is round; a rider should sit on a triangular base. For the layman, the latter should be easier to prove than the former and, yes, I am all for the proof of the pudding being in the eating. When the controversies first began about the three-point seat – a purely pictorial term – I found the only satisfactory way to settle most arguments was to demonstrate the classical seat on horseback. The moment people saw the control achieved by riding over the horse's centre of motion in this way, and perceived how, in movement, the three-point contact stabilised the rider, all argument evaporated.

What was more dramatic at these demonstrations was the very real and noticeable difference this simple mode of posture exerted on horses which had never before been ridden this way. As unbalanced horses came together and transformed, not only were people won over to the idea, they wanted to know more. Moreover, they were excited to find that such a seat could work for them and that it was not just 'my thing'.

It soon transpired that the only critics who seemed unconvinced or who wanted to argue further were those who had read about this seat but not seen it in practice. Clearly, they had little conception of the actuality and perhaps it was all too simple. There will always be those who wish to overcomplicate everything. Not for the first time I am reminded of the wise saying of Emerson: 'Nothing astonishes men so much as common sense and plain dealing.' This is so true when it comes to riding!

The other stumbling block for some was their saddles. Unless you have sat in a saddle which allows Xenophon's standing or straddling position, you cannot conceive just how such a seat might be possible. Unfortunately, we were coming up against people whose saddles forced them into a two-point position and, with the best will in the world, it is virtually impossible to sit with a vertical pelvis when the twist is designed like a ski slope.

My own first experience of the three-point seat was in a Portuguese bullfighting saddle, almost identical to the *manège* saddle of the seventeenth and eighteenth centuries and similar in feel to the ceremonial saddles of the Spanish Riding School. No longer tilted into the chair position, the difference in contact was a revelation. Once one had got over the the shock of being placed so much closer to the wither, it was an amazing experience. Suddenly one felt like a pilot instead of a passenger!

Some modern dressage saddles will do the same for riders; others will not. Giving newcomers an opportunity to feel exactly where all their seatbones are is paramount to understanding. The next stage is to point out the effects the new posture is having on their horse. Often it is a time of

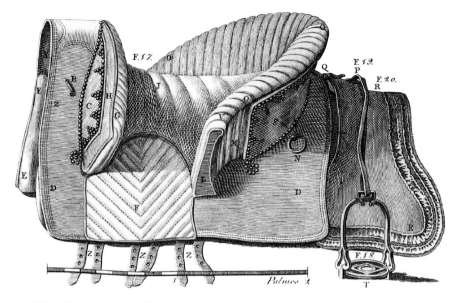

The traditional Portuguese saddle is a virtual replica of those classical saddles used in the time of La Guérinière and other eighteenth-century masters. They are similar to today's ceremonial saddles of the Spanish Riding School and enable the rider to straddle the horse with a full contact of the entire seat, forward and back, without discomfort.

(Engraving from *Luz da Liberal é Nobre Arte da Cavallaria*)

revelation even for the most obstinate die-hard. On so many occasions, I have heard the words: 'This is unbelievable; it's like magic.'

If this sounds patronising, I ought to point out that when I wrote my first articles on the classical seat, I undertook the work with great humility. Designed as a series of lectures to help our students, I doubt if I would ever have sent the manuscript away had it not been for those pupils pushing me and, in addition, the encouragement of Lucinda Green who told me firmly to 'get yourself published'. Again, she had come into my life at the right juncture and extended her generous time without reservation.

It was Kate and Marion O'Sullivan who accepted the first three articles on the seat for *Horse and Rider Magazine* and then commissioned a further nine; the rest is history. I have been writing for that thoughtful publication ever since and enormously admire the dedicated family who run it. The O'Sullivans truly love horses and have done a great deal for the horse world through publishing honest and searching articles, often, bravely, from comparative unknowns like myself.

What motivated me most to write in depth about the rider's seat was the vivid memory of how, for years as a teenager, I struggled, longing to know more only to find a dearth of information and certainly nothing in simple words about what one should or should not be doing in the saddle. For me, depth of knowledge came the hard way, from trial and error, first on unschooled ponies, later on flyaway Thoroughbreds and finally on kind but highly sensitive schoolmasters who showed me more than any human seemed to want to show. A natural progression from the whole process was the gradual turn to academic study but this was always conducted hand in hand with practical riding. One thing was certain, unlike some of my critics, I had not treated the subject lightly.

Since that time, far from being an armchair expert, my theory was and is, tested daily with the variety of different types of horse and pupil that enrol on my clinics. The latter are just as important as the former, for a correct riding formula has to work for everyone, not just the talented few.

I admit I work more at home with the hotblood breeds, the Thoroughbred, Arab, Anglo-Arab, Lusitano and so on, but I have had several big warmbloods, such as the Hanoverian, and also Irish Draught horses here in my stables for schooling and they too have responded to this seat and become very much lighter on the rein than I ever dreamt possible.

People are always saying that warmbloods 'need' a stronger seat, contact, approach and so on. I am not so sure I agree with this as I have found that once one can tune in to their centre of balance, these horses can be rendered as light and manoeuvrable as any Iberian or Anglo-Arab. Nevertheless, I believe the rider needs a stronger back and a bigger frame to achieve success for the simple reason that the warmbloods are themselves larger and, due to their longer strides, demand more muscular support from the rider's back if they are to be ridden from behind.

At home, most days I ride, teach with and school at least three horses. When I go abroad or teach around the UK, I have been known to ride up to eighteen horses a day. Concentrated work of this kind does not allow for fanciful theory or unworkable ideas. Taking private lessons from eight in the morning to eight at night with scarcely a break and still feeling physically fit at the end of it, without a single twinge of back or hip pain, must say a lot for the way in which one rides and deports oneself, especially over the age of 40!

Despite all the evidence to show that, in order to move freely, horses need to work as unencumbered as possible under the rider, it is sad that, even today, there are many dressage and general purpose saddles which are not designed to help either horse or rider. Some are so high in the pommel and cantle that they lock the rider into a position which may not necessarily be the right one; others spread the weight so successfully that it is spread back far beyond an acceptable level for the horse.

Like so many other expressions used in equitation, the term three-point seat is, of course, one of imagery. All clichés, of whatever nature, have to be taken with a degree of common sense so that advice such as 'drape your legs', 'soften your wrists', 'relax your stomach' do not mean abandon all tone, make your wrists floppy, collapse your stomach! In the same way 'maintain a contact through the seatbones and the fork' – the three 'points' of contact – does not mean come off everything else and sit on your pubic bone, as some people tried to make out; neither does it deny the existence of other connecting tissue or, indeed, padding and fat which exist around the seat area and which protect the seatbones.

Coming back to England from Portugal as the wife of a former British cavalry officer who used the term regularly, I was somewhat unprepared for the consternation and attacks which greeted those first articles which finally made it to publication after Henry's death. I was well aware that this description, which has been around in equestrian terminology for decades, had probably originated in Europe where it is familiar in all traditional dressage circles. However, as most British instructors had, at some time, been exposed or influenced by the ethos of the European cavalry schools such as Saumur, Hanover, Stockholm and so on, it was hard to understand what all the fuss was about. Yet my critics were not coming from among those former traditionalists, the whispering campaign against this perfectly natural way of riding was started among civilian ranks from a more modern influence.

It became obvious that people were rejecting the past and there was a new, independent mood about. Even logical precepts such as keeping your knees against the saddle, hands still or sitting up proudly were, all of a sudden, decidedly out of fashion.

In those days, I had less of a comprehensive equestrian library than I do today, but I remember taking heart from a small book belonging to my late husband which bemoaned the fact that the British were different from the Continentals when it came to riding and would never accept there was only one way which was correct and true. Perhaps significantly, this volume had been written anonymously, the writer only admitting to being an 'Officer of the Household Brigade of Cavalry'. The book was published by Edward Moxon of Dover Street, London in 1839 under the title *Hints on Horsemanship* and the author rued the fact that 'England is the only European country which admits of more than one style of riding. But in all Europe . . . there is but one style of riding taught, as a system; that style is the *manège*, or military style. The military style is, and must ever be, essentially a one-handed style, for the soldier must have his right hand at liberty for his weapons.' Suddenly, I realised that the author of this small, little known book had, in fact, hit the nail on the head most precisely.

The Moxon publication brought home with startling clarity the reason why the subject of the rider's seat has been so much neglected in recent times. It is, of course, because people are no longer required to ride one-handed, although in the army and the police force (and indeed the polo field) there is still some necessity. Until not so long ago, however, it was considered a life and death matter if you could not control your horse almost entirely from the seat, the legs and the upper body. As only one hand controlled the reins, the horse was expected to be light and hence the rightful preoccupation was with position and an understanding of the weight aids to achieve this end. Little wonder then that cattle ropers and bullfighters still ride from a seat which renders the horse well engaged and light on the forehand and I am not referring to those who mar the picture through overuse of the curb.

With two hands on the reins, there should be no excuse for dressage riders to resort to either rough-handed or bastardised methods. Sadly for many sport horses, however, people have become complacent and see no need to develop the type of mastery and technique promoted by the cavalry schools and those natural rural horsemen. Instead, they have rewritten the rulebooks. Lightness of the forehand is talked about but little understood. Contact is measured in terms of weight and denial of the old requisites of manoeuvrability from the saddle, such as the ability to pirouette the horse on a dinner plate radius or simply to make a 90 degree turn across the school without pulling on the inside rein. Unwittingly, new and modern ideas have allowed riders to become far more dependent on the reins than ever before. Thus ideas concerning the importance of teaching an effective controlling seat have diminished drastically with the disappearance of one-handed riding.

Even with the huge upsurge of interest in competitive dressage, people are all too keen to control the horse from the front end (see Chapters 14 and 15) and a preoccupation with 'outline' has merely accentuated this. For some, it is no longer enough to ride with two or four reins in two hands, they have to resort to draw reins, balancing reins and all forms of constricting nosebands to obtain, again from the front, the control they lack from the seat. If these contraptions were banned by every serious dressage instructor, particularly those in high places, we might see more desire to understand the use of the seat and to ride with a more thinking and feeling approach. It would also be refreshing to encourage one-handed riding in dressage competition as a proof of correct training and to reward it. If this were done, one could virtually guarantee a return to good posture and an understanding of the three-point seat.

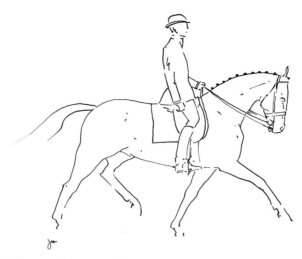

One-handed riding requires a very balanced three-point position and total confidence from both horse and rider, whatever the discipline.

Two-handed riding and a preoccupation with outline has led to the employment of the two-point dressage seat with certain riders. Here, to compensate for the lack of balance, there is greater tension on the reins, which shortens the horse's neck and produces a less flowing overall picture.

Fortunately, the traditional disciplines of classical or *manège* riding are still preserved in a few isolated regions or countries. Despite mounting pressures from outside, the Spanish Riding School continues to uphold the age-old principles of lightness, delicate aids and the need for a well-balanced seat. It is interesting that they, too, find it important to demonstrate one-handed riding in much of their display work.

In Portugal and Spain, Mexico and parts of the United States, where work with cattle still requires one-handed riding, it is inconceivable to ride with anything other than an independent, aiding classical seat and good riders scarcely touch the curb. It was by watching the Portuguese that I came to understand the weight aids we discussed in the last chapter, but these weight aids cannot be applied unless one sits with a full contact of all the seatbones to ensure quiet stability. Rocking on just two points under the buttocks leads to instability while sending out endless confusing signals to the horse.

I ought to add that correctly given weight aids are very fine and virtually invisible. They most certainly do not involve a drastic leaning in or out as one might expect to see in a children's bending race or in a bad demonstration of Western riding.

So why is the concept of the three-point seat so important? I have no intention of reiterating the full mechanics of this posture as it is more than adequately described and illustrated in my book *The Classical Seat* which has sold over 20,000 copies worldwide. I will, however, state that two theories of thought exist as to how this seat should be interpreted and they are probably much closer to each other than their advocates may wish to admit. In a general sense, however, the three-point contact merely implies that the rider feels they are sitting on *a full contact of the pelvic floor*.

Those people whose lack of centred posture or suitable saddlery still inclines them into the chair seat will basically be balanced only on the buttocks – the mythical two points or half seat. If the rider rounds or convexes the back, such a position may lead to the tail being turned under the trunk. Such action is essentially harmful to the spine for reasons already discussed and concentrates the rider's weight towards the horse's loins in a way not dissimilar to the old-fashioned hunting seat of the nineteenth century. Such a seat merely placed the horse on the forehand and flattened his outline, leaving, as Francis Dwyer wrote, 'the propellers out behind'.

Fortunately, not every hunting gentleman rode like that and when people began to adopt the forward seat and take the weight up and off the horse's back, there was noticeably less breakdown among horses. However, even this happy adaptation to common sense caused indignant rumblings in the Shires and the gentlemen's clubs of St James's. There has always been more invective from overnight experts in the riding world than in any other when change is threatened!

The main difficulty for the average rider seeking to acquire a full seat as opposed to the half seat is to be able to sit up while keeping the thighs and

Here, Emile Faurie displays a very centred position in the *piaffe*, demonstrating a clear three-point seat contact with the saddle

Christopher Bartle on Wily Trout again demonstrates the importance of the three-point seat to achieve balance in the half-pass.

knees sufficiently under the seat for the body weight to flow downwards and into the ankle joint. Pushing against the stirrup with an exaggerated deep heel creates stiffness in the hamstrings, causing the whole seat to slide back. It is the depth of the knee which is the secret to a balanced seat, as former cavalry instructor Gordon Wright points out in his book *Horsemanship & Horsemastership*[1]: 'The knees are forced down as low as the adjustment of the stirrups will permit, without causing the stirrup straps to hang in rear of the vertical. Knees are neither limp nor stiff, nor is there any effort to 'pinch' with them. Flexed and relaxed, they rest with their inner sides in continuous contact with the saddle.'

To achieve this, we should again consider the natural balance of our bodies as when we stand or move around on the ground. The knee is always under us and it is this perpendicular support of our bodyweight through firm, stretched quadriceps (the muscles at the front of the thigh) which helps to allow us to remain upright and over our own feet. In riding, we should have the sensation of letting go and extending these front thigh muscles so that the knee may take its rightful place against the saddle. This is a very different feeling from pushing down forcefully or tensing the hamstrings at the back of the thigh, which tends to block the horse by tensing the calf muscles. In my experience, there is also a good cosmetic reason for riding in a better posture as overuse of the wrong leg muscles tends to result in very muscular-looking legs; learning to let go with the leg and deepen through the front of the thigh tends to give a toned, streamlined look to the whole.

For riders who have difficulty in letting go and stretching through the front of the leg, I ask them to imagine they are about to kneel. This helps the feeling of letting the knee find its level and, as with the therapeutic kneeling chair (designed to help clerical staff sitting at their desks all day), such a posture places the lower back forward and supports the spine.

Apart from lack of tone and general stiffness, the greatest enemy to achieving a balanced seat is nervous tension which, even in a normally supple, athletic person, can create havoc. Novice riders should be helped to understand that every person's innate and natural reaction to fear and uncertainty will be to curl up to protect the vital organs, so they are not being foolish when they display these responses. However, once they can understand that the three-point seat actually unites them to the horse and that a three-legged stool is totally stable, whereas a two-legged one is not, confidence will grow. Logically, the deep seat which brings all the

---

[1] *The Cavalry Manual of Horsemanship & Horsemastership, Education of the Rider* (the official manual of the United States Cavalry School at Fort Riley, edited for today's civilian riders) by Gordon Wright.

connecting surfaces to bear without grip is going to be very much more adhesive than one which reduces that contact to a minimum. It is especially comforting when the rider begins to feel they can embrace the horse at every level rather than trying to balance on two points alone.

Until a couple of decades ago, the average British rider was considered by his European counterparts to have little seat at all. The Germans, the French, the Portuguese, the Spanish all employed the three-point seat, whereas the British were still locked into the hunting seat whether they hunted or not. While many modern European authors wrote of the merits of the three-point seat, and incorporated the term into their official manuals[2], there is surprisingly little literature from British writers on the subject. Hence the furore when I first put pen to paper.

Just to confuse the issue, one author had written of the coccyx as forming the third point of the triangle, instead of the crotch. Every doctor will warn us against ever sitting on our tail bone, which is not only virtually impossible but would, of course, be excruciatingly painful. It is possible, however, to understand how such a theory came about. When one rides in the classical three-point position there is a sensation, as one bends the small of the back forward, that one is pushing the coccyx towards the pommel at the same time. In actual fact, the coccyx is lifting well clear of the saddle as one does this, but the impression can be that the triangular feel of support stems from this point and spreads outwards and forward towards the two ischial ridges which eventually unite in front to form the fork. This is also described in Gordon Wright's book. Perhaps Veronica Ward got it right when, in a reader's letter to *Dressage Magazine* as these arguments were raging, she suggested that the classical rider's seat might be thought of as diamond shaped. This might well save a great deal of argument!

A nineteenth-century writer, Francis Dwyer, who wrote a very concise and in-depth book entitled *On Seats and Saddles*, subscribes to both concepts. 'To have a good seat, [the rider's] weight must be distributed equally between the three bones forming the triangle of his fork, and not on any two of these, or on the third alone.'

Dwyer goes on to expound the widely accepted theory that the seat should comprise as many adhesive surfaces as possible. Yet, further into the book, he somewhat confusingly brings the cocyx into the equation, which he amusingly names the 'Monboddo bone' and suggests that this may also form the third point, although 'the Monboddo bone must neither be overweighted nor made too conspicuous'.

---

[2] For example, The German National Equestrian Federation *Official Instruction Handbook*.

When I first wrote about the three-point seat, I confess to say I had not heard of Dwyer nor of many other venerable authors of the time. I had, however, read Hans Handler who merely confirmed my understanding of the seat by passing on the work of his superior, Colonel Podhajsky, and others before him in his great book *The Spanish Riding School* now sadly out of print. It was still some time before I would have the privilege to meet, to correspond with and to know his successor and compatriot, Brigadier General Kurt Albrecht.

Albrecht was to take over the directorship at Vienna after Handler's death and was not only at home in the rarified atmosphere of the Winter Riding School but, as an international FEI dressage judge, he well understood the problems that face riders out in the competitive field. The two books he has written are therefore destined to help people who may never necessarily have had the benefit of sound classical training to ride more efficiently, safely and in sympathy with their horses. Had his extremely lucid *Principles of Dressage* been available in English at the time my own articles and later book were under attack in the British equestrian press, one pertinent quote from him might well have silenced all the critics. This would have saved me a great deal of anguish at a time when I felt vulnerable following the death of a husband whose teachings I was determined to keep alive.

Albrecht is refreshingly unequivocal about the triangular base of the classical rider's position. He writes, 'The stability of the correct, properly balanced deep seat depends on the ability of the rider to maintain at all times an upright posture with the weight of his upper body resting on the three points . . . The three points of contact are at the junction of the two ischia (seat bones), the broad, fairly flat bones which form the posterior and lower border of the pelvis, with in front the inferior process of the pubic bone (the fork).'

I had written roughly the same but, having no knowledge of this highly respected authority's work at the time, was unable to draw on his book to support my own. Neither was I able to enlist the support of any public figure in Britain for, although many agreed with me in private, they were reluctant to put pen to paper. For a time I felt my back was against the wall but, nevertheless, remained true to my beliefs.

Later, when I remarried, Richard helped me to regain confidence and encouraged me to go on writing and to stick to my guns. Using this seat and demonstrating it in public, I began to discover that I seemed to be among the minority in Britain who had schooled several horses to *piaffe* and *passage* without having to resort to strong hands, permanent spurring or the necessity to teach the horse to engage and pick up his hind legs with constant smacks with a stick on the cannon bones.

In the final analysis I knew it was merely the judicious use of the weight aids of the seat which allowed this to happen and that a very gentle emphasis through the third point is as vital in its way for collection as more emphasis over the other two are for more forward movement and extension. Indeed, it is the subtle combination of all the facets of the seat which makes this way of riding so effective that one can happily ride the horse through almost every movement with either one hand or two on the reins.

On one occasion I gave an exhibition in the beautiful little indoor school at The Royal Mews showing shoulder-in, half-pass, *travers*, counter-canter, flying changes and *passage* and *piaffe* with one of my Portuguese stallions, Palomo Linares, with no bridle and just a silk cord in his mouth. When, later, someone accused me of trick riding, I could not help but smile. Richard had taught me to remain unfazed by such remarks and I quietly pointed out that there is no trick about a horse truly on the aids. The trick, if you can call it that, is to learn to ride with a seat which gives total control whatever the horse wears in his mouth.

Nevertheless, the classical seat argument was not destined to go away. A pamphlet was privately published by a rival, condemning my book, and, despite the support from home, I would scarcely have been human had I not been affected by it. I was much lifted, however, by a surprise review which arrived on my breakfast table when I was working in Kenya. Not only did the author write in glowing praise of the whole book, he also took the pamphleteer severely to task for his unwarranted criticism.

By this time, I was working on my third book, a history of dressage, and I shall never forget the moment when I opened the contents of that letter; my heart simply soared and my work took on new life and purpose. The review was from *Riding Magazine*, the reviewer no less an authority than Elwyn Hartley Edwards, known and respected by everyone in the horse world from the far reaches of Asia to the Rocky Mountains of Colorado and no doubt beyond. Author of over 30 best-selling titles on a multitude of subjects, the best known being his definitive book on saddlery, one could not have asked for more. Years later, I met Elwyn for the first time at the Lisbon Show. I found in him a singularly gentle and charming man, full of knowledge but, in that way of English gentlemen, very understated. When I tried to tell him then how much that review had meant to me and how it had given me the confidence to go on writing, he shrugged my thanks aside with a self-deprecating smile. Nevertheless, my gratitude remains to this day. For another author to give praise so unreservedly to someone starting out in the same jealous field shows a big heart and a generous spirit and, these days, such commodities are rare indeed. I shall never forget his kindness.

In the meantime, with book number three, I had begun to study the works of some of the traditional English dressage masters. The best known, with whom I was already familiar through my researches on the Spanish horse, was the illustrious Duke of Newcastle, fervent Royalist and tutor to Charles II. Newcastle, the breeder, High School practitioner and author is still highly regarded in Europe today but was never fully appreciated, either in his lifetime or even in later times, in Britain. There were many others, however, equally famous in their time, such as Berenger, Master of the Horse to George II, and the Earl of Pembroke who schooled cavalry officers for active service in the reign of George III. Philip Astley, a High School enthusiast who ran a riding school for the gentry in London in the late eighteenth century, also left a useful book, as did Colonel J. G. Peters who came later.

Over the years, I have saved up for and acquired some of these rare volumes which I count among my most treasured possessions. No serious author can be without his or her books with their faded engravings, the brown spots on the parchment pages and the smell of the leather. The integrity, the love and the care that have gone into these carefully worked chapters is almost tangible and, I am sure, exert a special influence. My own feeling of reverence was enormous when the Pembroke I waited for and eventually acquired turned out to have been the handbook of J. G. Peters. As well as bearing his bookplate, it also carries the beautiful black-inked copperplate signature of that author on the flyleaf. If Pembroke inspired him, and I admired Peters, who knew what might brush off on me?

By the time James Fillis went to instruct the Russian cavalry in St Petersburg at the end of the nineteenth century, the educated British rider was still a force to be reckoned with when it came to an understanding and mastery of advanced equitation. Nevertheless, it is also true to say that, even in Newcastle's time, only a very few specialists pursued the intricacies of *manège* work, most preferring to sit in whatever style they found easiest for themselves, regardless of the horse. Newcastle castigated these Corinthian gentlemen for their lack of concern, their lack of self-discipline and their lack of interest in the niceties of the *manège*. 'People of that character are good for nothing themselves and laugh at all the world, and at everything, they therefore strive to reduce everything to their own way of thinking, that it may resemble themselves.' In particular, he despised the way his fellow countrymen sat on a horse.

From these studies, it became increasingly clear to me that the seat which gives absolute control of the horse, whether with one or with two hands, and which I had had to go to Portugal to discover, had in fact been employed in England long before the more recent hunting seat ever evolved. Even in those days, however, few cared sufficiently to pursue it to any real depth of understanding. It was therefore hardly surprising to find that history was merely repeating itself all over again.

If one treads in the paths of the masters, I suppose one should not be too shocked when the masters seem to speak back to you. The following is a true account of what happened to me when I first visited the Duke of Newcastle's equestrian home at Bolsover in Derbyshire.

As the pre-eminent equestrian author of the seventeenth century, revered even by the great Sieur de La Guérinière of France, who based his work on the shoulder-in on Newcastle's shoulder-fore, I was eager to see where he had ridden his beautiful Barb, Neapolitan and Spanish horses, and where he had drawn the inspiration for his scholarship. I arrived on a bleak afternoon in October when scarcely a soul was about. The National Heritage employee who took my money at the kiosk at the entrance to the grounds warned me there was no guide that day and I would have to look around on my own but that I would find notices and a plan in each section of the castle telling me where to go next. Such freedom suited me fine as I wanted to linger and absorb the atmosphere of the riding school I had heard so much about, one of the earliest remaining indoor *manèges* in England.

Most of the main house, the banqueting hall and the gracious rooms where the Duke and Duchess received their guests in those elegant, opulent days prior to the English Civil War, had gone. Restoration work was being carried out but when I visited the castle in the mid 1980s all that remained in any good and recognisable order were the equestrian premises and the solid block of the castle keep where the Duke had his private quarters.

While the small indoor school and the forge were fascinating, the atmosphere was disappointing – mainly, I suppose, because there had been no horses there for hundreds of years. It was the castle keep which gripped me. Here was a real sense of passion, of desolation, of deep regret and of isolation. As I climbed the stone-flagged stairs from the kitchen quarters to the hall to the upper rooms, the feeling became more and more powerful. Even the murals on the panelled walls were hostile and forbidding.

I was high up now and the notice outside the door announced I was approaching the Star Chamber, the famous personal drawing room of William Cavendish, 1st Duke of Newcastle. Under the blue painted ceiling with its little gold stars, I felt infinitely depressed as I crossed the room to look out at the view. My eye swept over the deserted grounds, saw how the

201

William Cavendish, 1st Duke of Newcastle, was England's pre-eminent horseman in the seventeenth century. His teachings are still followed on the continent of Europe today and here he demonstrates the *ballotade* in front of the castle keep at Bolsover in Derbyshire. It was here that I had a strange experience of *déja vu*.

castle walls fell away into the steep precipice of black rock which holds the keep aloft over the town below and I remembered how this castle had sustained great bombardment from Cromwell's troops during the war and how sad its master must have been as he saw all that he had worked for and believed in under siege.

There was no one around, but suddenly I found myself speaking out loud: 'All is vanity!' I was looking out across the vale. Yes, I had said this, but I had never said it before and had no conscious memory of forming the words or indeed of any idea as to why I had uttered them. It was certainly not an expression of mine. Wondering, smiling a little and shaking my head at my own foolishness, I continued my pilgrimage. A notice told me the Duke's bedchamber lay on the next floor so up the stairs I went again. And then I saw it. On a painted scroll above the alcove for the bed, in a room in which I had never set foot in my life were echoed the words 'All is vanity'. *Ecclesiastes* I, verse 2. The hair stood up on the back of my neck.

As a native of the British Isles, one is surrounded by rich pictorial evidence of classical riders. One only has to look at Van Dyck's portrait of Charles I riding through an archway – there are four copies scattered throughout the kingdom, including one in Warwick Castle and one in Buckingham Palace – study the bronze statue of that same king on its plinth outside the Houses of Parliament, or even look at certain equestrian portraits by Stubbs, such as that memorable one of Lord Pigot of Patshull (1769) on his prancing grey stallion, to know that, once upon a time, Englishmen too had ridden proud and upright like the Prussians, the Austrians and our allies, the Portuguese.

Despite further positive reviews, the controversy over 'my' three-point seat continued unabated. Anthony Crossley, a knowledgeable horseman and writer, decided to write a humorous piece on the subject for his weekly dressage column in *Horse and Hound*[3]. Some tongue-in-cheek asides were made concerning the possible problem of a gentleman's virility and a lady's comfort if Sylvia's seat were to be employed.

Well travelled, Anthony had at one time visited Portugal and acknowledged that there was something spectacularly different about the way in which Nuno Oliveira rode. He had also written a stunning review of my book on the Lusitano and Andalusian horses so he well knew whence my influence had come. Nevertheless, according to Anthony, the whole subject of the classical seat was a touchy one and he found himself unable to agree with me.

Finally, it was Jane Kidd, highly regarded author and dressage judge, who took the bull by the horns and organised a seminar which was supposed to settle the argument once and for all. Entitled 'What Do We Sit Upon', other experts were invited. Mary Bromiley, well-known horse physiotherapist, would talk about the horse's back and John Gorman, an engineer, chiropractor and the inventor of an orthopaedic chair, whose views were similar to my own, would discuss the rider's back in relation to the correct posture in the saddle. Of the panel, I was the only person who insisted on bringing a live horse to the seminar (both Mary and John had brought equine and human skeletons) as discussion seemed quite irrelevant in my opinion without putting everything into practice. Nan Thurman of the Turville Valley Stud was kind enough to lend me one of her Lusitano stallions which had originally been owned and schooled by my late husband.

The gist of Colonel Crossley's argument was not concerned with the horse. He was much more interested in how the three-point seat – if it could be achieved – would affect the rider and whether, indeed, it was humanly

[3] 'The Mystery of the Magic Triangle', Colonel Anthony Crossley, *Horse and Hound*, January 2, 1987

It was once suggested to me that ladies could not possibly sit in the three-point classical seat position! Here, Anky van Grunsven adapts to Olympic Bonfire in a very harmonious way.

(Photo: Kit Houghton)

possible. I honestly believe he had not studied the human skeleton prior to all this, as he was convinced that the pubic bone lay well above the perineum instead of underneath. To be fair, many riders have little idea of the different bones which comprise their seat. Their seat is their seat and everyone has a slightly different conception of exactly what they are sitting on.

After both John Gorman and Mary Bromiley had given very learned expositions of how the position of the rider's pelvis affected both the human spine and that of the horse, I donned the radio mike and rode Monty the stallion to demonstrate collected, extended, sideways, backwards and forwards movement, all through minimal use of hand and leg and all in a three-point position of the seat. I had even applied bright sticky tape to the seam of my breeches to make the point about verticality. Despite not having worked together for a long time, all went happily and quietly between Monty and me and, with our programme over, I resumed my place with the rest of panel. During all this time, no one argued, indeed, no one said a word.

Now it was the turn of Anthony. Unimpressed, he stood up. He seemed convinced that what I was talking about was new and revolutionary and that what I had just shown on the horse bore little relation to what he believed to be the case – that the rider should sit on the two ischial tuberosities, in his opinion the only seatbones available to sit on. Without coming to blows, we both agreed to disagree.

The day ended in inconclusive discussion and some half-hearted audience participation. No one seemed to wish to resolve the argument one way or the other and a show of hands evened things out at about 50:50 for and against the three-point seat. It was only as people were filing out of the indoor school that I had a moment of inspiration. I asked Anthony to sit in my Portuguese saddle which, of course, is very different from the average English hunting or general purpose one. It is also quite different from the type of wedge-shaped German dressage saddle which was fashionable at the time. 'If you still think you have no bones to sit on in front, Anthony,' I chuckled, 'try sitting on this!'

Sportingly, he mounted the saddle horse and climbed into it. Suddenly his expression changed; in fact it was a study. He said nothing, but I swear, for the first time, perhaps in a lifetime of riding in a different type of saddle, he felt all his seatbones, back and front, and finally understood what we mean by the three-point seat. 'We'll continue this conversation another day,' he said thoughtfully.

Sadly, we never had the chance. This former army officer, who had come to love dressage rather late in his life, died shortly afterwards. I always wished we had had time for further discussion for I knew I could have learned from him and liked to think I could have helped him to understand the way of riding he had so admired in Nuno Oliveira. Not only was Anthony a true student of horsemanship but I believe he was an honourable man and I think we could have resolved our differences if time's jealous fingers had permitted. A grand old man, typical in his style of English sportsmanship, we still miss him.

Perhaps that insight illustrates more than any other why we do not, as a race, sit naturally in the three-point seat. Many of us do not walk like the Iberian peoples, with a firm upright pelvis. Too many prefer to move casually, understated and low key. Perhaps, too, we lack the discipline of the Germans to explore either the mechanics of the horse or, indeed, of our own bodies. We are naturally reticent, over modest and often even apologetic as a race.

Nevertheless, this should not prevent dialogue and discussion. I am all for opening up these matters with demonstrations, forums and displays, not just from the great and the good, but from riders of all disciplines. Classical riding and the classical seat should not just be about dressage; it is for everyone and for the benefit of all horses.

What riders today require more than at any other time in history is guidance towards establishing the same common language with which they may communicate better with their horses, a language that is clear, uncomplicated and logical. This can only come through openness, self-help and an attitude which does not preclude certain groups or people from being part of the overall system. This has happened before in history, when men of all cultures and nations came together to pursue an ideal during the Renaissance. If we are to encourage such a spirit into the twenty-first century, we need, above all, to reach out and use all those who have a talent for teaching and training. Only by pooling resources and spreading the word from a united front is there a real hope for the development of humane and correct riding worldwide.

CHAPTER 12

Opening the mind – teachers or trainers?

It is a well-known fact that some of the most successful riders in the world are not necessarily gifted teachers. Being at the very zenith of your particular field may not equip you to help others to achieve the same goals. This phenomenon applies to the pursuit and teaching of tennis, golf, snooker, boxing and many other activities as well as to riding. Indeed, of the most highly rated coaches in the various disciplines, without whom so many top competitors would be lost, comparatively few have made it to gold medal level themselves. Their strength lies in other directions, the power of observation being a priority, as is having a deep theoretical knowledge of their subject, an analytical mind and a real talent for communication and giving confidence.

As far as riders are concerned, what they need most, whether for jumping or for dressage, are first and foremost a pair of eyes on the ground and someone who is capable not only of being able to correct their horses but, more particularly, who is able to spot and correct the riders' own mistakes. For this reason it is scarcely surprising when one hears that so-and-so, a great competitor who has peaked early in their career and is invited to train others, turns out to be a disappointment. The old adage: 'If you can – do; if you can't – teach!' also works the other way round. Those who 'do', may not necessarily be able to teach.

Those few brilliant people who consistently make it to the top in the competitive field may ride more by instinct and individual feel than by technical knowledge. Unfortunately, you cannot teach talent, only pass on principles. Those who have worked hard to remain in the limelight may not have had the time and practice to develop their teaching skills. You have to be very singleminded to compete successfully and the idea of looking after and being number one is part of the strategy. With the best intentions in the world, it will be hard to consider others first.

To be a good dressage teacher, therefore, it is not sufficient only to ride well. Getting through to pupils in a way which clarifies and peels back the

Hands-on teaching and explanations prior to the work proper will help the rider to understand which areas need to be supported or worked on. As the horse generally mirrors the rider's posture, all teachers should take time to correct the smallest details.

mystique which surrounds the discipline also requires a deep knowledge of the science of riding as well as the more immediate practicalities. Added to this, the teacher must have the insight and confidence to be able to break down the more complicated techniques into simple language and explain them without bypassing the essentials. For this to be easily understood and assimilated by someone of less ability, a deep-rooted feel for the learning process, as well as a sympathy for what it is like to be on the receiving end of the lesson, are required. The best teachers are often people who have struggled at one time or another themselves. This gives them a sense of imagination and wisdom, a commodity which simply cannot be acquired in a few years.

There is also a vast difference between a riding trainer and a riding teacher. The trainer will tend to concentrate on the horse, pointing out to the rider what the animal is doing wrong in terms of mechanical virtuosity. Unless the pupil is also very knowledgeable, this will not necessarily help them to improve their horse there and then. It will point them towards areas to be highlighted but will not necessarily provide a solution.

Certain trainers have become so accustomed only to dealing with very well-bred and naturally athletic horses that they are fazed and at a loss to deal with less talented animals. They will tend to disdain a less than purpose-built horse and their antipathy is felt by the horse. It is very sad when one sees a trainer who is so involved with correcting the horse that they overlook and fail to correct the obvious – glaring postural mistakes from the rider which are merely mirrored by the horse. Unfortunately, this happens much too often so the root of the problem goes unchecked.

In consequence, the horse carries all the blame which, in its way, is equally hard on the rider, for how may the latter rectify their horse without improving at source? This neglect of the rider's mistakes shows a lack of care and observation which a true teacher could never countenance.

Sometimes one hears of a trainer who holds back on their pupils, happy to show them how well they can ride the horse but not necessarily willing to tell the pupils how to do it. There will always be the odd ungenerous trainer but fortunately they are rare. A dearth of good advice is usually caused by a lack of knowledge concerning rider problems.

Good teaching is therefore not so much having the gift of the gab – there are many trainers who produce an endless stream of meaningless patter – but knowing what words to use and when. Clichés can be dangerous for where one well-worn expression may seem crystal clear to the person who is uttering it, the phrase may imply something completely different to the person who is hearing it. To describe the succinct actions and feelings in high quality dressage is not easy.

While some instructors may blind one with science, becoming too pedagogic for the uninitiated to understand, others may dull the senses by repeating the same boring epithets again and again. While it takes an analytical mind to dissect and detect just where horse and rider are going wrong, one must always keep the interest and the human element alive. If something cannot be said simply, it is probably not worth saying at all. It is also healthy to cut through the gravitas, adding a little humour from time to time.

There have been many inspirational trainers over the ages but few in our lifetime who show signs of greatness thus qualifying for this special term of respect. Today, famous riders come and go and too often competition results depend as much, if not more, on the quality and athletic ability of the horse as on the artistry of the rider. Indeed, in some cases, the more refined the riding, the less the judges are impressed. A few prefer to see a picture where the rider appears to dominate and subdue the thrusting power

209

of the horse – the raw creature brought to heel by the superiority of the rider. It is almost a case of enacting one of the seven labours of Hercules. The greater the struggle, the more the performance is valued.

Those trainers who may toil behind the scenes and perfect the work of horses for others are not always recognised; there are many wonderful forgotten horsemen whose background derives from a more romantic, artistic age handed down from a heritage linked to the cavalry schools of the Austro-Hungarian Empire but, sadly, they are a dying breed.

One horseman who has successfully combined riding with training and teaching, and who, through his academic background, is particularly articulate and approachable, is the former Olympic gold medallist Reiner Klimke. Despite the pressures of remaining on the international circuit, he has remained faithful to the art of classical horsemanship throughout his career, despising any form of shortcut to success. His regard for the horse as a friend and partner is overwhelmingly clear not only from his riding but from his books and lectures. For him competition and pleasure are inseparable; the difference between his approach and that of others less harmonious to watch is that the horse is also included. 'It should be an absolute partnership, above all an enjoyable experience for both.'

Today's students are fortunate that they do not necessarily have to travel to Germany to see him ride. Through the medium of video, he has the ability to inspire and motivate and if more riders were prepared to emulate his quiet, controlled and elegant position in the saddle, we would hear of far fewer broken-down horses.

Those who have attended his schools and clinics have been impressed by his emphasis on feeling the horse underneath, knowing when to give and when to take, when to neutralise the aids. Klimke is a stickler for the *descent de main*, the giving of the hand also practised by Oliveira. The understanding of when to release the inside rein as the horse answers to the aids and comes into balance can only be established through feel and a knowledge of the mechanics of the horse. When this is not done, and the rider continues to ask to the inside, the horse will be overridden, brought backward by the hand, and blocked through the inside hind leg. This, in turn, will upset the balance and throw the horse on to his shoulders instead of keeping him engaged on his hocks.

Klimke also demonstrates the *descente des jambes*, the release with the legs to free the horse up as he moves through and under the rider. A master of feel and of the classical principles, Klimke is one of the few modern trainers who is a traditionalist in the best sense of the word.

Earlier in this book I wrote of the legendary figure and influence of Nuno

Oliveira. A great teacher to those who understood, he did not suffer fools, merely paying lip service to some of those visitors who had flown hundreds or thousands of miles to be taught by 'the Master'. Commercial from necessity, he treated some like clumsy puppies, smiled at others benignly as they basked in his glory or patted them on the head with soothing words of empty praise when their horse popped into *piaffe* as he growled a command from the corner of the school. It was the talented riders on whom he was hard, whom he often ignored and who had to work very diligently indeed to extract concrete help or secrets of technique from this complex man.

Because they recognised genius, it was those riders who stayed with him for years, sweating out the difficult days, the quirks and moods of his character, the sheer hard work of rising early to manage the young, unbroken horses and going on late into the night until he chose to stop. The man's horsemanship was so brilliant that it made up for anything that was lacking elsewhere and the discerning learned to learn from him by observation, practice and example.

A few years after his death, one of Nuno's former pupils approached me as I was packing up after a lecture I had given in Melbourne. I was tired and felt mildly irritated when she came forward with her question, for there had been ample question time earlier. Then I realised she was labouring to put her query into words and seemed very shamefaced. Could I please explain to her the concept of drawing the waist towards the hands? Previously, she had attended three days of lessons with the great man and this was all he kept telling her. To this day, she had been trying to follow what she perceived to be his advice by lying almost horizontally on the horse's back and trying to lift her stomach skyward but finding it impossible. When I showed her that all she had to do was sit tall, supported and upright, and push her tummy, her centre of gravity, towards her hands without collapsing down, she was mightily relieved. Laughable? Perhaps; I actually found it depressing. It demonstrated how pearls of wisdom are so easily misconstrued through a lack of good teaching worldwide and the lack of a common equestrian language.

Oliveira's greatest legacy is his books and those pupils he left behind who have gone on to become national and international horsemen and women and trainers of stature. In him they saw a revival of the tradition of their national heritage, for the Portuguese have always been thinking equestrians and far ahead of their time in terms of the academic study of their subject. These include men such as Oliveira's own son João, as well as Guilherme Borba, João Trigueiros de Aragão, Diogo de Braganza, Felipe Gracioso, Luis Valenca and Francisco Cancela d'Abreu. To become masters in their own right has not been easy in the shadow of such a man. As for his foreign students, Oliveira jealously protected his name and his talent, even overseeing the publishing of an advertisement in the United States to ensure that people did not claim to teach as though approved or qualified by him. Apart from his long-term Portuguese apprentices and M. Henriquet, a friend of many years' standing, only Bettina Drummond, the daughter of Phyllis Field, was recognised in America and Christine Farnier in Belgium. The others were, in his words: 'only students who have learned some equitation in Portugal during relatively short periods; good, bad or indifferent riders who are not qualified to give lessons in my name beyond helping beginners to sit in the saddle correctly'.

It was odd that he handed me a copy of this shortly before he died. Deeply religious, he suspected, perhaps, that people would soon be trading off his name, often undeservedly and dishonestly, and that he would not be around to protect it.

One of the most telling pieces ever written about Oliveira came from Bettina, a person for whom he had so much affection. 'Nuno's art was his song to God. That is why he told me to build my own indoor arena like a cathedral. As a child I really perceived that he was happy seeing one on his horses being quietly exuberant ... joyful, quiet, like in a church. That is how I also feel; this way of riding was his prayer to God, a song, a voice. That is why he loved the opera – the voice – a way of saying. "You gave me life; I give you this back, through art." Riding as an art is an intonation of how we all feel towards God.'

For me the greatest learning experience from Oliveira was to watch him ride. For those adherents who sat patiently in his small gallery day after day, the pilgrimage was also worthwhile. Earthbound stallions became airborne unicorns; stiff youngsters yielded into putty. His posture distinguished him from all others. Relatively slim of hip and slight of leg, he rode with bullish shoulders braced back and a powerful lower back which caused his chest to balloon upwards like that of the opera singers he so admired; there was a carved, very still quality about him.

Near the end of his life, he agreed that I might write a book about him. We had several discussions about the rider's seat, the rider's posture and his general demeanour but, before we had got much further than drafting the chapter headings and what the main emphasis would be, he died suddenly and tragically in Australia. The last time I saw him, I remember marvelling at how insignificant he could seem when off his horse and how, when riding, everything changed. It was as though he was charged with an inner force, but the power, whatever it was, never required to be switched on.

When, recently, I read the following story in a book about Zen[1], I was reminded so much of how he appeared to the outside world.

A certain king had asked his trainer to find the best fighting cock in the land to perform in a tournament against other trained birds. When the time came for him to request that his cock should be entered to fight, the trainer restrained his majesty, saying, 'No, no! Not yet. He's still too fierce, he's looking for a fight all the time.' So the king waited. After the third and final request, the trainer agreed that the bird could go: 'He no longer flies into a passion now, he remains calm when he hears another cock crowing. His posture is good, and he has a lot of power in reserve. Looking at him, you aren't even aware of his energy and strength.' It was therefore agreed that the fight could now be arranged.

'So a great many fighting cocks were assembled and the tournament began. But no bird would come anywhere near that one. They all ran away terrified and he never needed to fight. The fighting cock had become a cock of wood. He had gone beyond his technical training. He possessed enormous energy but it was all inside, he never showed it. That way, his power stayed within himself, and the others had no choice but to bow before his tranquil assurance and undisplayed strength.'

By the time I understood these things a little more, Oliveira was no longer with us but it was a small honour to be asked to write his obituary in *Horse and Hound*. Unlike my friend in Australia who organised his clinics, Joy Howley, a wonderful lady and publisher of his latter-day books, I never felt I really knew him. He did, however, bare his soul when he spoke of his concerns for the future of riding in a world where instant experts sprang up like mushrooms and where a deep committed love of the horse seemed a thing of the past.

As with many geniuses, he was hardest on those who achieved the most. He had the ability to make strong men weep, which I have seen with my own eyes – yet had it not been for him there would be no proud figurehead to give his people the will to pass on the classical tradition, neither would his followers have had the inspiration to revive the Portuguese School of Equestrian Art. As a result, even for those born too late to be taught by him, that carved, fighting cock, centaured way of riding is still alive and well in Portugal and Spain today.

It is this visual influence in the learning process which has been explained so well by writers and teachers such as Sally Swift from the USA. Right-brain learning tends to be visual and conceptual, where

---

[1] *The Zen Way to the Martial Arts*, Taisen Deshimaru, published by Arkana, Penguin Group, USA – a book given to me by Paul Belasik.

In all the times I watched my late husband ride, I never once saw him push at a horse with either seat or leg. Occasionally there was a quiet touch of the spur, but the real power came by riding from the waist to the hands, which perhaps has to be seen to be fully appreciated.

feelings blend with imagery to develop a very rounded and almost psychological way of riding. After all those years, my late husband Henry is still there in my right brain, looking so like Oliveira in his position on a horse that many people supposed him to be Portuguese. When in doubt as to how to ride a particular movement, I often visualise him doing it, and suddenly it works!

Those pupils who are humble enough and eager enough to watch every second, every small move, every nuance and shade made by great riders of calibre may sometimes take away as much or more than the rider who is actually having the lesson. Henry was a person of few words, but he exuded presence which horses felt as well as people. Moreover, he was generally mounted as he instructed and this seemed to influence all who came within his orbit in the riding school. It was almost as though they learned by osmosis.

Henry also gave riders a sense of feel. He would ride someone's horse,

Henry always believed in riding with his students as he taught. This inspired both
pupil and horse.
(Photo: Sylvia Loch)

lighten it within minutes, set it on its hocks, supple it, then give it back to
the owner and say, 'Now, feel your horse!'

When any trainer of talent rides a pupil's horse, a transformation can
take place before the eyes. The ignorant may ask, 'What good can this do
when as soon as I'm back in the saddle all will be lost?' But this is
generally not the case and a horse rendered light, engaged and collected
from ten minutes of knowledgeable riding should stay that way at least
for the duration of the lesson. In this manner, the trainer leaves his
imprint which will, in turn, benefit the owner. It gives them the taste of a
new balance, it renders the pleasure of a horse truly in the hand and it
brings a different magic into the spectrum which will not be forgotten.

Most horses rendered malleable in this way will enjoy the feeling so
much themselves that they will be more confident to offer something
similar again. For the rider, it will be easier when next they endeavour to
regain that balance because they will know what they are looking for. By
delving into that 'library of feelings', even for as little as five minutes, the
pupil will have gained as much if not more than they would in many hours
of indifferent lessons.

Alison Ure worked with my late husband for over two years at our Lusitano School in Suffolk and went on to compete internationally. She always claimed that he laid down the classical ethos in a way which continued to inspire her wherever she went.

Jane Hodge at sixteen. Jane trained with us in both Portugal and England. Later, as Henry's head girl she went on to become a very talented trainer and teacher in her own right and works today from East Anglia.

It is sad when a pupil does not realise the benefit of such a lesson. I have heard people grumble, 'I'm not going to him any more. All he does is ride my horse for half an hour, so I only get half a lesson!' The shortsightedness of such a remark is obvious. If the instructor is a good rider and has improved the horse during that half hour, then the money will have been well spent. Yet too often, as a spectator at other training sessions up and down Britain, I have been dismayed by the lack of respect certain pupils display when they retire to the sidelines and chat to their neighbour while their horse is being schooled by a superior.

The courtesies of the riding school still exist in certain countries like France, Portugal, Spain and Austria. There is an age-old tradition of respect from pupil to master. In the traditional *picadeiros* outside Lisbon, the master leads his horse to the gallery and utters the words: '*Da licenca?*' to the assembled company before he mounts, which means, 'Do you permit?' It is far more than a charming formality; it sets the tone. In such an atmosphere, it would be considered grossly rude to chat while a display, however humble, is being given. If you are there, it is expected you are there to watch, to learn, to consider. One does not chat in an art gallery; why do it in a *manège?*

What my late husband did for British dressage in his short spell in Britain with our schoolmaster horses was to inspire people. Regarded as a rebel by the establishment, sometimes difficult to live with because of alcoholism in the past, he nevertheless left a legacy. Visitors who have made their own impact in the world of dressage, who were made welcome at our house and who loved talking with him and watching him work, included the late Pam Dillingham from Canada with her daughter Desi. Previously an event rider, Desi became interested in dressage at our yard when she attended a number of courses and watched Henry's talents with the many young people who had joined the yard as working or residential students. Talented youngsters who had come under his spell included Johanna Beattie, Jane Hodge, Julie Hugo, Diane Thurman-Baker, Alison Ure, Julia Watkiss (Wetton) and Maggie Wilcox, all of whom went on to become serious teachers or to ride for Great Britain.

After generously sponsoring one of our working pupils, Desi then sponsored Britain's first dressage Olympic medallist, Jennie Loriston-Clarke; Richard and I were dining with Desi, Anthony and Jennie when the deal was clinched. From their successful partnership developed the idea of the British Dressage Supporters Club whose administrator, Margaret Clayton, had also attended residential courses at our home and been taught by Henry. Godmother to our only daughter, Desi once said to me, 'The great thing about Henry was things *happened* around him.'

Learning through academic study involves a different set of learning processes from the visual, intuitive methods described above. It is the left side of the brain which is activated by words. Charles de Kunffy is a regular visitor to England from the west coast of the USA, thanks to the organisational skills of The Training the Teachers of Tomorrow Trust based near Guildford. Born in Hungary, resident in California, his soft, slightly accented English reaches out to students through language, creating inspiration of another type. By explaining, suggesting, persuading, extolling rider and horse together, the partnership is given the confidence to produce very good movements through the powers of suggestion. With words, Charles is able to separate the functions of the various aids in the rider's mind, so that the body works in greater harmony, each component part understanding its role. This type of training, with a quick eye to spot the need for fine mechanical adjustments, is very valuable.

John Lasseter is another trainer, this time based in Britain, who uses language to get through to his pupils in a rather different way. Like Charles, his slightly accented English tones are soothing but compelling as he works the rider through various tasks set up around a series of cones strategically placed within the arena. This way of teaching through plausible

Pam Dillingham, a highly experienced event rider, came with her daughter
Desi to ride at Green Farm, Suffolk. Here she enjoys Castico, one of the
most sensitive and talented stallions we were fortunate enough to own.

explanations while keeping the rider mentally busy leaves no room or time
for negativity or doubt and heightens horse and rider concentration.

Other teacher trainers base their equestrian work on a deep knowledge of
good posture. Daniel Pevsner is also an Alexander Technique teacher, Paul
Belasik studies the techniques of Kyudo, a type of Zen, others base their
work on yoga. It is the postural aspect of teaching which has led to my own
enlightenment over the years, highlighted by the fact that, having to cope
with asthma and an allergy to horses, it has become vital for my health to
develop body control and correct breathing. The sense of well-being that
comes from standing, moving and riding in good balance and always
projecting one's centre of gravity while stretching up and opening the body
is, however, much more far-reaching than the purely physical. It stimulates
the psyche and focuses the mind. It also leads to inner composure,
increased confidence and the thrill of crossing new mental frontiers.

To illustrate just how developing good posture and a greater awareness of
symmetry can change one's life, I truly believe my ability to write came as
a result of my studies of the classical riding seat. Although I had tried to be
a writer all of my life and, from childhood, had dabbled with fiction in the
form of rarely finished novels and short stories, what ability I had only
seemed to find direction after Henry's death which brought about the sale
of our yard, leading to great changes in our lives. At last, no longer so
burdened with financial worries and the problems of how to meet the

I have never been a great person for trophies but the presentation of this
statue, from the President of the Portuguese Stud Book in 1986, very
nearly brought tears to my eyes.

(Photo: courtesy of *Horse & Rider Magazine*)

enormous bills of a big operational stable, I had time to pause and reflect.

With my young daughter crawling around my feet, I started to write
seriously about how to sit on a horse, how Henry had sat, how Nuno
Oliveira and Podhajsky sat. Subconsciously this improved my own
posture, not only in riding but about the yard and house, indeed, wherever I
went, whatever I was doing. Thus I became more aware of movement,
opening the body and, with it, opening the mind. Without realising it at
the time, I was becoming focused. This led to articles about the need
for schoolmasters on which to learn to sit correctly and it was a
natural progression to write about the beautiful horses we had brought
from Portugal and Spain. What started with an article in *Riding
Magazine* grew into an idea for a book. With encouragement from the
publishers J. A. Allen, slowly, quietly, my first big book, *The Royal Horse
of Europe*, began to emerge.

By now remarried, Richard was able to give me the confidence to write with conviction about something I understood. As a non-rider, he could look from a distance and see that the story of the Iberian horse was a fascinating one which needed telling, particularly from the historical perspective as well as the practical one. For this reason, he instilled in me the need for a disciplined academic approach and, in particular, the requirement for all my claims to be backed up with hard historical evidence.

Until this time, little accurate research had been made from outside the Iberian Peninsula into the origins and influence of these horses. Under my husband's guidance, therefore, I began to use the British Library, as well as tracking down records in stately homes and in private collections. Thus I learned my craft, developing a feeling as to where to discover source material and historical data as well as picture research.

In this way, everything I had learned in a practical way, from and with Henry, my years in Portugal, getting to know the old breeder families in Portugal and Spain, and with Richard all the time encouraging and pushing me on to greater goals, all my experiences with horses began to take on real meaning. As these thoughts took shape and, on paper, began to crystallise in an amazing way, the small book I originally visualised gave way to more words and more chapters and, finally, people began to speak of a sourced authoritative testament to the breed. As Caroline Burt and Mr Allen were now muttering, their publishing house was taking on a new, definitive book.

The support, both at home and across the water, was heartwarming. When, finally, the *oeuvre* was published in full glorious colour with over 100 plates sponsored by the Gulbenkian Foundation, the Mellon family and two dear friends in Portugal, I could scarcely believe the work was mine. The three years it had taken to write seemed to have passed like a dream and I felt as though there had been some divine intervention. Richard had been a wonderful mentor, but I believe my writing career was also helped by the arrival on my yard of Palomo. A teacher himself, there was something about the stallion that galvanised me to tell the story of his proud ancestors with more passion and urgency. It became compulsive to get the book finished so that, from now on, people would understand the Iberian horse and appreciate the part it had played in all our history.

Coming out just before Christmas 1986 and happily tying in with the sixth centennial celebration of the Treaty of Windsor[2], the book was

---

[2] This formed the first great alliance between England and Portugal in 1386. In 1986, celebrations between the two countries culminated in the Treaty of Windsor Ball which took place at Osterley Park, Middlesex where the Portuguese School of Equestrian Art gave a display in the presence of the Prince and Princess of Wales.

accorded a wonderful review in *Horse and Hound*. Involved to some extent in the equestrian arrangements at Osterley, I was deeply touched when the Ambassador of Portugal, João Hall Themido, arranged a dinner party for us at Belgrave Square. This was attended by the Ambassadors of Austria and South Africa, the Master of the Horse from the Royal Household, Richard and myself and several of our friends. Here, His Excellency made the most moving speech and toasted the book. Word drifted through to Portugal and a surprise party in Lisbon followed where Fernando d'Andrade, keeper of the Stud Book, awarded me the *cavalo d'or* or golden horse, his personal sculpture of a 15-inch-high *piaffing* Lusitano horse in burnished cast iron. What dreams can be realised when you allow them to happen!

Also moved and motivated by the classical horses which originally came to Vienna out of the Iberian Peninsula is one of the greatest riders and trainers of our times, Chief Rider Arthur Kottas. A regular visitor to Britain, originally at the invitation of Lady Joicey and more latterly through TTT, he displays a masterly use of the English language with his own, obviously unconscious, but very distinct body language and poise. A stickler for position, nothing out of line or rhythm escapes his eagle eye. His attention to detail is legendary, but corrections are always positive: 'Do this. Try that'; never: 'Don't do this. Don't do that'.

Such a positive attitude is absorbed equally by horse and rider. Of all the trainers I have watched, horses definitely notice and respond most to Arthur and invariably in a very rewarding way. The idle become motivated; the difficult and resistant become compliant and calm. In his lessons horses remain respectful, alert but also proud, happy and interested in his company because they know he is on their side. A true herd leader, his work in-hand is as virtuosic as his riding. He has the ability to inspire both horses and riders with his insistence on perfection, although at times he can be daunting. His combined abilities as trainer, teacher and rider elevate Kottas, and a very few like him, to the highest echelons of equitation.

Kyra Kyrkland from Finland is another thoroughly practical teacher trainer. To back up her experience and knowledge, she possesses a down to earth approach and there is no trace of patronage in her teaching. People like her, who genuinely want to help riders to understand their horses better, give all they can, without reservation. Riding pupils' horses in demonstration, she has the ability to think aloud, sharing little secrets of technique quite openly and talking through a problem without having to be seen to solve it all in a moment.

As a teacher myself, I find it hard to understand when I see a young, fit and able instructor handing out advice to a pupil without even having offered to sit on their horse's back. As this is such a vital side of teaching, one wonders why this occurs. With certain horses, watching is not enough. We have to *feel* it if we are to help, and looks can be deceptive. The horse has so much to tell us the moment we sit on his back and I am always suspicious of people who have worked with a particular rider over many sessions without ever having taken the trouble to become better acquainted with their horse. This is not the case with Malcolm Brown, a highly experienced dressage judge and trainer, who, to my mind, shows the best of traditional British equitation when, invariably, he gets the best out of all the horses he rides in a quiet, sympathetic manner. Disarmingly modest but effective in his approach, he is able to help pupils, not by showing them up but by working with their horses in such a way that he relaxes them, brings them together and makes it possible for them to offer more.

Unfortunately, there are still too many trainers who take the attitude that they have to prove something when they climb into the saddle. Perhaps owners are partly to blame for expecting too much. It should not at all be a question of bullying the horse into submission or showing how well one can ride. On the contrary, sometimes the trainer has to sacrifice composure and elegance in order to delve to the root of a difficulty. As a result of this probing, one may even have to change the whole strategy to suit that particular animal. Like people, horses should never be underestimated and can be full of contradictions and surprises.

There are many unsung teachers in the world, some quite hidden away and relatively unknown, yet it should not be hard to spot them. To teach is not for the instructor to show his superiority; it is to bring out the best in you, the pupil and the horse. Neither will a wise teacher try to stop you seeing other teachers; quality will always speak for itself and there is nothing wrong in being apprised of a different viewpoint occasionally. Genuine classical instructors will, in any case, teach on the same lines; it is only the emphasis or approach which may differ.

There have been times in my life when I have wondered why certain trainers have gone out of their way to discredit others. Generally, I believe this is caused by insecurity. Someone comes along and says something in a slightly different way from their way, which upsets them. Because they did not think of it, they feel threatened. I remember one trainer taking another to task publicly in a magazine for advocating a hand which gives by 'slightly opening the fingers'. Yet the writer professed to be a student of the school of Saumur. Proudly he quoted those masters of the French School, Decarpentry, Jousseaume, Licart and Paillard, to name but a few. Yet Decarpentry wrote of 'the vibrato on the rein', while Jousseaume advocated: 'at the slightest yielding, reward by loosening the fingers and a descent of the hands.' Different idea? Different language? I think not – only the odd word here and there. It is much too easy to take words out of context and fault-find but this does little for what all serious trainers and teachers should be looking for – a united front, a common language to produce more empathetic, cultured and thoughtful riders.

When Henry and I first returned to England, we were made to feel we were different and altogether rather foreign by certain British establishment figures. I well remember a senior dressage judge, Sarah Whitmore, bluntly asking if I was British when I took a Portuguese horse to be assessed by her for dressage points. As she clearly knew exactly who I was, the question seemed odd in the circumstances. Her next remark, that my horse might be better suited to the bull ring and ought perhaps to perform there, brought a smile to my lips. I responded that this was exactly what he had done in his past. I could have added that it was, in part, due to this disciplined training that he could now offer so much to students in Britain. Contrary to some assessors, I noticed she did not offer to ride him.

It seemed at that time somehow ironic and perverse that only the few who had trained at a classical establishment overseas seemed able to appreciate either our horses or what we were offering within the teaching profession. Charles Harris and Daniel Pevsner, both Fellows of the British Horse Society, clearly admired Henry's work and said so. Together with top riders such as Molly Sivewright and Alan Doxey, they all spoke a similar language. It was the faceless committee side of Stoneleigh which did not.

Nowadays, with the resurgence in classical riding, people are becoming much better informed, more open to aesthetic ideals and a uniform system. I often think how things might have turned out so very differently, not only for ourselves back in the late 1970s, but more for Britain's young riders, if we had come home a decade later. Leaving personalities aside, what an asset an academy of schoolmaster horses could have been to the country. It is no coincidence surely that those nations that win the most medals in international competition dressage today offer just such a facility for each new generation of riders. When governments are not prepared to finance such facilities, quality private enterprise should be encouraged by the relevant bodies with an open mind.

Over the years, I have been glad to discover that traditional German riding is no different, or very little different, from traditional French or Portuguese riding. The German riders whom I most admire ride upright, light and with regard for the horse's back in the same manner as I was taught in both Portugal and in France. Indeed, Reiner Klimke was an

After bullfighting and stud work in Portugal, my stallion Palomo very soon
settled into a new life in England as a learned professor. He has probably
inspired more people to ride dressage than any human teacher could possibly
hope to achieve since he started his secondary career at the age of fourteen.
(Photo: courtesy Fliss Gillott)

admirer of Oliveira, as is Egon Von Neindorff who studied there and who
later taught and influenced the Dutch trainer and writer Erik F.
Herbermann[3]. All, including the Austrian riders of the Spanish Riding
School of Vienna, were influenced by the writing of the French School
under La Guérinière, so everything comes full circle again.

There are also some very talented instructors in the Antipodes and from
South Africa. A few years ago, the British Horse Society launched a
seminar, taken by South African-born Emile Faurie, for dressage
enthusiasts in the east of England. A lovely, quiet, light-handed rider, Emile
rode and demonstrated with élan. When it came to question time, he was
asked the inevitable questions about his use of the aids. Someone remarked
they they had scarcely seen his legs move; the question was almost framed
as a criticism which made me smile as I remembered once being marked
down on a dressage test sheet for this very reason. The truth is that some
horses are so sensitive one can aid them from the thigh, again not a new
idea, but recommended by both La Guérinière and Newcastle. It is also
something which Emile clearly does with his lighter horses.

It made me smile even more when Emile cheerfully announced that he
did not need to use his legs. This reminded me of my late husband who

---

[3] The author highly recommends Herbermanns's book *The Dressage Formula*.

used to enjoy making remarks in a similar vein. The fact was, like Emile, he did use his legs, but he used them in such a feather-light way by knowing just when to touch a sensitive part and, more important, when to release, that it always seemed as though the horse moved through his own impulsion, framed by the legs but not because of the legs forever asking and asking.

Superior impulsion is when the horse moves through us with our legs merely defining how he moves. I think Emile relished being a little provocative with his answer because he wanted to get the same message across. He could have added more but he didn't. His reply sent shudders through a certain section of the crowd who had been raised on the idea of booting the horse in the ribs at every stride. Sometimes, it is very enjoyable to say the opposite of what everyone is expecting. People should never be complacent about riding; they need to question; they need to think.

We have discussed the different ways different instructors impart their message to pupils. All the methods I have mentioned so far have been positive. This does not mean that all trainers are positive. I know of some who are extremely negative both to people and their horses. There are even one or two who clearly do not like horses but find themselves in a job because of them. These are the ones whose main purpose in life is to dominate the horse, make him a slave, bend him to their will. If they do not like the actual animal itself, they enjoy what goes with horses, the glamour, the glory, the crowds, the top hat and tails, the hype, the fuss.

At the end of the day, you can always tell a trainer who has a deep love of horses. The most obvious facet will be their concern for the horse in the way they teach the rider. This will be the trainer who looks into the horse's eye, who touches his neck, who moves in close to the horse and gives confidence to the whole combination. This is the trainer who watches every move the horse makes and helps him with their own body language. Such a person will always find a reason why the horse could not do something and look to the rider to bring about change, not blame the horse.

A rider who genuinely loves horses will also welcome this approach. Such a rider will be mature enough to realise that when they are being corrected, the received wisdom will not only help that horse but all horses. If horsemanship is about partnership and we are expected to lead the dance, it makes no sense at all for the trainer only to work on the horse.

A good trainer gives the rider something to take away with them at the end of the lesson. They show the rider correctional exercises which work. They know their theory. They are not worried about giving away too much in the fear that the pupil will not need to come back to them for a long time. They are confident that what they have taught does and will work, and

Most horses need to stretch regularly throughout any working session. When you give the
rein, give it generously, but keep your position!

(Photo: courtesy *Horse & Rider Magazine*)

therefore, because of the success of their training, the pupil will hasten
back to taste more of the same splendid medicine.

This trainer is not jealous. They are delighted when they see other
trainers spooning out much of the same elixir, extolling the same
principles, confirming all that they themself believe in. They enjoy it when
the same advice is clothed in different expressions, different words,
different mannerisms and do not seek to destroy the work of others which
would be self-destructive to themselves in the end.

Such a trainer is not afraid to praise. They know that sometimes the
words of praise that they offer to the rider or the horse may not be as well
deserved as at other times but they also know that, often, praise to both
horse and rider, at a certain juncture, will buoy the spirits and renew the

effort. Encouragement of this type can make all the difference between failure and success.

They also know when enough is enough. They have the wit to see when the horse is tired and needs to stretch down, and when the pupil's brain is humming and unable to take in much more. They will not insist that a movement is ridden again and again. If it has been a difficult one to achieve, they will have the sense to stop the moment it happens correctly, lest horse and rider lose the feeling and the lesson ends on a bad note.

In relation to such an empathy for the horse, let me tell a rather sad little story from a few years back. I was involved in a clinic far away on the other side of the world where the co-trainer, a talented young man, was instructing on the other side of the arena and I was taking a break. The horse was a sensitive little Thoroughbred type, the rider a rather solid lady. They had come into the ring with the horse crooked, the rider tense, the horse on a fixed contact. During their session together, the trainer came up with all the tricks of the trade, all the techniques known in the profession, to work on straightening. Every movement, every combination and transition was used.

On and on went the lesson, the horse became sweatier, the rider became damper, and all the time the horse continued crooked. After 30 minutes I had to put my hands in my pockets to stop the nails digging into my palms with frustration; it was so clear what was needed. First, the rider was slightly crooked and, second, in all that time, the horse had been worked relentlessly on the bit and one could tangibly feel his discomfort. I wanted to call out, 'Let it stretch! It needs to stretch down! Let them both return to base camp and start again!'

But how could I? As a fellow trainer, waiting for my lesson, it would have been churlish and extremely bad manners to interfere. We did not know each other well and the young man, who was the resident trainer at the yard, probably resented my coming in the first place.

The lesson wore on; not once did the trainer correct the pupil's position, neither did he tell her to give the horse his head. A further fifteen minutes ensued and, by the end of that lesson, I too was covered in perspiration. Somehow I was feeling what the horse felt and it agitated me and I felt sick inside for not being able to intervene. Despite all the work, all of which was correct in its own way, the horse never straightened. I am not saying that it would have been easy to make that horse straight, but the first thing rider and horse needed to do when they came into that *manège* was to go forward on a long rein. If this had been allowed at consistent intervals throughout the schooling session, I believe the results would have been totally different. Mental relaxation and stretching are such an important part of the training process to all concerned.

Later, at lunchtime, I asked the trainer as impersonally as I could if stretching down might not have benefited that particular combination. 'Oh, we did that yesterday!' he replied enthusiastically. 'I wanted to show her some new techniques today.' My heart plummeted. He had entirely missed the point. Neither had he thought for a moment of the horse.

There is no athlete in the world who does not need a mental and a physical break in the middle of their work-out. Why do people withhold these logical interludes? Do they forget? Or do they simply not feel the needs of the horse within their bodies, within their soul? I know I would not be able to teach with half the conviction myself if the body language of the horse was not telling me about his rider. You have to get inside the skull of the horse if you are to help the person in the saddle. Watching the poll, feeling his back, feeling his mouth, feeling for any tension, even although you are on the ground you can become aware of these things and then, automatically, as it were, you know what needs to be done.

I learned my own lesson about relaxation several years back when hacking home with Dr Guilherme Borba, the Portuguese *chef d'équipe*. He had his horse on a long rein, mine was jogging slightly so I kept her on a half contact. 'Let the mare have her head!' he said abruptly. I let the rein out a few inches; my mare was still jogging. 'No, all!' I let more go, but not quite all. 'Why do you British do that?' he cried, clearly irritated. 'If you give it, give it *all* – to the buckle end. Never ride a horse half in, half out. Either it is in the hand, or you give everything.' I complied and the mare walked. The most valuable lessons in life and in riding need not be the longest.

CHAPTER 13

Straightness, squareness and some thoughts on shoulder-in

Straightness in the horse is a major preoccupation for most riders. While judges and instructors will be swift to pounce on such a lapse, few will take the trouble to explain the techniques involved to combat persistent crookedness and few seem brave enough to blame the rider. Yet as my good friend Shirley Renowden, chief examiner to the Association of British Riding Schools, once said to me, 'There would be few crooked horses if riders just learned to sit up, ride forward and look between their horses' ears.' It is all so very simple.

Unfortunately, it is the simplicity of good riding that seems to be overlooked these days. Dressage mark sheets tend to pinpoint the horse's faults, encouraging riders to make misguided corrections such as pushing the quarters this way and that instead of looking at themselves. Yet as Beudant[1] points out: 'A horse's habit of getting out of line, of not keeping straight, always come from poor training and from the annoyance of an unskilled rider.'

We all recognise that horses, like ourselves, are generally one-sided, and Udo Burger's book, *The Way to Perfect Horsemanship*, is particularly helpful in addressing the problems which arise out of crookedness. Nevertheless, while most horses will be less adept at certain movements on one rein it should not be beyond the capabilities of any rider – once they understand the technique – to straighten the horse on the school track or even cantering down the centre line. This is where real understanding is vital for, as Beudant continues, 'Traversed haunches are the result of a faulty distribution of weight on the shoulders. . . . To straighten a horse we should act on his forehand, not on his hindquarters.'

It is therefore by improving our own posture and working on the lightening of the forehand by bringing the weight of the horse more into his hocks that our job will be made so much easier. Weight in the hind end

---

[1] Captain E. Beudant, *Horse Training, Outdoor and High School*.

229

The old masters stressed time and again the importance of position in every movement. Here the rider's shoulders and inside leg position (deepening at the girth) lead the horse into the required direction.

(Engraving from *Luz da Liberal é Nobre Arte da Cavallaria*)

prevents the haunches from straying. When, indeed, the hocks are coming under and pushing instead of trailing, the horse should be straighter throughout and it is often just a nuance of position in the rider's own shoulders to bring about the slight encurvation of the forehand which will keep the horse correct through his corners and circles and during his progress around the arena. Arthur Kottas always makes this very clear when he teaches: 'Flex the forehand very slightly to the inside and the hind end will approach the track straight.'

For this, we have to understand the importance of our own shoulder position. Riding a corner with the shade of a feeling for shoulder-fore will have a far greater effect on the straightness of the horse than interfering with the hind end. The unsettling action of a busy lower leg merely fragments the forward thrust of the horse, pushing the forehand from behind. With my own pupils, the moment I see any form of crookedness, I ask them to sit up, deepen the inside leg at the girth, gently flex the horse to the same side, and, hey presto! the quarters are straight.

It is also important for them to understand the effect of a discreet indirect rein aid which can encourage the shoulders back into line with the hocks, rather than the other way round. For example, quarters straying to the right in half-pass right will immediately be helped by an indirect left-hand aid which brings the forehand back into its rightful place – in front of the quarters again.

Ideally, therefore, when riding on straight lines, there should be no question of the quarters straying. A horse ridden through from back to front is maintained in his forward progression from a proper distribution of the rider's weight through the seat and stirrups and a correct upper body position. Unfortunately, many riders are simply not forward pointing which, in turn, throws the weight awry. The natural inclination of any basically schooled horse will be to mirror the rider at every stage. We have already discussed the finer points of straightness in the rider's spine. What many riders do not appreciate is that to be forward pointing involves every small part of us for everything is connected to everything else and any divergence in forward projection can pull the energy of the horse off-course.

Thus, as well as shoulders, arms, elbows, hands, chest, stomach, hip bones, knees and feet all directing forward through symmetrical balance, we need to remember that our eyes and face govern where the horse looks. The horse that 'falls' off the track or into the circle is one who has merely responded to the gravitational pull of a rider who may not even realise what it is they have asked with their body. We have already spoken of the slack knee, the collapsed hip; equally bad is the head that turns too much too early – as strong a weight aid as any other. As the human head may weigh anything up to 8 kg, we should turn it only as much as we want to turn our horse's head.

Then there is the problem of the hand which opens but is not regulated by the opposing hand. On a circle, too many riders open the inside rein, forgetting that it is the outside rein which affects the degree of opening. Again, when the horse falls inward, he is blamed, but how can he know how much to bend or turn if there is no rein of opposition? Riders have to be reminded time and again that every aid we give requires a counter-aid if the horse is to interpret our requirements correctly. Turning to the right therefore requires counter-aiding from the left! As Beudant writes: 'our efforts to keep the horse straight are usually illogical'.

Nevertheless, from a purely mechanical point of view the age-old principles are not so hard to understand. What we can never afford to do is to learn them parrot-fashion, otherwise all our work with horses will be fraught with difficulty. For example, in the turn to the right, when the conventional aid is right leg supporting forward on the girth, left leg back, riders must take care not to push overtly against the horse with the right leg. Too many riders confuse what should be an inviting aid into a pushing one with the result that the horse moves left! One really cannot blame the horse.

This also happens in the strike-off to canter and the only way to correct it is to think of letting the weight down more into the stirrup rather than nudging against the horse and putting him on to the opposite lead. Horses do what they *feel* we have asked them to do, not what they guess we are trying to say. How can a horse know we want right lead when our body is actually saying something else?

Similarly, in the rein-back many riders forget to take their own centre of gravity back so, again, the horse is receiving conflicting aids if we show no difference through our seat as to when we mean forward and when we mean back. In a lateral movement, we must learn to take our weight a little sideways if we mean that, but we should also know that too much weight one way or the other will simply unbalance the horse so that he is afraid to try anything. Very little works in riding unless it is subtle.

Logically, if we wish our horse to bring his forehand right in a lateral movement, we must make sure we have also turned our own 'forehand' to the right to take up precisely the same angle as that which we require in our horse so that, again, our weight complements him. Similar to the horse, the 'forehand' of the rider is comprised of the entire upper body, which includes head, shoulders and breast, and it is important that in making the lateral depart we do not leave some part of us behind. Once we ride from our solar plexus, everything generally becomes much easier and the aids can become much more refined.

All this sounds very simple but too often riders give their horses conflicting aids because it has never been explained to them *why* the conventional aids work. They should also understand that nothing will work unless it is correctly synchronised. In riding lessons, there is much confusion about where the rider's eyes should be. You would think that to keep the head balanced in a straight upward line over the shoulders would be elementary and that if the shoulders turn, the head should go with them. Yet, unbelievably, riders are still being taught to contort their bodies by twisting

Good modern dressage riders also understand the importance of the shoulder and inside leg position, as demonstrated here by John Lasseter. Note again the depth of the inside leg at the girth to support the horse and bend and direct him into the *travers*.

the head and neck one way while turning the body another. The classical rule is simple: always look forward between the horse's ears if the horse is to move forward and in equilibrium.

This precept is as old as the hills, written in every manual, every lavish tome from the classical period of the Greeks to the present day. Even my old 1961 *Manual of Horsemanship* mentions it and when, recently, I updated this delapidated volume and bought the latest edition, I presumed it would still be there. However, somewhere along the way a discrepancy has crept in which would account for the flaws which are appearing in the riding of certain movements today. Instead of seeing riders looking between their horses' ears; too often they are looking away to where they wish the horse to end up seven or eight strides later. The old precept: 'the rider should be erect and the eyes looking between the horse's ears'[2] has been replaced with: 'You must be straight; you should look in the direction in which you are going.'[3] It is the last part of the sentence which is so misleading, particularly as the horse himself seems to have been left out of the equation.

Perhaps we should pause here to consider the implications of this worthy advice, for no doubt the author may well have meant the same as before, but, by omitting the all-important point of looking through the horse's ears, readers may have been led to draw quite different conclusions. Nowhere is this more obvious than in the riding of circles and particularly in the execution of the shoulder-in.

The shoulder-in was first introduced by England's own Duke of Newcastle in the seventeenth century as a suppling exercise for cavalry and *manège* horses. The exercise was modified, polished and honed into today's dressage movement in the mid-eighteenth century by the Frenchman La Guérinière who rated Newcastle as the greatest exponent of his time. For many classical riders the shoulder-in is considered the singularly most important lateral movement for the development of the horse's elasticity and weight-bearing ability behind. As Nuno Oliveira writes in *Reflections on Equestrian Art*: 'I never begin the training of a horse by giving him a lesson other than the shoulder-in.'

The real value of the exercise is that it leads to the activation and bending of the horse's hind legs which gives greater elevation to the forehand from lowering and suppling the quarters, strengthening the back and stabilising the neck. If, however, the rider does not put himself into a position where the horse can carry out this gymnastic feat correctly, the whole exercise

---

[2] 1961 edition of *The Manual of Horsemanship*, published by The British Horse Society, Kenilworth, Warwickshire.
[3] 1993 edition of *The Manual of Horsemanship*.

The shoulder-in evolved as a suppling exercise to aid collection and engagement. Here, its inventor, La Guérinière, demonstrates the required posture of the rider who advances his outside shoulder and turns his head and upper body into the direction of the movement.

(Engraving from *École de Cavalerie*)

Too many riders twist their bodies in the shoulder-in by dropping through the inside waist.
This is often caused by pulling back on the inside rein, which merely tilts the horse's head
and pushes it on to the outside shoulder.

becomes counter-productive. Oliveira warns against the 'so-called shoulder-in, so frequently seen, in which the rider pulls on the inside rein while leaning on the same side, with his leg drawn back to jab the horse with the spur, which forces the poor animal to move while remaining twisted, and which takes all impulsion away from the horse'.

It is my belief that the commonest underlying cause behind the detrimental overuse of the rider's inside hand is a misunderstanding concerning the rider's head and shoulder position. Too many riders drop a shoulder to the inside, thus forgetting to turn the whole upper body. Others twist, by bringing one shoulder back instead of two and forgetting to turn from the sternum or breastbone which will bring the outer shoulder round as well. For this reason, shoulder-in would better be named shoulders-in.

As shoulder-in requires the horse to look to the inside of the school but to remain in a three-trace position on the track, clearly the rider must look in the same direction. On the left rein, for example, the first requirement is that the forehand of the horse looks left and the inside fore makes a new track. This is brought about by displacing the weight to the left which is helped and made possible by the rider deepening the inside seatbone momentarily and bringing their own 'forehand' to the left, thus mirroring exactly what they require of the horse. Having set the movement up

Here Carl Hester rides a four-track shoulder-in. The rider's body position is exemplary, the angle of the shoulders, chest and waist giving guidance to the horse who will want to mirror image his partner. The face of the rider too is turned in the direction of the movement, while the eyes look up the track. The rider's inside leg could be a little deeper to ask for a bend to the inside, but the emphasis of weight depends on the level of the horse's training and is obviously correct for this horse. (Photo: courtesy Bob Langrish)

237

correctly in this way, the rider then requires the horse to move right, up the track. It is the rider's lower body, from the waist downward, which literally takes the horse up the track, and the horse soon begins to respond to the sideways aiding or nudge of the rider's inside leg by engaging his inside hind leg which moves deeper under the belly and into the trace of the outside fore.

All, however, will be spoiled if, at the same time, the rider does not support the horse with the outside leg and if they turn their head to look in the direction in which they wish to go rather than looking into the movement itself, i.e. between the horse's ears. As the weight of the head also affects the whole upper body, the feeling to the horse would, in such a case, be one of being drawn back to the track and out of the lateral movement. Unreasonably, then, the rider is irritated, pulls more on the inside rein and kicks the horse in the rib to achieve the sideways feel again. The result is a twisted horse struggling to carry out a movement incorrectly ridden which generally ends up as a contorted quarters-out. Once the rider's head is out of sync, the whole picture is marred.

To be fair to the latest edition of *The Manual of Horsemanship*, this very point concerning the shoulder-in is admirably stressed further on in a section concerning 'Advanced Movements'. Under aids for shoulder-in we read: 'The rider sits centrally in the saddle and looks between the horse's ears. He will be able to see where he is going by looking up the track out of the corners of his eyes. If his head and shoulders are not in line with the horse's head and shoulders, he will unbalance the horse and spoil the movement.'

How sad, therefore, that in addressing the basic position of the rider in the saddle, earlier in the book, the same care was not taken to enforce the principle of always looking between the horse's ears whatever we are doing. Updating perfectly adequate instruction is a dangerous business and a clever use of words may cause misinterpretations which, when gradually absorbed into common usage, can undo so much good advice from the past. For this reason, I have always been a little suspicious of trainers who claim to have a 'more modern' approach.

A similar instance is encountered in the execution of the canter circle. If the rider's head is looking to the centre of the circle instead of towards the next segment of the circumference, the horse may very well strike off on the wrong leg or fall into the circle with the hind end swivelling outwards. The greatest obstacle to a good canter circle is when the rider's upper body turns too much to the inside or too strong an aid is given with the inside rein. This has the effect of blocking the horse through the shoulders and

The riding of the counter-canter will generally only be effective if the rider continues to look over the horse's leading leg. Turning the upper body (as illustrated) in the opposite direction may achieve a change when you least want it. On the other hand, this a common sight in the jumping arena, when riders expect their horse to change for them!

may prevent the horse from engaging his inside hind, an absolute requisite of a balanced circle. As in the pirouette, it is the pivoting leg which has to take the greatest load of weight.

Some horses are so sensitive to the weight of the rider's head that they will literally change legs just by a quiet change in direction from the head alone. We hear of others, more sensitive still, which change according to where the rider's eyes are looking. When teaching, I often ask riders to imagine that they too have a poll like the horse (the top of their hat being the imaginary point) and that they too must stretch up from the neck to allow the poll to become the highest point of their body. This stops all the unbalancing turkey nodding which we have already discussed, but it has the added advantage of helping the horse to keep straight when he is required to be straight, and just a very gentle inclination of the rider's head to right or left should achieve the same result through poll flexion in the horse.

Thus, in counter-canter along the track, provided riders continue to look and turn their head very slightly to the outside of the arena, the horse will be unlikely to try to change. Generally, when a horse is going nicely in counter-canter, even for the first time, he will remain in this mode unless the rider suddenly alters their head and shoulder position. The telling time is when one approaches a corner. Nine times out of ten, even quite experienced riders involuntarily move their head to the inside. Nine times out of ten, the horse will do the same and, of course, the counter-canter will be lost, by a change, the horse going disunited or making a hurried downward transition. You can never blame the horse when you made it impossible for him to give you what you wanted in the first place.

To appreciate how these intentional or unintentional weight changes work and how each may effectively open little sluice-gates (see Chapter 10) for the horse to slip through, I believe that it is very important to introduce novices in dressage to some form of lateral work at a fairly early stage in order to improve their more basic work. Once the rider feels on a schooled horse how every misalignment or change from the conventional forward-pointing affects the horse, they may begin to ride the three gaits with much more awareness and respect for the horse's balance generally. All this is very logical and the rider soon respects the difference between offering purposeful openings and those which previously they might have given inadvertently and which need to be closed.

Again, the concept of the river encased by straight, forward-facing banks is helpful. The rib cage is too often forgotten in riding and as both sides of the waist (as well as the front and back) give support to the spine, it is important that riders become aware of the necessity to concentrate on keeping their sides firm and upright if the banks of the river are not to cave in and give way. There is a very real difference between rigidity and the necessary tone and support upon which our horses rely. Too often, in turns and circles, riders tend to collapse to one side, which will create huge problems for the horse if he is to keep turning correctly so that his hind feet continue to step into the tracks of the forefeet.

As children are less prone to this mistake than adults, I blame this tendency on the fact that we all drive cars and the body has become inured to the concept of leaning this way and that as one turns the wheel. But riding is not like steering a car. If the driver's waist droops or collapses to one side, it matters not one jot in a car; for a horse it is truly threatening if the rider does this. How can a horse keep his balance on a circle when the rider's weight is actually pulling him in the opposite direction? Trapped in the middle of opposing forces, the reins fighting the bodyweight, most horses do a pretty miraculous job. To help eradicate collapsing on a circle, I find imagery is of paramount importance. For some riders I say, 'Sit taller to the inside!'. Others need something more positive, such as, 'Imagine an extra rib to the inside'.

Having discussed the shoulder-in from the upper body position, let us now examine it in relation to the lower body. There are two schools of thought concerning how to apply the weight aids. The competitive school teaches that the rider should deepen their weight slightly into the inside seatbone throughout the movement, which, in theory, would necessitate that the rider's inside hip should remain forward (as though on a circle) while the horse steps laterally away from the press of the inside leg drawn just behind the girth. A more individualistic overview from Nuno Oliveira suggests that the rider's weight should be taken a little more to the outside. This would necessitate bringing the inside hip a little back to turn both hips slightly into the movement in the same way as the shoulders have turned. Such action would tend to throw the rider's weight more toward their outside seatbone. The issue is difficult.

If we think of the shoulder-in as an extension of the circle, then we would remain with the inside hip forward but must be careful not to deepen it to the extent of blocking the incoming inside hind as it reaches through. Nevertheless, many horses respond better to a slight sitting into the outside seatbone as they are moving towards the outside hand, and this way can particularly help a novice horse to understand in which direction he should be flowing.

The way I look at it is this. To initiate the shoulder-in, I always think 'circle' by deepening the inside leg on the girth and slightly advancing the inside hip to complement the inside leg position which prepares the horse for the movement as I approach the track on the long side. Unless he is fairly advanced in lateral work, I then generally ride a 10-metre circle first. Having completed this, the first step of the lateral movement is ridden in the same way as the first step of a new circle to take the forehand forward and off the track. After that I am looking to free the horse away from the circle and take him up the long side of the arena. In so doing, I am thinking sideways and more central with my weight, making sure that the inside leg is giving the horse more of a nudge feeling against his side, rather than over-deepening and leading him around and into another circle. The horse is also helped to understand that he is to remain on the track by the outside hand momentarily checking and possibly opening a little to lead him away.

After this careful setting up of the movement (shoulder-in is the only classical movement[4] where the horse is moving in a different direction from the way in which he is bending), I generally find a correct position of the upper body, with the outside shoulder advanced, is sufficient to maintain the movement provided the seat and leg just flow with the horse. I also find that the outside thigh is most important to aid the shoulder-in by supporting

---

[4] I do not regard leg yield as a classical movement as it tends to push the horse on to his outside shoulder and generally confuses the horse for the half-pass.

the forehand and encouraging it to remain in its correct tracking. Of all the movements, shoulder-in is perhaps the most contradictory one in terms of correctly aiding the horse. It is definitely the most personal one when it comes to knowing how to ride it and which way will be best for your particular horse.

Every horse is a little different. Some horses find it exceedingly difficult to bend one way and move away in the other direction; others find it easy. Some riders grasp the concept quickly; others struggle for years. The main point about all this is to have an open mind. Feel your horse; work with him; go with the flow. Respect the fact that he simply cannot keep his head and shoulders left (or right) if your head and shoulders do not take up the same angle. Remember that, throughout the shoulder-in, you are riding the horse mainly from your inside leg into your outside hand. It is the outside hand which gently leads you and the horse up the track but the rider must be careful not to lose the flexion from the poll to the inside.

There is, however, a legitimate exercise which can enhance the shoulder-in and which, indeed, does require changing the direction of the flexion. As the horse becomes more proficient in the shoulder-in, it is often helpful to make another 10-metre circle halfway down the track and to change the exercise to *renvers*. This helps to confirm the stability of the horse's neck and to ensure he can soften and bend to the opposite side. By asking the inside hind pushing under to turn into an outside hind, also engaging under, the two movements can complement each other. As the greatest fault of the shoulder-in is generally too much lateral neck bend in the horse, riding some steps of *renvers* when the horse is fully confirmed in shoulder-in can be very beneficial. The rider, however, must take great care not to muddle the horse through a lack of understanding of the purpose of the movement as well as of the correct aids and how to apply them.

At all times, whatever the exercise, it is important that the horse can feel through your weight and how you use your legs what you are trying to do. There is all the difference in the world between the feeling for circle and the feeling for sideways. Always think 'supporting downward' with the inside leg in the circle (or later in the half-pass) for the horse to bend *around* it; always think 'nudge', 'press' or 'supporting against' with the leg if you wish to move the horse laterally and *away* from it.

Any tightness of the inside rein or – worse – pulling back towards the waist with the inside hand will prevent the horse from stepping through with the inside hind leg and he will tend to jack-knife on to the outside shoulder. Instead, keep the inside hand asking softly at the wither or, if you require to give a more definite opening aid, make sure you take it forward a

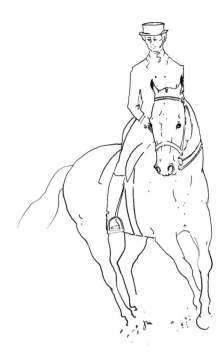

In the canter pirouette, the rider looks sympathetically into the movement, which will help her horse. Unfortunately, this picture is slightly marred by the rider's inside leg moving backward instead of supporting the horse more through the forehand.

little rather than back. If the quarters are curving in too much, use the inside aid against the wither as an indirect hand aid. Riders must stay firm and supported upwards through the waist, especially to the inside so that they do not collapse downward to stifle the in-coming stride of the inside hind as it steps through. Above all, look into the movement, never where you wish it to end up or you may never get there – at least not in shoulder-in.

Nowhere is the uprightness of the waist more important than in the canter pirouette. Leaning in makes it virtually impossible for the horse to retain his balance and encurve correctly around the rider's inside leg. Instead, the outside hind leg falls out and the horse loses the forward impulsion so necessary for the collection required if he is to canter in an ever-decreasing circle.

These inconsistencies will also be shown up in the quarter- or half-piroutte at the walk. The horse simply cannot turn on his hocks on a small radius if the rider is not sitting tall and deep with the weight dropping into the inside stirrup from upright hips and an upright waist. Again, riders can be helped by hands-on assistance to ensure they are allowing the leg to support the horse in the turn rather than pushing against him, which will impede the turn and push the quarters away. Quite apart from the value to the horse as a gymnastic exercise to supple the quarters, walk pirouettes (quarter and half) are wonderful for improving the rider's understanding of support, straightness and forwardness, particularly as preparation for better canter work. After a few experiences on a sensitive horse which shows up the common faults, the rider will begin to appreciate how, by embracing the horse, the lower body also gives structure and form to every movement. Riders need to be clear in their own minds that the head and upper body basically affect the forehand, while the seat and legs take charge of the quarters.

If there is anything more confusing for the horse than a rider's flopping, unstable upper body, it is the instability of a floppy lower body where the weight is being pulled about in all directions in a confusing mish-mash of instructions. Horses need to be ridden between clear parameters and riders who have always prided themselves on being relaxed in the lower regions may get a sharp reminder from a well-schooled horse that he cannot be expected to travel forward and straight when everything is on the move. There is a real difference between the supple, spongy quality of an adhesive seat and legs and the sloppiness of untoned limbs and wobbling hips.

To educate such riders, I ask them first to exaggerate the hip movement on a schoolmaster and then to try sitting still with quiet open hips and to feel the difference. It can be quite a psychological shock to find oneself in a much more commanding position simply by appearing to do nothing. To find that this, in turn, can give the horse a more collected, balanced feel can be mindboggling. Yet all this can be achieved in one lesson, even with riders who have never had a dressage lesson in their lives before. Of course, it will take many more lessons, perhaps over years, for the same people to become so balanced and controlled that they no longer induce crookedness or can correct it before it happens, but at least a positive start will have been made.

Riders who have not been made aware of inconsistencies in connection with their weight and the necessity to provide a proper framework through which the horse's impulsion may flow, often find that their bodies have a very good way of lying to them. They have become comfortable in a certain position which may not be the true one and this feeling of comfort has led to the brain being convinced that all is square when it it not. This leads to the horse being 'corrected' when it is really a rider problem. By leading the dance from a faultless position, the horse at least has a chance to travel more forward or laterally as required and any stiffness will be minimised.

Wanting the best for one's horse is a very different philosophy from wanting the best for oneself. Indeed, it has been a salutory lesson all through my life that what I have often thought I wanted has somehow eluded me. Why this should be so, I do not know – perhaps it is the same for everyone, although I must admit I have often thought things come more easily to some than to others.

It started as a child, when, for years, I longed for a little sister; instead I had two big, sometimes rough brothers but was surrounded by animals. As a teenager, I longed to be dainty, small and boast an hour-glass figure like my best friend; instead I shot up three extra inches at the age of sixteen to become long-legged and look more like a boy than a girl with hips the same size as my singularly unpromising top. At school, I dreamt of the glory of winning goals in school teams; I was never picked but I was in every play, generally Shakespeare, with the longest speaking part and more work. During A Levels, I dreamed of Oxford where my mother's family had gone; instead, I was offered a place at Leeds, which, foolishly, I disdained. Nevertheless, if I had not enrolled on the excellent secretarial course my parents arranged for me in Edinburgh, before going south to work in London, I might never have been able to run an equestrian business and might not now be writing books.

Looking back now, I see that all these things, although not what I wanted or planned for at the time, had a pattern to them and led in many ways to the life I am leading now. Even in my riding career there have been many false hopes and disappointments, yet, equally, and for which I am very grateful, there have been wonderful surprises, all the more appreciated as they have generally been totally unexpected.

I have already spoken of my book *The Royal Horse of Europe*. Back in the early eighties, out of deference to Henry's and my own love and commitment to the Portuguese horse, I had founded the Lusitano Breed Society of Great Britain. After seven years as chairman and a further two years as president, with a wonderful team behind me, I was unexpectedly sponsored for a horsebox by Vista Alegre, the world famous Portuguese porcelain company whose equestrian links are well known in the Peninsula. Not only do Vista Alegre support various shows and equestrian events in Portugal, they also manufacture the most stunning and delicate porcelain horse statues as well as a series of specialist plates showing the baroque horse in High School poses. As I was the first person in England consistently to demonstrate Lusitano horses in public at clinics as well as to compete them regularly in affiliated dressage, I believe they felt I should have a worthy vehicle in which to transport my precious cargo. Having access to such a box has transformed my life in recent years.

The story does not end quite there. One day in 1993 an important-looking envelope stamped EIIR, addressed in thick black copperplate writing, plopped through the letter box. The invitation was to attend a state banquet at Buckingham Palace which Her Majesty the Queen was giving for Mario Soares, the President of Portugal, at the end of April. Once over the shock, I set off to Cambridge with my daughter, who, at the age of ten, succeeded in picking out the most wonderful shimmering dress which could have been created for the occasion. Out of the bank came the cabuchon rubies which one day will go to Allegra and which were originally made up into a pendant, earrings and a small tiara for her great grandmother from jewels relieved by the British during the Boxer Rebellion from the Summer Palace in Peking under the command of her great grandfather.

With a sense of history and awe in my heart for how things can turn out, Richard and I were driven down the Mall, with Portuguese and British standards flying, on a balmy late spring evening to a reception which surpassed all my wildest dreams and made me feel very humble. When, later, after dinner, the Lord Chamberlain whispered in my husband's ear that, after coffee I should please be ready to talk with Her Majesty in a withdrawing room for some minutes on the subject of the Lusitano horse, in which she was particularly interested, I admit I was floating on air.

When eventually we were summoned and I made my curtsey, all nervousness fled as I looked into a pair of very sharp blue eyes and realised just how much the Queen already knew about these horses and how much she understood. I am convinced no words of mine told her more than she already knew and, as many people have before me, I marvelled at her interest, knowledge and research. It was a testimony to her ability to make people feel at ease that, at one point, I found myself interrupting her when discussing how comfortable these horses are in their collected work. 'It's partly because they are built for it,' I said, 'and also because they love their work and give themselves so willingly.' Of course, I need not really have told her because at one time she had owned a fine purebred stallion herself, a gift from a former president. Nevertheless, I think she enjoyed being reminded. If not, she was much too gracious to show anything other than genuine interest.

One might imagine that such golden and surprise interludes in one's life would make one complacent and want to take life easier. Somehow, however, at least for me, it does not work that way. Today, I am busier than ever before, particularly in my desire to promote a more humane approach to equitation in general. If it is the Lusitano horse who has shown me the way and helped to give me recognition, it is to all horses that I owe my loyalty and that is more important than anything.

One of the organisations I have enjoyed a close relationship with in Britain is the Anglo-Austrian Society, based in London. Originally, they were extremely helpful in arranging a visit I made to Vienna to interview the Director of the Spanish Riding School, and of the Piber Stud, Dr Jaromir Oulehla, when I was writing my book on the history of dressage. This, in turn, led to an invitation to lecture for Friends of the Society and other cultural groups. Finally, it culminated in my writing some of the publicity for the School's programme on the last two occasions when the Lipizzaners came to Britain. What was refreshing about their approach was that, far from being reluctant to use the services of someone specifically interested in Portuguese horses, the Anglo-Austrians recognised how well this background complemented their own dedication to the Lipizzaner. In this spirit, we all worked together for the good of the horses – their horse, my horse, indeed, all horses.

Of late it has become fashionable in certain circles to denouce the work of the traditional baroque academies. On one occasion, when the editor of an Australian horse magazine criticised the work at Vienna as out of date and out of step with the world of competition riding, I wrote a very strong letter to him to argue the point. As a result, having been a regular contributor to that same magazine for several years, the door slammed shut and I was never asked to write for them again. Even the Christmas cards stopped!

Yet there is so much to learn from those establishments which have upheld traditional values for the sake of art for art's sake. Where money, prizes and material rewards do not enter the picture, it is so much easier for proven principles to be upheld and I shudder to think what would have happened to dressage today had those centres of excellence not continued. What a debt we owe to figureheads like Colonel Podhajsky and those who followed in his wake who refused to bow to commercial pressures and change their image for something more flashy, more modern and undoubtedly far less pure.

Talking to friends and pupils I am only too aware of how the vast majority of thinking riders still need a Mecca to which they may turn their eyes for inspiration and clarification. We all need direction and, in the words of the Bible, a straightening of the way before us. For me and for many others the Spanish Riding School of Vienna magnificently fulfils that purpose.

In this context, the Vienna Academy has always taught that when we ride our hips should be square to the horse's hips and our shoulders to the horses's shoulders. This is reiterated in both the German *Instructor's Handbook* and the British *Manual of Horsemanship*. This precept is a sound and important one yet, sadly, it also appears to be out of fashion among too many schools of thought.

In circle work, many riders align their hips and shoulders correctly at the onset but lose the inside hip at the furthest point of the circle, generally due to pulling back on the inside rein. Instead, the rider must think of solidifying the inside leg from a deep, supporting and forward inside hip to encourage encurvation; only then can they feed the horse to the outside rein to complement the outside lateral stretching. It is virtually impossible for the horse to engage his inside hind leg on the circle if the rider does not mirror him.

Sometimes one feels ashamed when an instructor of the calibre of Arthur Kottas, chief instructor and rider at Vienna, still has to remind British riders of this elementary fact when he teaches in Britain. 'Bring your outside shoulder round! Deepen your inside seatbone forward!' is said time and time again. How can a horse bring his shoulders round when the rider leaves theirs behind?

Some years ago a pamphlet was published by a dressage teacher who took the British Horse Society to task for promoting the classical 'shoulders to horses' shoulder, hips to horses' hips' concept. Much damage was done through what amounted to scaremongering and, to this day, people are concerned about twisting their spines if required to move a shoulder or a hip back or forward to complement the horse.

There is no truth in the idea that the rider's spine can be twisted if the pectoral region and pelvic girdle work independently of each other, provided we always support our backs through balanced upright posture. Independent movement of hips and shoulders is both natural and normal and every time we walk, skip, run or march we are swinging the hips and shoulders forward and back in diametric opposition one to the other.

Anyone who schools horses regularly will know that it is working against the horse to ignore the shoulders to horses' shoulders, hips to horses' hips precept. Indeed, we would lurch drunkenly from side to side if we ignored this traditional advice on a serpentine. Any natural action which involves advancing, squaring or regressing the various component parts of the human frame in the same way as we would on the ground should be possible on horseback. However, this is why it is so important not to be caught in a sedentary position. It is the supportive upright spine which is capable of independent movement. If one slouches and treats the body with contempt, one can rick one's back standing at the kitchen sink!

It is an understanding of the influence of weight through good posture

Remember that independent movement of shoulders and hips should be perfectly natural and safe for a fit rider provided that she supports herself through the waist, back and abdomen. We are built to move!

that is so often lacking in modern riding. For those fortunate enough to grow up in the countryside or at least to have access to hacking, hunting or cross-country riding, the lessons of weight develop naturally out of self-preservation and a need to balance the horse. The turns, twists and loops of even the most novice horse trials course require at all times that the rider remains square to the horse and goes with him. Unity of balance and direction, stimulated through the eyes and looking for the next stride, is a gift for the taking.

In any sport there will always be those who use their weight and balance more efficiently than others, which is why we have such brilliant jockeys and eventers as well as the talented tennis players, skaters and footballers of whom we all know. Nevertheless, we can all learn to develop greater feel by riding exercises which stimulate both us and the horse together.

Nowhere is the shoulders-hips concept more apt and important than in riding a good serpentine. Serpentines are wonderful for confirming balance and making sure the horse understands your aids. They involve bends and straightening on both reins and at the same time they encourage impulsion and pushing from behind. As every loop of the serpentine requires a change of weight and direction as one approaches and leaves the centre line, refinement of the aids is an absolute prerequisite of the movement. Subtlety is important if we are not to push the horse the wrong way as we bend him, and it requires real concentration on squareness to approach and depart from the centre line with the horse truly straight.

Control of this nature should never be physically tiring; on the other hand it should be mentally stimulating and one can always be forgiven for getting off the horse feeling brain-weary. I well remember what that talented South African rider Emile Faurie, who attained so many successes for Great Britain on his effervescent, beautifully fluid horse Virtu, had to say on the subject of concentration. Someone had said, 'You ride so quietly, you make it look so easy, you obviously never have to think about what you're doing.'

As quick as a flash, he replied, 'I'm afraid you are incorrect. I never stop thinking about what we are doing for one second when I ride. You have to think – *all* the time.'

This reminded me of the first few months after Henry died. My lovely daughter Allegra was born only eight weeks before his death and, being an 'older mum', I was advised during my pregnancy to give up riding. I only started again after Henry's funeral. It was a very therapeutic and healing process being back on a horse, although looking after my tiny baby had also helped me greatly. I remember, about two months later, some close friends coming down to visit me and watching from the gallery of the indoor school while I worked with one little Thoroughbred mare, Little Cass, who, through her sensitivity, was extremely challenging despite her kind personality. They were not particularly horsy people but I had known them a long time and the wife, in particular, had always been outspoken. Later she confessed she was shocked by my attitude when they arrived. 'You looked so content and absorbed in your work,' she said. 'I expected to find you abstracted and sad.'

'But that's what so wonderful about horses,' I said. 'They take you completely out of yourself and if you are involved with a discipline, as I am, you can have thoughts for nothing else while you are doing it. There simply isn't time to be sad.'

She looked even more shocked. 'But surely riding is the one area where you miss him most?'

'Of course,' I said. 'I miss him in the yard, in the school, teaching and telling us all what to do and generally inspiring us and the horses. Of course – there is a huge gap. But when you're alone with a horse and you know what you want to achieve and are feeling its body through every fibre of your own body so that every tiny movement and turn it makes are influenced by you there is a very real sense of responsibility with no time to think of anything else – you have to ride for the moment, every moment, otherwise you are not giving it your all.'

I suspect many people like myself have been helped through a bereavement or terrible shock through their horses. The closeness, the affection, the contact are all part of the healing process, but it is the mental side, the brain work which goes with classical riding, which actually eradicates all pain, all worry, all depression for that period of time. Any break or respite from one's troubles has to be good for you, and for me, personally, Cassie was as good as any trained counsellor. Not only was she fond of me but she challenged me, she stretched me and she kept me mentally aware and thinking – a wonderful combination of cerebral support during a difficult time. That, together with the gift of my wonderful daughter, certainly kept me going. Besides, I knew Henry was behind me.

Perhaps, had it not been for Little Cass and horses like her, I would not have been ready for the next horse that was to come into my life and alter it forever two years later. But although I have alluded to him a little in these chapters, the full story of Palomo Linares is probably another book in itself.

CHAPTER 14
Outline and rounding

In January 1995 I started what was intended to be a small club for friends, pupils and readers of my books, which I called the Classical Riding Club. The idea was to bring together like-minded people in order to promote, through self-help, a more consistent approach to training. By highlighting all that we believed to be correct yet thoroughly humane, and emphasising this aspect of riding through demonstrations, clinics and seminars in a spirit of harmony, it was felt we could spread enthusiasm and enlightenment. This would be fuelled by articles, viewpoints and shared experiences from a quarterly newsletter which would promote the ethos of the Club's Charter. With over 500 registered international members by the end of the first year, the club was definitely creating a more thinking atmosphere within several riding disciplines.

It was the members themselves who encouraged me to introduce new dressage training tests which could be used at any competition alongside the conventional ones. We all felt the time was ripe for placing greater emphasis on the skills of the rider, irrespective of their breed or type of horse. In recent times, it is sad but true that competition results have often became more important than the means by which they were attained, which somehow takes the art out of riding and reduces it to just another sport.

Putting my first draft tests together for the club and trying them out among pupils, friends and fellow teachers, I became aware of a worrying trend in riding philosophy. It seemed that some of the most hallowed precepts of classical dressage, which I had long taken for granted, no longer appeared to mean to others what they had always meant to me. In my assumption that others shared my understanding, I had used a number of terms which, as far as the educated horseman or woman is concerned, should leave no room for doubt. Indeed, their intrinsic meaning is generally left to us – if we care to look – in the writings of the traditional masters. Sadly, however, insufficient numbers of today's riders read these works in any real depth, and when one begins to consider the implications, particularly how in recent times so many people seem to have grasped the wrong end of the stick, it seems all too obvious that true understanding can only be attained over many years of study and practical horsemanship.

One of the concepts that seemed most noticeably to have lost its original interpretation was the idea of 'roundness' or 'rounding' and this came as a profound shock. Indeed, so different was the modern interpretation of these two simple terms from the traditional viewpoint that I had to admit to myself that some of us were actually speaking a different language one from the other.

Somewhat surprisingly, I found that among people who bred horses or who jumped them, the concept of rounding was far closer to what I had always understood it to mean than what was perceived among the modern dressage fraternity. Perhaps this was due to the fact that the former were primarily concerned with the correct function of the horse rather than a cosmetic idea of what 'looked' correct. I know I am not the only person to rue the subjectivity of dressage judging, particularly at times by people who are not able to ride, let alone school to the level they are judging. Nowhere were attitudes more confused than in the area of the horse's profile or outline.

To the traditionalists the whole idea of roundness comes from the shape and muscling of the horse's back, loins and quarters, both at rest and in movement. While there are clearly horses that are born with a rounded morphology, such as the close-coupled Iberian breeds, the Irish Draught, Welsh Cob and some hunter jumper types (horses of more curvilinear appearance than rectangular), the determining factor is not always so much one of conformation but of how the horse uses himself behind the saddle. It is when the thrust comes from engaged hocks and quarters, emanating from an elastic use of the back, that the whole dorsal frame is elevated to give a convex or rounded effect. This will be in sharp contrast to the horse who props himself up on the rider's hand, leaves the hind legs trailing and hollows his back to show a concave profile.

To return to the ideal, the more the horse is able to flex the lumbo-sacral joint to bring his hocks underneath the body mass, the more the withers and neck appear to rise, culminating in the poll which becomes the highest point. This posture not only looks natural, balanced and poised, but leads to increased athleticism and manoeuvrability. The overall effect, therefore, is of one continuous, arching, rounding line forever moving forward and upward from well-engaged quarters and deep, actively flexing stifles, hocks and fetlocks.

This whole gathering process, known as collection, or *ramener* in the French school, combines flexion with elevation and the one simply cannot

Roundness is represented by the tone and muscling of the horse's back, loins and quarters. Only from strong, gathered hind legs and a liberated forehand can the horse coil and uncoil like a spring. (Engraving from *Luz da Liberal é Nobre Arte da Cavellaria*)

False roundness involves a forcing down of the horse's natural head carriage, a hollowing through the back and the subsequent loss of engagement behind. Unfortunately, such abusive riding is not sufficiently penalised in today's dressage arenas.

exist without the other. The appearance of rounding through the topline is due, therefore, to the greater support underneath the belly which lifts the whole. When the horse ultimately bends or flexes through the poll, with a subsequent softening of the jaw (the end result of the gathering process), the illusion of a more short-coupled curvilinear frame is given. Things are rarely as they appear in equitation, for it is this closing of the angles of the joints which actually involves more pliability and stretching of the various muscle systems. The final proof of correct rounding, as one trainer said to me recently, is when every horse looks like a baroque horse.

What concerned me about the viewpoint expressed by many of the regular dressage competitors with whom I was talking, was that roundness had little to do with the rear end of the horse lowering and coming under to raise the forehand, but was focused almost entirely on the setting and lowering of the horse's head and neck through the hands. As long as the horse's muzzle was in the required place (and there was conflict as to where this should be), many paid little heed to what was happening behind the saddle. Yet in the classical school the acceptance of the bit and the position of the horse's head are not so much the core of the issue but the end result. The more the horse engages, the higher subsequently the raising of the poll, neck and wither. Only then will he be in a position to flex and soften down correctly.

This effect, more often described as 'on the bit', is clearly explained in the FEI handbook for dressage under 'Object and General Principles', clause 6.

> A horse is said to be 'on the bit' when the hocks are *correctly* placed, the neck is more or less *raised and arched* according to the stage of training and the extension or collection of the pace, and he accepts the bridle with a *light and soft contact* and submissiveness throughout. The head should remain in a steady position, as a rule *slightly in front of the vertical, with a supple poll as the highest point of the neck* and no resistance should be offered to the rider.

The italics are mine and it is these highlighted aspects of the horse's general posture which contribute to the visual concept of roundness, one of nature's wonderful phenomena which no doubt inspired many equestrian artists over the centuries to capture the flowing, rounded lines of the collected horse with just a few simple brushstrokes. True roundness not only gives the illusion of freedom and elevation, it actually allows the horse to move more freely due to the increased engagement behind.

How different this is from the earthbound aspect of all too many dressage horses! How can it be that to so many roundness concerns the fixing of the head into a vertical posture, often long before the horse is ready to do this, and driving the horse downward and into this contact? Too often this results in the horse dropping the wither or 'breaking' at the crest, with the face inclining towards the chest, and coming behind the bit simply because the hocks are not sufficiently under nor the back supple or strong enough to support such action.

This had led to many uninitiated riders not only believing that roundness *per se* allows for a broken crest, a head behind the vertical and a shortened neck but, indeed, that it is desirable! For many, this is a 'good outline'! Despite the clearly stated FEI directive that the poll should always remain the highest point, a number of trainers have simply ignored this long-established precept. Certainly one sees this at all levels of competition, even in many so-called classical yards.

To my sadness, an article was published in *Dressage and CT*[1], written by a fashionable trainer, Christian Thiess, who stated that there was a legitimate argument for the horse departing from the (required) classical posture of maintaining the poll as the highest point of the horse's neck. He suggested that, by adhering to such 'rules', there could be a tendency 'to push the horse into a rigid, mechanical frame'. Quite the opposite, surely? The rules were there to protect the horse!

---

[1] 'The Great Controversy', *Dressage and CT*, January 1994 issue, published at Cleveland Heights, Ohio.

In the double bridle, riders must take care to lighten the rein and send the horse more forward and in front of the leg. Any compromise to the correct position of the poll will tend to create tension both in front and behind the saddle and to stymie the horse's natural movement.

While Mr Thiess is a thoughtful and educated writer and trainer, clearly he believed a little bending of the rules – as well as a bending of the horse's neck in the incorrect place – could be acceptable. After all, as the article pointed out, what about stallions whose crest is highly muscled and pronounced? I could see his point that, in collection, the muscular tissue covering the second and third vertebral process might, indeed, protrude a little higher than the poll. Surely, in this case, the situation could be rectified by allowing the head to be less angled?

There will always be small exceptions to almost every rule under the sun, particularly when exceptional circumstances present themselves. Horses are no different from humans in this respect and if we may diverge for a moment in order to illustrate this point, let me tell the reader about a pupil whose arms are so short that she simply cannot keep her hands at the base of the wither without leaning forward and jeopardising her position. Does this mean we change the text of every riding manual and remove the requirement for riders to keep their hands in place or their shoulders back? I think not; imagine the consequences if we did!

As it is, there are too many who are only too willing to ignore the rules without us making it easier for them to do so. There are also those who seek innovation, seriously believe they can re-invent the wheel or who simply just disdain the classical ethos. To disregard the principle of the poll of the horse remaining the highest point in any schooling programme, would, in my opinion, encourage further ignorant practices in the name of outline. In particular, the quest for lightness, which should be the ultimate aim of all riders, might be even more neglected.

If nature had intended for the horse to bend from the head from a different part of the body other than in the atlanto-occipital or atlas-axis joint (poll) and particularly from further down the neck, she would have designed horses that way. No horse moving energetically in freedom will bend from the second or third vertebra; all bend to varying degrees from the poll. As this leads to the vast majority (from Shetland ponies to Arabs to Hanoverians) all displaying the poll as the highest point in movement, it is clear that this is simply a question of biomechanics and, like it or not, we must learn to work with it.

As with the human being, once the synchronisation and interplay of the vertebrae with their attendant muscle groups is upset, the horse becomes uncomfortable in much the same way as we would ourselves if made to run around with our chins tucked into our chests – people should seriously try it. When the equine spine is denied its freedom to stretch, for example in overbending, the current or flow of impulsion from the hind legs to the forehand will be interrupted or fractured and the horse will lose much of his potential for fluidity, rhythm and lightness.

With very short, thick-necked horses, there is some excuse for a mild compromise of position, with the horse bending from just behind the poll, between the second and third vertebrae. This is not due to an inability of the topline to sustain any raising, rounding or arching, rather it is the heaviness of the jowl which may prevent sufficient flexion being achieved through the junction of the head and neck. In a finely conformed horse, however, there is little excuse for such a 'breaking' through the crest and such thoughtless action can only place the horse on his shoulders and make him very much harder and heavier to ride.

Politely defending the necessity, therefore, to keep this precept firmly in place, I am glad to say that my letter in defence[2] of the traditional viewpoint was also published and several readers wrote in to express their agreement.

Nevertheless, it became obvious that Thiess was not alone in wishing to depart from cast-iron principles. To me, his article only highlighted the concern that, while he himself clearly understood the difference between a correct and an incorrect outline, others do not. Unhappily for the horse, not

---

[2] Readers' letters, *Dressage & CT*, July 1994.

only is there a growing number of dressage riders for whom the idea of roundness starts with the front end of the horse instead of the rear, but, in thinking this way, many make it impossible for him ever to achieve roundness.

Instead of working towards an upwardly mobile horse, with a light, airy forehand, such a preoccupation with dropping the chin too early has led to discomfort and pain for too many animals. By insisting through the hands that the head remains in the vertical when the horse is simply not physically or gymnastically able to sustain this, the rider displays appalling ignorance.

Unfortunately, insufficient dressage riders, instructors and judges understand even the most simple facts concerning the muscle systems of the horse. There is no need for people to become experts about such matters, but all who teach or judge dressage should be aware of the necessity to stretch the equine frame before attempting to position the head. This can only be achieved when the horse is actively pushing from behind from engaged hind legs, which initially requires a certain freedom in the forehand. The angle of the horse's face to the ground, whether in front of or into the vertical, should only be considered when all the joints are sufficiently supple and yielding to sustain such bending.

From these observations, the hitherto unspoken thought occurred to me that, for the uninitiated, the eye was invariably drawn to the position of the horse's muzzle as a starting point for assessing roundness when, clearly, it should be looking at the base of the quarters. This would truly typify the case for putting the cart before the horse if ever there was one. Indeed, were some of today's judges guilty of this? And if so, why, when the directives for the art of equitation are so clearly laid down, happily surviving for over 200 years to be enshrined in today's national rule books? When the nub of the matter of the horse's posture is all to do with the engagement behind, how could people remain in doubt?

As I talked to more people, I began to see why such confusion reigned. Dressage riders were *not* familiar with the rule book; precious few had ever studied or considered the hallowed principles despite the relatively simple language of the FEI's 'Object and General Principles of Dressage'. Rather, most remained in oblivion of those requirements, relying instead on their trainers to inform them. Here again, there was ignorance. While some instructors adhered to the classical principles based on the horse's natural way of going, others did not. With a singular lack of reverence for the time-honoured, painstaking work, many were only interested in obtaining a quick result by whatever means possible.

After all, it is comparatively easy to fake an illusion of good outline through the hands and if some judges are not sufficiently educated to spot

Familiar sights like this have led to people becoming totally confused as to where rounding should commence. Until judges penalise riders whose contact 'shortens' their horses in this way, we can never hope to attain lightness.

(Photo: Bob Langrish)

the difference, why worry? Once people are in the habit of seeing something performed in a certain way, however incorrect, it may only be a matter of time before it becomes accepted as the norm. The transition from what is unacceptable to what is acceptable will obviously be hastened if those same people who are producing horses schooled in this way are also involved in the interpretation of how they should be judged.

Thankfully, there are still riders, trainers and judges who know the difference between correct practice and parody. Nevertheless, in today's harsh financial climate it becomes increasingly difficult to remain true to one's craft when time is at a premium and the work is long and painstaking. The undeniable truth, that it may involve years of patience and hard work to build up the muscles in the back and quarters through increased engagement of the hind end to produce proper rounding, is not always popular. What may be even less acceptable is that no horse can be forced to give his back if he does not want to. An illusion of rounding may indeed be achieved mechanically but lightness has also to involve a giving of his mind.

No wonder, therefore, that many still cling to the theory that the horse should take the bit with a contact to be measured in terms of so many kilos, with the pressure remaining constant irrespective of the level of training or what the horse might be doing. This philosophy effectively denies the horse the space to grow and lighten through deeper engagement, thus contravening the whole object of superior training 'so that the horse thus gives the impression of doing of his own accord what is required of him'[3].

It particularly worried me that adherents to the modernist school of thought were often looking for evidence of the horse fully on the bit as early as Preliminary and Novice level. As a result, during the final edit of my tests I deliberately omitted the words 'roundness' and 'outline' not only from my lower-level tests, but altogether. Even at Elementary level and above, I asked that the judges look for and mark 'lightness of the forehand' and 'engagement behind' so that there could be no confusion. This would, of course, bring roundness into the equation but at least then we would not be seeing artificial rounding rewarded by judges whose concept differed so much from the traditional classical one.

As regards the lower-level tests, obviously none of these requirements should be asked for when the young horse is still learning to balance himself and naturally relies on sufficient freedom of the head and neck to help him to do so. Again, so that there could be no misconceptions, I settled for 'acceptance of contact' and a 'lack of tension'; the word 'outline' being counter-productive in my opinion to freedom, straightness, forwardness, suppleness and looseness through the back and shoulder.

One of the great malaises in dressage training today is that the freedom and stretching stage of schooling is often missed out because riders are restricting the horse long before he is confidently coming to the bit as a result of the forward aids. Judging for shape too early can lay the horse open to abuse from gadgets which fix the front end when the back is insufficiently developed to sustain a constant frame. Trying to hold themselves in an outline not only creates tension in young horses, but may build up areas of real discomfort behind the saddle which, in turn, leads to chronic back problems which often go unnoticed until it is too late.

For a long time now I have spoken out against the use of draw reins and balancing reins as, invariably, they are used on immature or unmuscled

---

[3] Clause 3 from the FEI 'Object and General Principles'.

Young riders should be encouraged to understand that young horses may not be sufficiently muscled to work 'into an outline' at the onset of training. They should, therefore, be encouraged at lower-level tests to ride forward, calm and straight as in this pleasant combination winning at Stoneleigh in 1987 in the days when people were less preoccupied with false roundness. (Photo: courtesy *Horse and Rider Magazine*)

horses who are simply not ready to be shaped in this way. Worse, they are generally made to be worn for much too long at a time and through quite rigorous exercise which will cause real pain. The argument that they are safe in the hands of experts makes one wonder just how good these experts are if they need to resort to artificial aids of such an unyielding nature. The whole ethos of good training is to work on precepts of reward through good sensations, and this can only be achieved in a lasting, satisfactory way if we teach the horse to yield by degrees. Demanding forcefully with a gadget which requires everything at once has to place stress on muscles and joints.

As every experienced horseman and woman knows, the training of a horse is a progressive, step-by-step seduction. We are well equipped with our own natural aids to ask for submission in a way which allows us to feel and read the state of the horse underneath us stage by gentle stage. Forcing may give us a quick fix but it may also bring pain and discomfort. I have heard more sad stories from veterinary surgeons and back specialists than could possibly be recounted here. Just one, however, might be worthy of repetition because we all know what it is like to have a headache and few people realise that horses too can suffer headaches.

A friend with considerably neurological knowledge, who stables her horse at livery, was concerned to see one particular pony at the yard standing with lowered head while tied up in the yard one Saturday afternoon. The pony had a bright chirpy personality and would normally take a keen interest in the goings on around him, yet on this occasion he held his head fixed as if unable to move it. He belonged to a small child who was, indeed, far too small for him and who was taught by her mother, a woman who subscribed to the kick and pull school of thought, with an apparent ignorance of suppleness and correct contact. Yet, despite all this, the child had a natural feeling for balance and often presented a pleasing picture, despite being obviously over-horsed.

Later, during my friend's evening visit, she noticed the pony back in its box, standing dejectedly in a far corner, its head pressed against the cold stone wall. My friend became even more concerned as this behaviour indicated symptoms of headache and depression. She determined to talk to the owners the next day.

Before she had a chance to do so, the answer came on the Sunday. The previous day's jumping lesson was being repeated and, for an entire 30 minutes, she saw the pony being worked in a gadget which forced its head almost between its knees every time the rider pulled on the balancing rein in response to the mother's exhortations to 'Keep its head down and under control!' Needless to say, the symptoms of headache disappeared shortly after the child returned to school.

There is no doubt that the character of the horse will deteriorate as a result of his suffering. As, however, he cannot speak out, except through body language, which, sadly, is not always as obvious as in the above case, the cause of the ensuing resistance and nappiness is misunderstood. Too often it is put down to the quirky and irrational behaviour of horses.

In addition to localised and often immediate pain, the creation of false roundness in front of the saddle through draw reins and other restrictive gadgets produces a longer-term physical affect. After a few weeks there will be some muscle wastage at the base of the neck where the trapezius muscles are located but which are prevented from doing their job of supporting the neck naturally from above. This will become more pronounced as the work continues. Gradually, this leads to an overdevelopment of the splenius muscles at the side of the upper neck, which shows a horse that has held himself in tension as he has been blocked through the longissimus dorsi, which runs the length of the horse's spine. Bulging splenius muscle and muscle wastage in front and under the saddle expose the fact that the horse has had to pull himself forward from the neck and shoulders instead of the forehand being pushed naturally forward from active hind legs and a strong, elastic back.

I am constantly amazed by the generosity of the average dressage horse who, despite all the odds being stacked against him, still does his best to comply with the rider's requests even though he is so often ridden from front to back. Far from encouraging bigger strides behind, such a preoccupation with shape and a forcing of outline stifle forward movement and athleticism.

Unfortunately for those competitors who know their theory, feel their horses and play by the rules, insufficient lower level judges today have the knowledge to reward correct rounding. 'Tense in the back' or 'too high in front' is sometimes the remark doled out by ignorant adjudicators in response to their first sight of a horse who has begun to elevate upwards through the wither and suspend himself from true rounding in the frame. Too many judges have become inured to the sight of horses working croup-high with hollow backs, shortened necks and hind legs which straighten and punt rather than flex and engage; thus when a really correct horse is presented, it all looks rather different and foreign to the eye.

This reminds me of an amusing story told to me by my friend Eleanor Taylor, a highly successful advanced dressage rider who, with her husband Roger, runs a classical dressage academy near Aberdeen. She has now given up competition, not only due to the inconsistencies of judging, but because, in her own words, she just wants to enjoy her horses and improve for her own and their sake rather than to please someone else whose values may differ.

A couple of years ago, she had one particular Intermediare horse who had a superb walk. At one important qualifier he was awarded a 9 for his walk by Nick Williams, an international judge. At his next event, a far less experienced judge gave him 4 when the horse had performed equally well. When Eleanor questioned the result, she was brusquely told, 'His walk is not normal – I could not give him more.' How sad when brilliance is not recognised as such because it does not subscribe to the common denominator.

In the early work, therefore, the rider must never think of any more than providing a quiet, fairly passive hand which allows the horse to find a steady support from the bit as he reaches forward with his head and neck. It is not so much a question of following the horse's head. The rider's hand

'Being at one with the horse.' Nowadays, former competitor Eleanor Taylor just enjoys her horse, Vivaldi, at The Grove Riding Centre, Aberdeen.
(Photo: courtesy Roger Taylor)

should 'think' a little ahead of the horse so the legs may ask him to step into and to take the contact. If the contact is not steady, the horse will feel an unpleasant bumping in the mouth and be discouraged. The bit should never pull back nor be dropped against his teeth, so the rider should ensure that the hand remains in place. There is nothing wrong and everything right (from the horse's point of view) about bridging the reins or leaning the knuckles a little into the neck to confirm stability. One may also test the horse's forwardness into the bridle by taking one hand up and forward – as though pushing the rein – while still keeping a feel of contact through the fingers.

Both hands should remain sufficiently forward of the rider's body so that they may work with the sensation that they are taking the body and that of the horse towards the hands – never the other way round. In other words, the horse comes to the hand and chews the bit of his own volition and in response to the forward aids of the rider's leg and seat. Once the horse begins to seek, and remain confident into, the contact which is always there for him in the same place and in the same way, the rider may then soften the fingers in each stride. This is a way of acknowledging the horse's efforts of keeping up to the hand and this quiet rewarding forms a secret bond of trust between horse and rider.

Later, as the horse supples and strengthens behind the saddle, we can begin to look for the first evidence of rounding. The traditional school looks first to the hindquarters and the loins to make sure that both are supple and yielding. True engagement cannot come from stiff, tense muscles and, again, it is the stretching ability of the longissimus dorsi which is so important for collection. This is where a sympathetic seat is so important. If the rider does not have the ability to ease their weight forward through a three-point contact so that they relieve those muscle sections under the back of the saddle, thus allowing them to stretch, the horse will find it very hard indeed to round his back and lower his croup by flexing the lumbo-sacral joint.

Once, however, the hind end is able to engage from unencumbered, elastic dorsal muscles, the loins and quarters free up while taking on a rounder, bulkier image. It is this natural appearance of curving, with the muscles more highly defined, which continues right up and through the horse's back. Although in part masked by the saddle, the entire topline of the horse should portray lift, lightness and roundness so that the whole horse looks taller and prouder.

It need not take a very experienced pair of eyes to judge from the way in which the quarters deepen and the withers rise up in front of the saddle as to whether or not the back is thus truly rounding, provided the judge knows what to look for. It should also be obvious that it is the hollow-backed horse which shows flat withers, a shortened, telescoped neck, with the face inclining backwards, which demonstrates unnatural tension and tightness throughout the equine frame.

An unnaturally high carriage of the neck, where the horse opposes his rider with a pronounced brachiocephalic muscle showing under the gullet, instead of softening down into the bridle from well-engaged hocks reaching under the body mass, is also relatively simple to spot. Riders should be made more aware of the ring of muscles which flex, stretch and support the frame from underneath as well as on top, by working in pairs, never in isolation. It is this natural and inbuilt support of the whole marvellously intricate mechanism of the equine body which is so often damaged by too strong a contact, the employment of artificial aids or by a heavy, interfering seat.

Once the back is elastic enough to connect the push and flow from the hind legs to the forelimbs, the rounding effect of a harmoniously working muscle system continues through the neck as it stretches forward and upwards. There is all the difference in the world between a stiff, peacock neck and an arching, cresting neck ending in a supple flexed poll. One again we are reminded of the importance of correct bending from the correct place.

The many gadgets currently in use to promote artificial rounding often

While preparing for *piaffe*, it is important to ask the hind legs to step more underneath the horse's body to raise the forehand and lower the croup. Here Palomo begins to lift up through the wither with a soft underneck muscle and a very light acceptance of the bit, the proof of engagement.

(Photo: Madeleine McCurley)

create just such an incorrect effect, irrespective of the breed of horse, yet their prolific spawning on the market should not be blamed on the manufacturers alone. It is the riding public who are at fault for ignoring nature's rules and demanding these potential instruments of distortion, even of torture. What has made me feel angry on behalf of the horse is how so much ignorance can abound when, today, the availability of real learning and profound scientific knowledge is so much more accessible than ever before. There are the classic books, the videos from the most illustrious academies, the workshops, seminars and wise words from those whose methods have been proven over several decades of practical work in the field. One can almost imagine riders of the calibre of Podhajsky and Wynmalen turning in their graves if they saw how some dressage is ridden today, with the desire for instant gratification taking the place of years of scholarship and practical hard work.

For a glimpse of sanity, I turned to an old book, my copy being the fifth edition, published in 1905 and written by the famous Captain M. Horace

Hayes FRCVS 'late Captain of the Buffs' who is probably better known for his *Veterinary Notes for Horse Owners*. His lesser known book *Illustrated Horse-Breaking*, as its title suggests, deals with all aspects of starting the young horse correctly and methodically but in a way which complements his natural way of going. For general schooling purposes, Hayes emphasises the requirement to extend the neck as much as possible. Verticality of the horse's head must never be demanded before the horse can carry himself in full balance, and certainly not when he is still working on the forehand. As for shortening the horse's neck at a later stage or allowing overbending, this is totally counter-productive.

> The chief muscle which draws the fore limb to the front, is attached to the head in such a manner that it acts best during movement, when the head is carried more or less at right angles to the neck . . . Neither for control nor for movement, is it well for the head to be flexed to a greater extent than this. The more the chin is drawn in beyond this limit, the more will the pull of the reins be transferred (from the bars of the lower jaws) to the animal's head; the more oblique will become the direction of the pressure of the mouthpiece on the bars, and the more will the horse be obliged to lower his head, thereby unduly increasing the weight on the forehand.

If readers are not already convinced of the danger of shortening and lowering the neck to bring the horse's head behind the vertical and 'on to' the bit – so often seen in dressage today – the following paragraph from the same section of Hayes's book is important.

> Thus by bringing his chin into his chest, the horse first – more or less deprives his rider of control over him; second – disturbs the proper distribution of weight between his fore and hind legs; and third – hampers the movements of his forelimbs.

Looking at the execution of even the most advanced tests, and certainly going behind the scenes in the average competitive training yard in Britain and abroad, one is led to admit that the general thinking on outline and roundness is fundamentally flawed. No wonder that in recent years of teaching, I have found quite competent riders more bewildered about contact and the use of the hands as an aid than ever before. A subject which used to be treated as a matter of common sense, black and white, has become wrapped in mystique, with so many grey areas that people have become utterly confused. Without clear direction in this area, it is scarcely surprising that newcomers to the various disciplines are tempted by contraptions which promise all things to all men. If only the horse could speak!

CHAPTER 15
Feeling hands and thinking around the piaffe

W hen I was young, for all the faults which did exist in the system, the use of the hands was never a controversial subject. You either had good hands or you had bad. If they were good, it was generally deemed that you and your horse should be left alone to get on with things; if they were bad, you were yelled at until things improved.

Perhaps because I played the piano, one of the few things my riding teachers did not correct were my hands. To play an instrument you have to learn flexible finger control; this is only possible once you have learned to support the wrists and that takes time. Indeed, the wrist cannot be easily supported unless the elbows are bent and remain close to the body line while the shoulders support the whole. I seem to remember someone in the distant past telling my father when I was about twelve that I had good hands when I rode, and I slept very happy that night. 'Good hands' was the highest compliment and, from then on, I was determined to preserve this asset. I doubt that many children today would care whether they had good hands or not. It is something which is not much talked about these days, which is sad for the horse.

At that time, even in schooling sessions, the word 'contact' was rarely used. 'On the bit' was another expression that scarcely entered one's jargon; the horse was either a puller or he was light on your hands. Indeed, the idea of placing the horse *on* the bit was quite foreign. Books written at the time discussed the horse coming *to* the bit, or being *in* the hand, expressions which imply receiving rather than the more currently fashionable one of placing or putting down.

What was also discussed, even at basic levels, were the words to 'bridle' and to 'flex', actions which were understood to emanate mainly from a supple poll through very subtle actions of the fingers which could either ask or give. These flexions should never be obtained by bending the horse lower down the neck as is too often seen nowadays, and especially not from side to side which is damaging. Yet, poll flexions *per se* have become taboo

269

Direct flexion simply means the ability of the horse to bend his head downward from the poll. If we remain faithful to the classical ethos, the head should remain just in front of the vertical. (Photo: courtesy Kate Austin)

The old masters placed much importance on poll flexion. Here, lateral flexion is demonstrated without overbending or lovering the neck.

(Engraving, Pembroke)

in some circles today, which seems extraordinary since, as Colonel Patterson explains in his book *Sympathetic Training of Horse and Man*, 'the word merely denotes flexibility which is exactly what we want'.

This was the basic philosophy understood by all thinking cavalry officers of the time who not only rode on parade and required total obedience and manoeuvrability in close formation with others, but who were encouraged to improve their expertise and general knowledge of horses by playing polo, competing across country and, of course, hunting.

My own husband, Henry, who also spoke of flexions and had hands of silk, had hunted three days a week in the army when going through the Royal Military training course at Sandhurst. It was rather frowned upon if young officers did not fully participate in all the equestrian sports.

For this reason, it can scarcely be argued that to teach the horse to flex or to yield from the poll will hamper forward movement. The whole thrust of asking the horse to flex from a light, asking hand coupled with a light, asking leg was in order to make him more balanced and controllable in these outdoor pursuits. This action had nothing to do with prettifying the gaits, but was simply to stop him from falling on to his shoulders and overloading the forelegs.

As Patterson goes on:

Flexion is bridling – a term which has been used and understood by every class of English people connected with horse for hundreds of years . . . Flexion (or bridling) is the rendering of the head and neck light and flexible by teaching the horse to bend his neck *at the poll and to relax his lower jaw*. This lightness of the head and neck reacts on the shoulders and, through them, on the entire forehand. If our horse is not flexed, the rider feels as if he were dealing with a log of wood with all its deadness and heaviness . . . a flexed or bridled horse on the other hand resembles a fishing-rod in which flexibility becomes greater as you go forward.

In those days, the double bridle was the accepted norm for more refined riding once the horse had been correctly mouthed, broken and was working confidently forward in all three gaits in the snaffle. Once into two bits, when the horse was five or six years of age, the rider encouraged his horse to extend his neck forward and maintain stability by keeping a positive but quiet contact on the bridoon. Finger pressure, applied gently and only intermittently by squeezing the curb rein and in combination with the aids of seat and leg, then taught the horse to yield through both the poll and the jaw.

Such action exerted mild poll pressure from the lever effect of the weymouth, while the chain, acting on the groove of the horse's chin, created a similar involuntary response, causing the horse to move the jaw lightly and, in consequence, relax it. The effects of the two bits were taught and practised with feeling and understanding.

Today's double bridle is virtually the same as it was then, but not everyone is familiar with its action or, indeed, the action of the fingers in bringing about change. It should be recognised that the dropping of the horse's chin and subsequent softening down into the bit constitutes a direct flexion. Initially, some horses may actually open the jaw slightly as they do this but, provided the rider has feeling hands and rewards their horse by immediately easing the rein again, the horse should learn to close the mouth but in a more relaxed way, so the jaw is no longer clamped against the two bits. This therefore meets the FEI requirement that the horse should 'accept the bridle with a light and *soft* contact and submissiveness throughout'.

Obtaining a direct flexion in this way is obviously more difficult with a snaffle bridle, which exerts no poll pressure, than practising an indirect flexion to right or left, accomplished by normal bit pressure on the bars of the horse's mouth to the required side. Nevertheless, both methods of yielding or bending can be achieved with patience and understanding in a way that is pleasant for the horse in either bridle once the rider has learned to use their seat and legs more thoughtfully. For example, dropping the nose is immediately made easier by applying both legs lightly on the girth to help to free the horse's back as described in a previous chapter. Flexing the horse laterally will, again, be made easier by applying the appropriate leg at the girth, with the opposite leg a little back.

To eradicate the propensity of some riders to bend the horse (incorrectly) lower down the neck instead of concentrating on the poll area, I sometimes ask pupils to improve their understanding by first testing these techniques out on themselves. By placing a finger close to the atlas-axle joint at the base of their skull, which represents a similar articulation point as in the poll of the horse, I then ask them to drop their own chin. When they have done this, I ask for a turn of their head to look sideways or even back over their shoulder. Very soon it becomes apparent that everything is very much easier when the neck is steady and extended upward from behind (similar to the topline in the horse) with the jaw relaxed. As with the horse, the sideways turn is more far-reaching with the chin down. In nature, there is generally a logical echo all the way down the line in the different species.

One of the greatest proponents of outdoor riding from the French School, Jean Saint-Fort Paillard, who became an instructor at the Cadre Noir of Saumur, reminds us that the hand must never 'exert a greater traction on the reins than that exerted by the horse itself. Doing so would tend to justify the horse's reaction of pulling even more strongly against it. On the contrary, once the [yielding] process has been started by the first action of the hand, the rider should leave the entire initiative of the performance to the horse and merely adapt his own behaviour to that of the horse.'[1]

The problem for so many riders working their horse in the snaffle but expecting a far higher degree of control for dressage than would be expected in the old days without the double bridle, is obvious. Asking the horse to flex and soften to the bit through finger pressure alone, rather than the often crude movements so often seen, requires a higher all round standard of riding. In particular, it requires an understanding of how to use the upper body, as well as the seat and legs, to complement any rein aid. Lack of knowledge too often leads to frustration when the horse fails to bridle, leans hard against the hands, pokes his nose forward and appears not to answer to any of the aids.

An unbalanced horse, generally referred to as a horse that 'is not on the bit', can neither be flexible not manoeuvrable until he can be taught to yield directly and laterally, but in bringing this about no action of the hand alone can work. *It is the combined effect of all the aids working the horse into the*

---

[1] *Understanding Equitation* by Comm. Jean Saint-Fort Paillard, Pitman Publishing, London, 1975.

hand which renders the horse flexible. The hands themselves should remain quiet and do very little. As for turning, when a horse is pulled around by the neck, the result of a hand pulling outward and backward, he will merely throw his quarters out so the balance will be made worse.

To rectify these problems, many modern trainers resort to the use of flash or drop nosebands to achieve some form of yielding. This is a good schooling aid if the horse opens his mouth and yaws against the snaffle, but if fitted too tightly[2] such a noseband can be counter-productive as it restricts the horse in the jaw so that he is more likely to fight against it rather than soften down by dropping his chin. Generally, any means which involves discomfort or force, and takes away from the rider the ability to give and reward, has to be condemned out of hand. I have even known non-rearing horses learn to go up rather than submit to an overtightened flash or grakle, mainly because, whatever they do, they can never be rewarded – short of the rider jumping off their back and loosening the offending contraption.

This is not to say that the feeling in the rider's hand should never be one of firmness. Indeed, fixity or resistance momentarily applied, and in combination with legs and seat, is one of the great aids for teaching the more experienced horse to soften through the jaw and poll and to flex into the hand. The kindest hands in the world are not those which droop; on the contrary a good pair of hands know just when and to what degree they must set and create a frame for the horse to work into with fluidity and impulsion. Once the hands take their position at the base of the horse's neck, the horse quickly learns that to pull back against the hand is counter-productive because immediately the rider will put more leg on and he will come up, as it were, against himself. Instead, the horse learns that if he works forward and into the contact, at the same time yielding through the poll and jaw, he can enjoy the support of the hand without being punished by it.

Gradually, as he transfers more weight to his hind end, he finds the feeling in his mouth becomes lighter still; in response, the empathetic rider will also have lightened. These nuances between horse and rider form part of a living process which simply cannot be replaced by gadgets. Buckles and leather cannot be made to feel; with the human body nothing is dead or irrevocable. One moment the wrists, elbows and shoulders may act as though set in concrete, the following moment, as the horse yields, the whole framework can soften and ease so that the horse may flow through, confident of his just reward. This comprises the whole philosophy behind

[2] See also Chapter 16.

the statement: 'when the horse gives, the hands give' and Xenophon's method of training through discipline and reward. In this way, the obedient horse learns how to lighten and reward himself.

I was at the osteopath's the other day, receiving some treatment after tripping and ricking my back. We discussed how so many people, including myself, have tension around the shoulder area, which is often caused by working at typewriters or WPs when one has to hold the shoulders and arms in one position for long periods of time. My osteopath, also a physician, suggested it might be the same for riding. I explained that we all try our best to ride without tension. 'But surely', he said, 'you have to fix your shoulders? Any fine work with the hands absolutely demands that you fix the shoulders and to a lesser extent the elbow and wrist, otherwise you would have no real control over what the hands are doing. All precision work requires this basic control. You can't finger a keyboard or a fine machine tool if you allow the shoulders and arms to become loose and floppy.'

I was astounded. I had been working on this chapter all morning, concerned that people would not understand how fixing allows for finer rein pressure (provided, of course, the rider remains supple in the joints). Now, in the afternoon, a learned non-rider was confirming it all.

Correcting overforceful riders is one thing. At the other end of the scale, and among the kindest people in the world, there are just as many closed minds! I am continually having to re-educate pupils who believe the idea of fixing or resisting with the hands, elbows and shoulders is somehow cruel. Preoccupied with the idea that the hands must always follow the horse, one of the primary and most important functions of the hands is altogether disregarded by this school of thought. Bewitched by photographs of great masters riding with washing-line reins, they earnestly believe that, from day one, the only way to ride a horse is to throw away the contact. 'Fine,' I tell them. 'Show me your horse in self-carriage and then by all means throw away the reins. I must warn you, however, there are very few people and horses who are talented enough to work in that manner for long periods. Of the former, Nuno Oliveira was one in our lifetime – there have not been many of that calibre since.'

You cannot altogether blame people for thinking this way. A glimpse of the end product does not tell us of the preparation over many years which went into the work. Horse manuals are also profoundly confusing. Every other book will tell us how the hands must follow the movement of the horse at all times. This is wonderful advice for the first two to three weeks of riding a completely green horse, to give him confidence in the mouth or during the walk on a long rein (although even in the latter there should be some idea of asking at the same time). It is also good advice to follow during the process of jumping, to allow the horse to stretch his neck to the full if required in order to extend or bascule; it is also allowable at full gallop or on the racecourse when the hands are basically taking up a position of total non-interference while the horse carries himself on the forehand. When, however, this tired old phrase is trotted out again and again to the readers of sophisticated dressage books, it is quite inexcusable and totally misleading.

The hands should *not* move independently of the body once the horse is working forward from behind. When all is as it should be, the 'give' through the rein comes through a fine easing of the fingers and of the rider's shoulders and elbow joints when the hand is *in place*. To a less obvious extent, but equally important, 'give' also comes from the suppleness of the rider's lower back and the subsequent projection of their waist (see Chapter 8). Jiggling to and fro with the hands, as though they have a life of their own, is counter-productive in every way and people who set out to 'follow the movement' usually promote far too much movement and disturb the balance of the horse's neck as well as being a constant irritant to his mouth.

In the words of Blaque Belair of the Cadre Noir, the horse requires a 'steady equal feeling'[3] if he is to transmit impulsion from the quarters to the forehand. As for the hand which draws the neck from side to side as we see from the training methods of some showjumpers, a great deal of damage may be done. As Seunig writes in his definitive book *Horsemanship*[4]: 'the unsteady or sawing hand, which pulls the neck to the right and to the left from its base (the part that should be steadiest), this weakens the scalenus muscle, interfering with it to such an extent that it grows limp and is unable to do one of its jobs, holding the ribs and sternum up to the front'.

Sadly, riders have become so steeped in the idea of moving their hands to follow the horse that they are absolutely horrified at the suggestion of bringing the horse together and actually feeling the horse's mouth at the end of the rein. Riders must be educated to communicate more through their fingers in order to say, 'No, I don't want you on the forehand; this is the contact I wish you to take; please work into this frame,' or 'Thank you for coming together, now you may stretch down and forward again.' It is too easy to forget that communication is about interaction. As well as permanent passivity, which can be read by the horse as easy compliance, we are quite entitled to make polite requests.

---

[3] from *Cavalry Horsemanship*, Col. Blaque Belair.
[4] *Horsemanship* Waldemar Seunig.

Whatever the movement or gait, the hands remain in place. The moment of 'give' in every stride is transmitted through the fingers, elbow and shoulders. It is the support of the rider's seat which allows the hand to fix ahead of the movement. This pleasing combination of Michael Klimke riding Raikito at Gothenburg (1996) shows an attentive horse softly on the bit and correctly flexed through the poll.

(Photo: Bob Langrish)

In order to accomplish the latter, particulary through the transitions, the rider must learn to take up a fairly exacting contact where the horse can accept the hand without contracting the neck. At the same time, however, there must be sufficient asking or resisting through the fingers and seat to prevent the horse wanting to pass through the hand and drop on to the forehand. It is the ability to combine all these requirements which brings out the true artist in equitation. Riders need to be aware that the more one gives, the more the horse will take – and that a properly mouthed horse will, indeed, always try to follow the rider's hand. The old adage, 'You give the hand, and it's not enough, he'll take your arm!' could easily be applied to horsemanship.

It is up to the rider, therefore, to establish the parameters within which the horse is to work. Giving and giving and giving only results in taking and taking and taking and, in the way of rude, uneducated people, the unschooled horse may take to such an extent that he spoils things for

A soft lateral flexion is shown here in the canter pirouette ridden by M. Michel Henriquet
at his *manège* in Versailles. The inside leg is supporting the horse in his bend to the right.
The hands remain in place – whatever the movement.

(Photo: courtesy M. Henriquet)

himself. If he is not to spend the rest of his life miserably on the forehand,
it is for us to show intelligence and establish the guidelines. Although
initially difficult, this will eventually lead to the horse regaining his natural
carriage and grace so that his life can be prolonged in a healthy and useful
state. There is no benefit to either horse or rider in remaining forever on the
forehand. On the contrary, it generally guarantees early arthritis or
breakdown in the horse's forelimbs and is totally in opposition to nature's
way of organising his natural locomotion.

The point of fixing the hand, therefore, is not to block the movement of the horse but rather to guide and restore it into a proper balance. The object is not to bring the horse's head behind the vertical, rather to encourage it just forward of the vertical which encourages correct rounding by setting all the articulations of the spine into synchronisation. When these are working correctly, the horse will often produce foam or cream at the mouth, the result of the jaw being sufficiently flexed to stimulate the parotoid glands. I like to say that this is nature's sign that all is being lubricated from within and the horse is working like a well-oiled machine.

As feel or contact is such a hard thing to describe, I find the best way to help pupils to understand what is required is to suggest the drink tray concept. From a confirmed upper body posture (light or full seat should make no difference provided that it is stable and balanced) the rider should quietly fix the hands in the same way as one would if carrying a light, but precious object. Fixing implies making steady, making sure, retaining in place – there should be no hint of heaviness. If one thinks about this logically, particularly unrelated to riding, this could not be more different from pulling back, putting down or dropping the contact.

Imagine you are carrying a tray of champagne glasses; the hand fixes, the tray is secure, the drinks do not spill. There is sufficient movement through the elbow to prevent jarring, the back and hips are supple, while the hand remains steady. There is no pulling back against the tray otherwise the whole caboodle would be upset; instead, it is just a feeling of taking the tray forward as we ourselves progress forward with it. That is the picture riders should have in mind as they take up a proper contact; not how to make the horse stay on the bit, but how to carry the tray forward without spilling the champagne!

Whether we are working forward in extension or preparing for very collected work, towards *piaffe* and *passage*, the principle remains the same. Establishing a contact must be backed up by sending the horse into that contact in each and every stride. The feel is the same for rein-back.

In their attempts to put the horse on the bit, too many people struggle or draw back with the hands and succeed merely in shortening the horse through the wither and neck because they forget to ride the horse off the leg. Hand alone causes the horse to 'break' at the crest, deepening the forehand and coming behind the bit. Hands which have difficulty in remaining in place are nearly always caused by the rider rounding the shoulders, collapsing through the waist and failing to project from the centre.

Competition can cause enormous stress at the highest level. This hand has lost its position and is pulling back. Too much hand action may ground the hind legs, and here, for a moment, the horse shows his displeasure.

(Photo: Kit Houghton)

Nowhere are the above faults more noticeable than in a bad *piaffe*. There are many Grand Prix horses which have learned to perform *piaffe* with a light rear end instead of a light forehand. I blame this entirely on hands which pull back or sharply upward from a seat which has never learned to ease or to take the horse with it. Next time you watch a top-level test, look to see if the forelegs are raised higher than the hind legs. Too often they scarcely leave the ground and we see the horse shuffling in front with the forelegs overloaded and bending backwards, while the hind legs, with insufficient flexion, hop and bounce up and down like stiff pogosticks. The lightness is all in the wrong end, and it is little wonder that this is often accompanied by crookedness. Yet, despite this, the horse is too often awarded high marks because almost everyone is doing it and so it has become acceptable.

How can this state of affairs be allowed to happened when we read the following definition of the movement in the FEI rules?

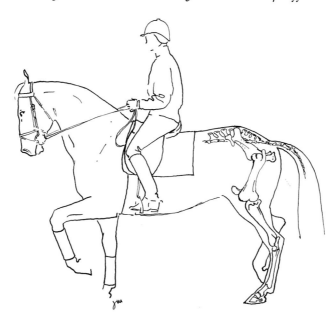

Invariably the *piaffe* is taught nowadays with a strong and often heavy seat, which may flatten the loins. No amount of spurring will therefore help the horse engage once he is strung out behind and riders must rethink their position if they are to help their horse.

The *piaffe* is a highly collected, cadenced, elevated diagonal movement giving the impression of being in place. The horse's back is supple and vibrating. The quarters are slightly lowered, the haunches with active hocks are well engaged, giving great freedom, lightness and mobility to the shoulder and forehand. Each diagonal pair of feet is raised and returned to the ground alternately with an even cadence and a slightly prolonged suspension. In principle, the height of the toe of the raised foreleg should be level with the middle of the cannon bone of the other foreleg. The toe of the raised hind leg should reach just above the fetlock joint of the other hind leg . . .

Yet, despite the ground rules so clearly laid, this movement, which comprises the culmination of roundness and contained energy, is so often performed *volte face*. Instead of the hindquarters lowering to take the weight back, we see the grounding of the forehand. As a result it is the hind legs which elevate to the height of the cannon bone, and not the forelegs as required by definition. This makes a mockery of the *piaffe*, demonstrating incorrect schooling and allowing false rounding from front to back. The horse is not off the leg, he is not united, he is merely a prisoner hopping from diagonal to diagonal between tugging reins.

I believe one of the reasons we see so many flawed *piaffes* is because the rider has not learned to concentrate their body weight over the horse's strongest point[5] in order to alleviate the longissimus dorsi and the quarters and to allow sufficient lowering of the croup to take place. If there is ever a time when the horse most needs his freedom under the saddle, it is now. Squashing or flattening the loins is disastrous for *piaffe*, but as the movement itself is a natural one and, indeed, one which many horses enjoy, the highly schooled dressage mount will often try his best to oblige the rider despite being hampered in this way. The result is all too often a mere parody of the movement, resulting in choppy staccato steps emanating from stiff hind legs.

I believe another reason for the abundance of poor *piaffes*, particularly in competition, is the lack of preparation undertaken nowadays in collecting and lightening the walk. I can honestly say that every horse which I have schooled to *piaffe* has initially volunteered the work himself after consistent suppling exercises in walk. *Piaffe* is, after all, just a natural progression in the consistent gathering of the horse so that he steps more energetically under himself, going from four-time to two-time. *Passage* is nothing more or less than a very elevated, very cadenced, suspended trot, again vibrating with contained energy.

I learned the importance of collecting the walk in Portugal, its habitual and uncontroversial practice no doubt stemming from the advice of the old masters such as Marialva and La Guérinière. Both of the latter had paid great attention to the collection of the walk before seeking to establish collection in the other gaits. Yet, the mere mention of collected walk has often horrified trainers at home who seem unable to understand its lightening and engaging qualities and I was therefore glad to read what Bettina Drummond had to say on this subject in a recent magazine interview[6] from her home in Potomac, Maryland.

Bettina, a lifelong protegée of Nuno's, explained: 'Oliveira's training techniques either left people mesmerized by their beauty or frustrated from being unable to comprehend them since he taught a great deal by true feel. Anyone used to "driving" the horse forward found it hard to understand Oliveira as he spent countless hours perfecting the walk, using slow lateral work to supple the horse, to redistribute its weight in order to enable it to move in true balance and collection.'

The Portuguese have always looked to the French School for inspiration in their High School work. Oliveira's two favourite writers were Baucher and Beudant. Not surprisingly, therefore, we find that the old French masters also placed great importance on the refinement and lightness of the walk. Baucher called the walk the 'mother of the gaits' and his second,

---

[5] See Chapter 7 and, more specifically for the *piaffe*, Chapter 9.
[6] Interview in *Horses Monthly*, June 1996 entitled 'Does Classical Training have a Place Today' by Jodi Ann Axtell.

Riding the *piaffe* with a lighter, more forward seat will invariably help both the younger and the older horse to lower through the croup and to bend through the joints sufficiently to give spring and ease to the movement. Although care must be taken not to place the horse on the forehand as shown here.

gentler method of obtaining flexion is still much admired on the continent today.

In his book *Piaffer and Passage*, General Decarpentry insists on absolute submission of the jaw in the gathering of the horse, which cannot take place without '*the poll always being the highest point of the head and neck*' (sic). The preparatory half-halt is given with a firm upward movement on 'tightened reins, with fingers well closed, quickly followed by a progressive opening of the fingers and *giving* with the hand'. Virtually all the pictures show the *descent de main* in the *piaffe* and *passage*.

I have felt much vindicated by these wise words, having been taken to task by certain fellow writers over the wisdom of teaching the 'giving' with the fingers in the more collected airs as well as the redistribution of the weight of the seat forward towards the pommel and off the back of the saddle. Likewise, in both his books Decarpentry calls for more weight into the stirrups and less in the seat even at the expense of bringing the shoulders a little more forward to sit more into the crotch and thigh and to retain the natural hollow of the back so that 'the loins are arched'.

In *Piaffer and Passage*, a series of photographs is shown to demonstrate, step by step, how the rider's posture affects the performance of the horse. Decarpentry criticises: 'The torso of the rider [who] is too far back, which adds weight to the hindleg off the ground' or 'the rider [who] is stiff, his torso tips back'. The best photograph, where the horse's croup is more rounded and the haunches lowered, shows a much more vertical position of the rider's hips with deepened knees and thighs and the crotch in contact.

There are further helpful pictures of *piaffe* in *Academic Equitation*. In examining the riding posture of the then Chief Instructor to Saumur, General Wattel, it is interesting to note that his exemplary position differs not one iota from that of Oberbereiter Brigadiers Gebhart and Lindenbauer of the Spanish Riding School in Vienna and of those famous Germans Professor Lörke and Colonel Gherhardt. All ride upright, all demonstrate a three-point seat, in each case the horse is high in the poll, the neck stretches freely forward, the reins show no tension, the profile is round and the hocks are well engaged, so important for the transitions.

Brigadier General Kurt Albrecht also insists on a three-point contact if the rider is to sit deep and to collect their horse. In *Principles of Dressage* he explains how the empathetic rider must be sufficiently disciplined to 'be able to produce the required seat effects by minute changes of inclination in his pelvis'. He explains how 'disengaging the *kreuz*'[7] is achieved by increasing the pelvic inclination and pulling up the ribs, putting more weight on the fork than the seatbones. However, 'these shifts of weight must be slight and the "three point contact" must always be preserved'.

How sad that today's dressage riders are not always taught to emulate those classical masters! Visual teaching by using photographs or projected slides with clear explanations is very effective as I know from recent lecture tours I have given in New Zealand, Australia and in several parts of the USA. Participants generally say the same – their trainers pay insufficient attention to the detail of the actual body posture for the riding of movements. They are told all about what the horse should be doing, but insufficient advice is given concerning the nuances and adjustments of weight required by the rider to allow or encourage the correct biomechanical response. It is surely no coincidence that with a lapse worldwide in a disciplined, uniform posture, movements such as the *piaffe* and *passage* have declined in quality. Yet, as Decarpentry proves time and again, only when the rider is correct will these high-precision movements be correct. Only with classical riding will we see the classical movements harmoniously performed.

---

[7] See also Chapter 9 re the section on Müseler.

Hands that block, bodies which block in the wrong places, and blocked minds concerning lightness certainly do not facilitate the motivation of the horse towards the higher airs. Motivation! I use this word intentionally, for a well-schooled horse who is gathered in hand will discover the delight of these movements for himself and, in the words of Xenophon, 'assume all the graces which he puts on of himself when showing off voluntarily'.

A last word on the *piaffe* demands that the rider understands the absolute gathering or *ramener* of the horse. This cannot be accomplished if the hand aids are crude or the horse too much 'on' the bit. Instead, the horse must be light *in* the hand through increased engagement and power behind.

At home, I have an autographed and well-thumbed, privately published book[8] by Jean-Claude Racinet, former officer of the Cadre Noir, who now teaches in the United States. One particular paragraph stood out when I was browsing through the section on collection and lightness recently. Although not specifically about *piaffe*, these thoughts could well be applied to the riding of *piaffe* or, rather, explain why so many *piaffes* are flawed. 'One must bear in mind that gracefully arching a horse's neck has never set him on the haunches, whereas a horse set on the haunches regardless of the prior position of his head is much more likely to come gently onto his bit, provided that the rider gives subsequently the hand and leaves the horse in "liberty on parole" . . . Complementary actions of the fingers may then be waged in order to perfect the *ramener* so obtained.'

Racinet is a great admirer of Oliveira but he is first and foremost a Frenchman and tells an amusing but true story of how a group of French riders spotted Nuno riding at an exhibition while holidaying around Portugal in the 1950s. In those days, Oliveira was scarcely known outside his own country. Amazed by his brilliance and at the lightness of his High School work, particularly the *piaffe* and *passage*, the Frenchmen asked, 'What kind of horsemanship is this marvellous one that you practise?'

Equally stunned, Oliveira replied, 'But . . . yours, of course; the traditional French horsemanship.'

In his book a rather sad aside is made by the author: 'For it is another tragedy of our time that even the French have forsaken their own heritage.'

Of course, it is futile to give with the rein unless the horse has first been united or brought together through the influences of the seat and leg into the rein. How many teachers remind their pupils that 'hands together bring the horse together'? Too few, yet the rein lightly against the neck is an

---

[8] *Another Horsemanship* by Jean-Claude Racinet, 1991. For further information write to the author at 1091 Mountain Spring Road, Anderson, SC 29621, USA.

important aid in itself and I well remember the feeling of elation when I heard these words reiterated on the lips of Dr Reiner Klimke as he addressed an audience of over 2,000 people at the 1994 ABRS Conference in Essex. In one breath, he confirmed something I have believed with all my heart for several years and which I have tried to teach my pupils. 'Only with hands together can you truly unite the horse'. A year later, I heard similar words from Charles de Kunffy at a TTT clinic. 'Hands together form the eye of a needle. Thread the energy of the horse through it!

Quite apart from the fact that centring the hands centres our entire body and thus helps to keep us square, we should also never forget the unifying effect of the reins against either side of the horse's neck. For this reason, I have always thought the word 'collect' in relation to the hands is a very good term and says it all. Riders should think of collecting the horse's energy with body and hands as it is offered up to them from behind. This is the feeling of the true *piaffe*, *passage* or collected gait. Separating the hands may allow all that lovely power to drift away.

The significance of keeping the hands together and united was something which my old stallion Palomo taught me long ago when he first arrived in England after a history of bullfighting which requires enormous impulsion yet absolute precision from collection. With him I learned that any dropping of the rein, other than the softness he created himself through deeper engagement, was not appreciated. Also, he could not tolerate even the tiniest jerk of the wrist and, however careful I was, it was hard not to make the odd error with the hands in what might be described as a 'normal' dressage position.

I soon learned that the only way I could correct my human failings to gain the respect and happiness of my horse was to ride with my hands in the usual supported wrists position but, instead of keeping each fist apart by the width of a bit, I had far more control by allowing the knuckles just to touch each other. In other words an involuntary movement by one hand would be dissipated against the contact with the other hand rather than felt by the horse in the mouth.

There is nothing new about bringing the hands together in this way, particularly on the more advanced horse. Nevertheless, even the younger horse may appreciate such a 'steadying' of the hand once he is working forward and acceptant of the bit. Indeed, it often gives him a greater feeling of security and it is very much easier for the rider to relax the elbows and the shoulders, while keeping them in place, when the hands lightly touch in this way. Such fine-tuning may work wonders with any horse which is sensitive in the mouth, provided it is not inclined to an overhigh head carriage.

Today's fashion to take up a position where you can 'drive a bus between the reins' has largely come about because it does have its uses for certain work. Riding with open hands opens the door for the horse to travel forward and through with a low head carriage which can be very useful with the young horse. It is also useful to correct a horse whose head carriage is too high, or for the more experienced horse to take the rein down, chew the bit and stretch as a reward after the more collected work. (See Chapter 16.)

Nevertheless, if we wish to correct a rider's position, this is much easier when the hands remain together. A horse, too, is brought to a better posture with the hands together and *in place*. This helps to settle the horse in place, the natural progression for the work towards *piaffe*. Countless masters have written of the vibrato of the fingers, like the 'violinist on the strings of his instrument' which 'must be skilfully graded without appreciably moving the hand or the wrist' (Beudant). Softly bent around the rein, the fingers speak to the horse through nuances of pressure. These actions do not disturb the position of the hand whatsoever, but exert sufficient feel to be noticed by the horse.

Closing firmly when the horse is to make a downward transition, the fingers should soften immediately after the transition is completed to say 'Thank you for obeying me'. They give and take a little in swift alternating actions when the horse feels heavy, dull or inattentive to say, 'Hey! I'm talking to you! Please attend!' They open fractionally more to encourage the flow of a more extended gait, saying. 'That's right, Go on! Stretch! That's right . . . Take a little more!' As the horse improves, it is sometimes more effective to give this aid unilaterally to free the shoulder of each particular side. With the hands acting one at a time the fingers may check, momentarily close – outside hand only – to steady the horse on a corner; to warn of a transition; to collect the canter; or to support the shoulder-in. An inside unilateral aid is the one which can give a little to the inside to encourage softening and flexion on a turn or circle or to free the inside shoulder in the canter.

Riders should be made aware that to take with the inside rein generally causes the very opposite of what they desire. It takes real control and willpower to make those fingers yield, soften, release, let go, yet by doing so we will achieve superior flexion to the inside. We will free and allow the inside hind leg to come through on a circle or in the shoulder-in, achieve better bending in half-pass and so on. Whether working bilaterally or unilaterally, it is the judicious use of the fingers of the hands which makes the rider and, ultimately, makes the horse.

It should go without saying that the hands must never, ever move

A fair *piaffe* performed on Palomo at the age of 23. Palamo's heels are in the perfect
position; ruefully the author admits hers are not.
(Photo: courtesy Richard Weller-Poley)

backwards. If the hand is fixed with soft fingers but a firm wrist at the
optimum place at the base of the horse's neck it is just a question of always
riding towards and into that hand at all times, whether increasing or
decreasing the gait. As Racinet writes: The 'fixed hand' is 'realised by a
pressure of the fist on the rein, without any help from any arm traction . . .
Since there is no recoil at all, yielding, for the horse, becomes "self-
rewarding" and will therefore become easier and easier.'

Fixing the hand in this way should not prevent us from stroking the horse's neck from time to time, moving one or both hands forward to check the evenness of the horse or the fact that he still seeks the bit and to ensure that he is not leaning on a particular rein. It can also serve to free up the gait. Only from a supported upper body position, with the hands placed in a predetermined position, will the fingers be able to give or take sufficiently to allow for nuances of change in gait or within the gait.

Even when the horse pulls, it would be counter-productive to move the hands back as this would merely result in a pulling match. Pulling may be resisted by resting the hands a little more firmly against the same spot on the horse's neck and bearing down slightly with the fist, while at the same time riding forward vigorously with legs, back and seat into that immovable contact. This action has exactly the same effect on the horse as when lungeing a horse in side reins and sending him on with the schooling whip.

We must therefore realise that our hands represent similar parameters as the side reins to the lunge horse. If we ride him forward into that predetermined frame, he will realise that it is useless to pull against himself. However, any deviation on our part away from those guidelines, either by pulling or by becoming floppy-wristed, may spoil the picture. The horse is quick to spot an inconsistency and the fidgeting, shifting hand will produce an unsettled, fidgety horse whose shifting balance will make him most uncomfortable for the rider.

Pupils often ask me how to ensure that they are not taking too strong a contact when asking the horse to work into a frame. The horse himself should give us the answer to this sensible question. Provided that the horse is able to retain the poll as the highest point, the result of extending and arching the neck naturally forwards to connect from the hind legs to the bit, it will be obvious that no overrestriction has taken place. On the other hand, the rider should not be fooled by a horse which is not sufficiently responsive to the leg to bring the forehand up. Too many lazy horses drop on to the shoulders or behind the bit simply because they have not been educated to move forward, up and 'off the leg'. The rider must be discerning enough to see the difference.

Once riding from back to front is understood and put into practice at all times, it should not be too long before the happy day dawns when the horse no longer leans, pulls, resists or makes himself heavy in front. Finally, the rider discovers that pleasant sensation when the hands merely receive the horse. When he can be rewarded with a lighter rein without losing rhythm, the rider is well on the way to discovering the *descente de main* to acknowledge and to thank the horse for his efforts and particularly for placing his impulsion at the rider's disposal.

Giving in this way must never be confused with dropping the contact. When students move their hand to and fro, forward and back, the first thing I ask them, somewhat sharply (and intentionally so), is why they are throwing my horse's energy away. If this does not work, I become a little sterner. 'What he is offering is a precious gift! Why are you throwing the rein back at him like that? He has offered you himself; now you reject him. Please ride my horse with better manners. Sit still, keep your hands still and receive him!'

This lesson in manners may sound a little harsh but it has far better results than chiding people that their hands are bad, they are moving too much, their wrist is limp and soggy, they are banging the horse in the mouth every time they drop the contact and then take it again. It is a different way of looking at things, but it is a logical way and it works.

For people who really cannot keep their hands together, I place soft elastic bands around both of their wrists. This allows the fists to part to roughly the width of a bit, an acceptable level, but the bands will snap if a sudden jerk is made so there is no risk to safety. Generally, however, it is the sensation of the rubber against their skin which encourages riders to remain focused on quieter hands and to keep them more central. Gradually, they find they no longer feel the need to separate the hands to such an extent. They think twice about pulling back on the rein or, where once their opening aids were too extreme, they become more refined. By centring the hands, they learn to develop and centre their body aids and this leads to increased confidence.

I have found that everything in riding has its parallel in other disciplines; playing good tennis is utterly dependent on a firm wrist and forearm and the most featherlight but accurate strokes come from the ability to maintain a strictly uniform line from the elbow through the wrist to the hand. Hence the expression 'the iron hand in the velvet glove'; only from a steady forearm and steady hand will we find soft, treacly fingers which can act on the rein with the finest of aids which are so small, so hidden, that no one is aware of them except the horse.

CHAPTER 16

Loosening, stretching and lengthening of the horse – the ins and outs of deep work

Freedom! Stretch! On parole! As it is such a lovely feeling to allow the horse his head and to let him carry himself freely, it constantly puzzles me that we do not see the walk on the long rein performed more often and to more advantage.

From the competitive viewpoint, this is even more surprising as a whole section of marks in a dressage test is devoted to the free walk, generally asked for across the diagonal of the school. A faultless performance here should be an easy way of picking up maximum marks. As dressage judging is so subjective, this single exercise is also more likely to be fairly marked (whatever the type, shape or size of horse) than any other movement where factors such as presence and grandeur may prejudice the result. Indeed, the very nature of the free walk lends itself to objectivity provided, of course, it is executed correctly. And perhaps here lies the rub; for unless we have trained the horse to work from back to front, the free walk will be poor and stunted.

Indeed, time and again we observe horses losing marks in the walk section through inattentiveness, crookedness, inactivity, lack of stretch, falling on to the forehand or the fact that they simply do not seek, chew and take the rein forward and down. One may only conclude, therefore, that this work is not regularly introduced into their schooling at home, and this begs the question – why not? The stretch on the long rein has always been one of the absolute cornerstones of good schooling and is vital in the preparation of putting the horse to the aids.

Unfortunately, there exists some confusion between whether the free walk is simply a reward or an exercise in its own right. Although it acts as a welcome relief to many horses needing to stretch their heads and necks after working into the hand, it should never be underestimated for the good it exerts on the entire dorsal musculature. For this reason, it should continue to be asked for at frequent intervals during any work-out, even when the horse has mastered superior extension as well as collection.

291

Free, forward and extended! This young colt moves extravagantly in trot due to the complete lack of restriction through his head, neck and body. This is what we have to try to emulate when we begin work with the young horse.

(Photo courtesy Jim Goff, USA)

If this exercise is not included, those muscles which are destined to extend the most in self-carriage may become tight and jammed, leading eventually to muscle spasm. This is particularly prevalent in horses working at high degrees of collection, including *piaffe* and pirouette when they tend to 'hold' themselves just behind the saddle rather than lowering. Indeed, the greater the *ramener* required in the various movements, the more important it becomes for the horse to stretch forward in the free walk in between times.

Longitudinal suppling and stretching do not only involve the topline of the horse. There is far more to consider below, and the thorax and belly of the horse play an important role in sustaining and supporting the stretching and collecting ability of the back. Back and neck muscles do not build by magic. Only through exercises which involve the opening and closing of the entire 'ring of muscles' which frame the horse, will the horse grow in muscular power. Muscles develop from functioning both ways – shortening and lengthening. This involves lateral bending and stretching in circle work and turns (part of a circle) as well as in all the lateral movements. In all these exercises therefore, the horse shortens and bends to

292

the inside of his body and lengthens and extends to the outside.

As with the human, every equine muscle is designed to contract or shorten in order to exert a form of leverage on a bone or part of a bone or a joint. Muscles work in pairs, so for any muscle to carry out a particular action, there has to be a second muscle that is able to achieve the opposite effect. In this way, the two types complement each other by alternating their roles. Just as a muscle cannot pull if it is permanently relaxed, neither can a muscle let go if under permanent tension. The result of two muscles incorrectly pulling against each other at the same time would be a locked joint. Unfortunately, fear and tension can cause horses to become so tight in their muscles that they virtually seize up in their movement and this is something we have to guard against through better understanding. Nevertheless, total relaxation would result in no activation whatsoever.

When in doubt, it is very helpful to return to the human analogy. To extend the lower arm, for example, and to hold it out horizontally in front of us, the biceps at the front of the upper arm must let go and stretch while the triceps at the back will exert pull and tension by shortening. With the arm extended in this way, the only way to lift it up again will be for the biceps to shorten, causing the elbow to bend and raise the lower arm while the triceps at the back will passively let go and lengthen. To extend the whole arm out again, however, the triceps must once again exert their pull by shortening again. This is not so different from the concept of extension and rounding or lifting in the horse. The more these opposing sets of muscles are employed in their dual functions, the more elastic and pliant they become. This enables them to sustain movement over longer and longer periods without tiring.

With both the human back and the equine back, many vertebrae are involved. The equine back is a far more rigid structure than our own and all the driving of the rider's seat in the world cannot cause it to move beyond its very limited scope. Neither can the equine spine be manipulated; what is important is the building and suppling of the muscles which clothe the spinal processes and ligaments over the quarters, loins, back and neck for, without this bridging effect, the horse cannot remain connected through the back and respond correctly to the rider's forward aids of seat and legs.

As we encourage the horse's topline to sustain more controlled movement by raising, stretching and rounding, no back can cope with these demands if it is not correctly exercised through constant changes of mode, gait, direction and emphasis. Sadly, riders seem unaware of this as they work their horse in the same mode for too long without respite or change. This leads to many horses working in defensive mode where they contract themselves against the rider instead of becoming permeable and fluid in movement. Incorrect tension of this type shows up as a very different state from soft cresting roundness through correct and fluid lengthening and shortening. It is easiest of all to spot in the neck area which demonstrates as a short tight neck not in proportion to the rest of the horse's body and much too prevalent in dressage horses even at the highest training levels.

For the horse to move in what seems to be a loose and relaxed way, we should recognise that both sets of muscles have to be well toned and able to shorten and lengthen at will and at a moment's notice without getting stuck. This gives the feeling of fluidity (*durchlässigkeit*) leading to *schwung* so sought after by the dressage trainer. It is the concentration and employment of all his impulsive forces which leads to the highly schooled horse working in what is often termed a 'relaxed' way of going.

Yet superior collection and impressive extension require anything but a total relaxation of the actual muscles involved. With all the muscle groups working, stretching, bending, flexing, opening, letting go, coming together, it is their perfect synchronisation and their ability to change from one mode to another which give the look of looseness or permeability.

To achieve this ease, in very simple terms it is imperative that a horse is allowed to open and stretch his entire frame if he is also to understand about being 'brought together'. The Portuguese describe this latter mode as 'closing' the horse, i.e. lowering the croup by bringing the hind legs more underneath to close the angles of the joints of the hind legs. As for extension, this can only be accomplished correctly once the horse understands and has experienced the feeling of being united or connected.

This employment of all the muscle functions is best achieved through transitional work, not just from gait to gait, but within the gaits and from time to time using the halt as well as one or two steps of rein-back. If these two latter movements are not performed on soft reins, however, with the horse's head and neck reaching decontracted and forward into the bridle, the horse may again tighten and hold himself against the rider. To be of benefit, therefore, the execution of these movements must be meticulously correct.

This brings us to another factor. There is a very great difference between the sudden release of kinetic power, those lengthened strides required in extension, and the contained feeling of potential power realised in collection. This is where the correct execution of the free walk on the long rein can help the horse to understand what will be required of him in the medium or extended trot, for example. The reason that so many horses fall on to the forehand in a rush for freedom during the lengthened strides is because they have never been taught to retain power while following the rider's hand forward and down on the long rein in walk, which requires maintaining an active push from behind.

True lengthening is never about falling apart. It has to come from exuberance behind and a desire to move and to push forward from strong hocks and quarters. Needless to say, extension should not be asked for too early in the education of a novice horse. There should be at least a degree of self-carriage through collection, and the free walk on a long rein must necessarily have been perfected first.

As well as physical fine-tuning, lengthening also requires a definite degree of mental understanding. An association of ideas born of sensation brings us back to Xenophon's ancient rules for the training of the horse. Again, the free walk will have helped to confirm this.

Young or stiff horses, like people, must be introduced to exercise thoughtfully and slowly. Thus baby horses, like young children, should not be overcorrected in their first strugglings to carry us; rather they should be encouraged in every step they take and frequently rested and rewarded. As the horse becomes physically stronger, more is asked, but common sense should warn the rider if things are not as they should be and that perhaps they have asked for something before the horse is ready to give it. Contrary to popular opinion, most resistances are not caused by bloodymindedness.

The young horse's introduction to stretching forward should first be encouraged on the lunge in walk. The side reins must never restrict the horse's natural head carriage, but he must be encouraged to step up to the hand from day one, with skilful use of the lunge whip aiding behind.

295

Weak-backed. the young horse drops his wither when first mounted, so the rider must soften the back and urge the hind legs on with her own legs to help him to push from behind as he did on the lunge. The rein must be positive but allowing so the horse can balance himself with an unconstricted head and neck and seek the bit.

Trot will only be asked for when the horse begins to push from behind. Here there is a little tension but as the horse continues to seek the hand through the top line, the back begins naturally to rise.

A year later, the horse has developed through the topline but must continue to be allowed to stretch his neck in all gaits in response to increased engagement behind. A light seat is maintained to encourage fluidity.

Finally, the horse lightens through the forehand; a result of his increased athleticism under and behind the saddle and the rider sits full-seated. (Photos: T. Burlace)

While there are, of course, lazy horses, one sharp tap on the rump with a schooling whip should ensure respect for the leg for the rest of the lesson. If not, the rider may be applying the aids incorrectly. When it comes to working the mature dressage horse, as every successful athlete or sportsperson knows, sustained performance in any athletic demand requires a proper warm-up which includes stretching down, and this does not mean charging round the arena in a spanking sitting trot to 'work' the back. Muscles and joints need a softly-softly approach if they are to free up, so the work should be careful and gradual.

For me, personally, and for many others, particularly those brought up in the Portuguese tradition, all the suppling, bending and lateral exercises are first done in walk. Even with the most hotheaded horse, this has a calming effect. Moreover, it gives the horse time to think as well as the rider and is very beneficial to the mental equilibrium of an explosive, tense or unwilling animal. Once the work proper is embarked upon, no set of muscles should be expected to maintain the same degree of flexion or extension in the same mode without a break at regular intervals. Following on from this principle, it can be assumed that the most athletic horse in the world also needs his moments of passivity, as well as his active working exercises.

As well as developing the free walk on the long rein to develop straightness, stretch, freedom of the shoulder and pushing from behind, most dressage trainers nowadays advocate either the 'long low' approach to working the trot, or the 'deep and round' programme. The proficient then go on to work the canter in the same way but this requires more balance and confidence on the horse's part. Whichever words are used to describe this method, the end result should be the same. This is that the horse stretches through the back and neck, that he carries his hind legs well underneath him to increase the bascule, that the head stretches down to follow the rider's hand on a steady but allowing contact and that the horse's nose is never pulled in to shorten the neck.

Unfortunately, not everyone understands how to set up the deep work. There are the many who allow the horse to fall apart and on to the forehand, thus disconnecting the back so the exercise not only becomes a major waste of time but is actually damaging. Then there are the relative few who have sufficient feel and knowledge to know how and when the horse is able to push effectively from behind so that his footfalls come deep enough under the body mass to lift and round the back to facilitate the stretching. When correctly done in this latter way, the method can be very beneficial for certain horses, encouraging much more pliability and freedom through the various muscle structures and a greater degree of self-carriage in general.

Nevertheless, as with all things, 'the razor in the hands of a monkey' syndrome continues to worry people. Should one attempt something about which one is unclear? Does one have to be an expert? In the same way that collection can do irrevocable harm if incorrectly executed with the hand pulling the horse back and telescoping him down into himself, the increasingly popular long and low method can also be detrimental.

What should the average rider do? The first thing is to understand just what is being asked of the horse and to ask the question: 'Is my horse ready for it?' Let us deal with the second question first.

My maxim has always been that whether introducing the horse to the collected exercises or whether introducing the horse to the round and deep work (as I personally prefer to call it) the criteria have to remain the same. They are:

- Do not ask until all three gaits are well understood by the horse and established on both reins.
- Do not ask until the horse is able to move actively and obediently forward from the leg into a quiet and steady contact of the hand.

A horse with a very tense mouth and high neck carriage
(supported from the underside of the neck rather than the topline)
will benefit from deep work.

299

Initially, we try to give with the inside rein to prevent the horse from leaning on it. This demands that he take responsibility for his own weight by engaging behind on a turn or circle.

Commencing the deep work requires a light, inviting rein to encourage the horse to fill the vacuum. The leg on the girth maintains forward impulsion and helps to encourage the back to rise, although the neck remains too short.

With the hands lower and more apart, the horse begins to uncoil the neck and reach down to seek the bit.

Now the corner can be ridden with good engagement and support behind, and with the horse lighter on the rein and in a better posture.

(Photos: courtesy T. Burlace)

301

- Do not ask until the horse is able to carry himself forward while evenly bending in the circle without leaning in.
- Do not ask if the horse's back is hollowed; wait until the horse is strong enough in the back not to want to drop it when asked to lengthen through the frame.
- Do not ask if the horse has an unnaturally low head carriage and is still on the forehand.

Many instructors will tell you that working deep and round will improve the forward thrust of the hind legs so one can start right away. Yes, forward thrust is improved, but only when the back is already coming up and the horse shows no inclination to lean on the hand. The main benefit to the already connected horse is that working deep creates greater elasticity and a greater desire in the horse to work forward, stretch and bascule the whole spine. It unblocks areas of muscle tension, it releases joints which, in the more collected work, tend to become a little tight. It removes the tendency of some horses to want to bore on the rein in the medium or extended gaits, and it teaches the horse a greater degree of self-reliance.

In short, it is a superb exercise when knowledgeably and sensitively done and, most importantly, when all the work is directed from behind. Long and low, deep and round should never, ever involve pulling the horse's head and neck down with the rein or fixing it into position, particularly far behind the vertical, so gadgets are out.

Sadly, however, as with all things, people see good work, do not understand, copy it and abuse the whole system. This has led to tremendous controversy and, for a time, in Germany, where the idea originated, the arguments for and against the deep method were orchestrated and whipped up almost to fever pitch in the various equestrian magazines. Not surprisingly these were selling record numbers of issues to a horsy public intrigued to see who was for and who against.

In the end, this academic argument focused on two successful international riders who were known to employ it. These were Nicole Uphoff-Becker and Isabel Werth, both highly acclaimed in their own right, not just as world champion riders but largely as trainers of their own horses, although they both had their mentors. The main thrust of the argument ran between 1992 and 1994. Many great horsemen and women and trainers became involved and their opinions were sought by a number of journalists.

Two of those to come out strongly against the method were George Wahl[1]

---

[1] *Dressage and CT* magazine, January 1994.

and Reiner Klimke. In an interview with Christian Theiss, Mr Wahl, a former *bereiter* of the Spanish Riding School and trainer to Christine Stuckelburger, had this to say about the method. 'In my opinion this has nothing to do with the classical art of riding. . . . I don't believe that this has a future, it is perhaps a fashion that will disappear in the course of time. It will disappear when the judges again look out more for throughness, for collection with the nose forward, rather than looking for collection of pulled together horses with their noses backwards. This is the mistake. The judges evaluate things like this much too well when virtually they are not classical.'

During a 1994 visit to England, Reiner Klimke stated, 'People are always trying to discover new things but in riding there are no shortcuts. Judges have forgotten to look at the whole horse, they look at steps – tic-tac . . . forgetting more important things like the back and the neck. Today we should be trying to get judges to look at the whole horse; they should punish overbending and the head behind the vertical in all their marking.' Dr Klimke strongly felt that the long, low method led to further overbending and therefore had no value.

Yet, while some well-known competitors were, and still are, riding deep work with their horse harshly pulled in well behind the vertical, others are not. Unfortunately, however, it always seems to be the bad which gets copied, the mediocre which finds its populist level. In Britain, it is disheartening to see many people who should know better shortening the horse's neck through overuse of the hands, which is the very opposite of what the exercise is supposed to be about. Correctly done, deep work should stretch and lengthen the neck, liberate the shoulder, free the back and encourage the horse to push more from behind to fill the vacuum that a more rounded frame should have provided. That is the ideal.

Unfortunately, it takes a very talented rider to be able to feel for all these facets functioning correctly and it has to be faced that, ignorantly performed, this method can have very detrimental effects.

How, therefore, can the inexperienced be assured of success when two of the world's greatest trainers riders disapprove? Firstly, they would be foolish to try without a pair of eyes on the ground. Basically, Georg Wahl and Reiner Klimke are both correct. In many of the photographs one does see horses being ridden in the warm-up arena with the horse's head pulled well behind the vertical and the neck in an overbent position on taut reins. Yet this is not at all what either Nicole or Isabel subscribes to in theory. Isabel was candidly honest when she explained that she would never purposely fix the horse in such a position. 'You can't always be perfect,' she said, when interviewed. 'If I have done that, I was not aware of it at the moment. I must say honestly, it was not intended. That is not the objective of the matter, to fidget about with one's hands, that was a mistake on my part, not an issue of training. Using one's hands in excess is a mistake that must be fought every day.'

Nearly all the top trainers of the world who use the deep method agree that the horse's head should never be forced in this way. As Klaus Balkenhol remarked: 'What Nicole is doing is, in my opinion, absolutely legitimate . . . she is always watching that the acceptance of the bit and the going through the back are maintained correctly. It is definitely much better to work the horse this way rather than not allowing them any personality at all, like riding them with running [draw] reins . . . The bad thing is that many want to imitate it, but are doing it wrong.'

This, therefore, has to be the preoccupation of any rider who decides to work with a friend or trainer and ride their horse deep. Are they allowing the horse to follow the hand down because of his increased engagement behind, or have they dragged it down with the hand? Between them, do trainer and rider have sufficient knowledge to know when the horse's back remains up, arching forward and over through a supported frame without breaking through the neck? Can they feel or see if and when the horse drops behind the bit, loses support and falls on to the forehand? All these questions need to be addressed, and anyone who is unsure of the answers would be better not to attempt the work.

If, however, satisfactory answers can be given, then the rider should proceed quietly, never asking too much as this work, as in all matters equestrian, should be progressive. Even lowering the head and neck by two inches is a step forward. The horse needs to be very strong behind to lower the whole structure of head and neck to a point below the chest in the early stages while still keeping up the momentum from behind. Any lowering in front should be matched by lowering behind the saddle, i.e. the quarters pushing under and through, the hocks bending and reaching deeply forward, which, of course, raises the back.

Erik F. Herbermann who, in his book *The Dressage Formula* explains so well the importance of work on the loose rein in walk as a means of 're-naturalising' the horse within work periods, wrote a very good article on deep work for the American magazine *Dressage and CT*, entitled 'Forward and Downward Riding'[2]. Here the benefits of the method are thoroughly explained. 'The exercise epitomizes one of the most important fundamentals of riding; that the horse learns to stretch its whole spine forward in order to reach for and find the bit correctly *in response to the*

[2] *Dressage and CT*, April 1994.

forward driving aids. In conjunction with this, it is an excellent avenue for assisting the rider to raise and fill the horse's back and neck, which should bow upward elastically both under the saddle and in front of the wither.'

Later in the article, perhaps the most important aspect of how the work should be ridden is emphasised. . . . 'It achieves these results because it is (other than needing to provide for the necessary forward urge) largely *a passive, unforced approach which helps to balance out the horse's entire muscular system of extensors and flexors*' (my italics).

This, therefore, has to be the overriding factor. We must always nurture and encourage that idea of the push and the demand coming from the hind end. When we focus on the front end, this should only be as a feeling, visual barometer of what the hind end is doing. We may read the forehand, we may receive it through our fingers, but it has to offer itself. Only in this way can we prove that the horse is moving purposely forward off our aids, not because we have set or dictated to the forehand but because we have addressed the source of our horse's energy.

A horse correctly mouthed and bitted in this way will always want to follow the rider's hand. A horse which moves fluidly and impulsively from behind, pushing through and under the bridge of the rider's body without being diverted like a wayward stream, will seek the contact to reconnect to the pilot. To him the hand is a comforter, a link with his rider, something to be accepted and cherished – something not easily relinquished.

If this sounds overromantic, so be it – but perhaps the time has come again for riders to think more in this way. Too much is mundane and ugly in today's world. Let us return to the pleasant images. One which is as old as the hills is the idea of holding the reins as you would a captive bird. The fingers close softly around the leather in the same way that you would carry the living creature, not tight enough to crush it, but not so open that it can fly away.

I have already spoken of my Portuguese stallion Palomo who somehow found me in a dusty paddock near Sintra in 1986. An ex-bullfighting horse ridden on a severe curb for most of his early life, he showed me a very delicate mouth from the beginning and, even today, under any pressure, anticipation or excitement, he has a tendency to open it or to curl his tongue up at the back. We have worked through these problems but when his original breeder and rider told me I would never totally cure him, I accepted it. Some things cannot be perfect and his past history had taken its toll. There is nothing so shortsighted as to nag a noble horse when he is clearly giving his all.

Nevertheless, this small matter does not prevent him being one of the

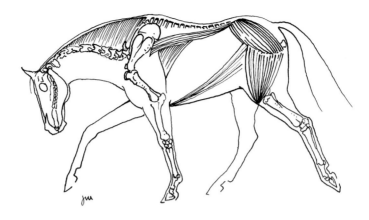

Rounding down correctly, performed on light reins, will help to build the muscles of the topline of the horse through stretching and flexion. It is this vital natural support system in the horse which must be developed if he is to carry us with ease.

finest horses I have ever ridden. His spirit is indomitable, his generosity humbling. Every step he takes is made in the pursuit of excellence. Nothing is shoddy; he tries with all his might to make each movement perfect and often gives riders the benefit of the doubt because, in his wise old way, he knows how it should be done and how it should be ridden. Even now, as he approaches his mid-twenties, he will, on request, pump himself up into full collection through the strength of his quarters, the elasticity of his hocks and perhaps even more on the strength of his own pride and determination. He will also open up into a longer frame if the rider asks, but there are few people I can trust to let him work deep.

A horse that can only be ridden from behind gives a wonderful feeling to a dressage rider who has never experienced in the flesh all the things that one reads about in books. Without a thought for the support of the front end, it is quite simply there as a result of his engagement. Nevertheless, Palomo depends absolutely on that invisible thread of contact from the hand whether it be through the bridle or a mere cord. Take that link away and he is lost.

So we work through the various exercises and when the time comes for such a horse to stretch down, long and low, I remind the rider that even though he is to lengthen his neck and lengthen his back, the hand must still be there, taking the horse down and forward with it. 'Take the hand forward, make the *descente de main* but don't abandon your horse!' Those who feel for the horse understand immediately.

If only more would take the time to study the horse, watch him in all his attitudes, they would see beyond the obvious, the first impression. People marvel at pictures of horses working on the lightest of reins, yet if they looked further they would see the firmness of the hand *in place*, a hand totally supported by the rider's posture, a hand which remains there quietly at the base of an arching neck, a hand which receives the horse. There is all the difference in the world between a horse floating away aimlessly from undisciplined, moving hands and the horse that has been placed *into* the hand by the legs and seat.

There are still insufficient riders who understand the difference between letting go with the horse and letting go with their own bodies. A horse who is on parole, as it were, still needs a supportive body and legs which send him forward. A sensitive horse will feel lost, even threatened, when his rider no longer sends him into his bridle. Unfortunately, there are many riders who see no difference between giving with the hand and giving everything away. Yet, if we train the horse to answer every small request made by our bodies, it is scarcely surprising if, when suddenly we let go, he falls apart. I have seen the most athletic horses suddenly trip and hurt themselves simply because the rider has been distracted and dropped them.

Riding deep work requires rather more tone in the rider than riding normal work. To create sufficient energy to show the horse the way to the ground with confidence requires good upper body posture, a supple lumbar spine, loose, flexible hips and asking legs which, nevertheless, seem to melt into the saddle. With the hands held lower and wider apart, the rider should think of riding up and over and through the contact. Long and low should never be thought of as flat. Whether we are collecting the horse or opening the frame, the principles of rounding, as discussed in Chapter 12, remain the same. The feeling must always be of the horse coming up to meet the rider, cresting the wave, moving off the leg.

The horse is erect in his deep work. The rider is erect and must continue to take the waist and chest to the hands, even more so now that they have opened the whole equine frame. It is too easy to become distracted by the concept of moving centres of gravity. As long as we ourselves recognise that, for all work, we owe it to the horse to sit in the centre, to be centred ourselves, and that we have mastery over that centre, we cannot go far wrong. Many authors write of the weight of the horse being divided into a 60 per cent: 40 per cent ratio. This is generally deemed to be divided so that the heavier part rests in the forehand. On the contrary, Reiner Klimke tells us to think of the 60 per cent remaining in the quarters. This is sound advice in all the gaits, except the gallop, and, even in deep work, we should still feel the hind end is the loaded end.

In riding the horse long and low, he should certainly feel no heavier in the hand. It may take some persuasion, with the fingers inviting him down in response to the asking leg, to put him there, but he should feel as light and submissive in the mouth as he does in full collection.

One last word about training methods. One should never be too proud to change one's views. The first time I saw a professional working a horse long and low, I was horrified. The horse was definitely on the forehand and not just 60 per cent but probably 80 per cent of the horse's weight seemed thrust into his shoulders. As the horse concerned was a Thoroughbred type, already built downhill, it logically seemed to me the very worst kind of exercise to give a horse. I stand by that gut feeling today and know I was right on that particular occasion.

Unfortunately, because I had seen the exercise first performed with so little regard to the type of horse and the way the horse moved naturally, as well as the fact that the hands which were in control were tugging at the rein with a lack of leg to back up the whole exercise, I was put off. For years I spoke out against the exercise and felt that, for British horses, it was the very last thing that our riders should be attempting to do.

Everything changed for me with my last two horses. One was a somewhat stubborn youngster who had been extremely difficult to back. He had an excellent mouth but, like many young horses, had a weak back and was rather rubbery through the neck and shoulder, always snaking out of good sound forward work and finding excuses to evade sideways. Poles on the ground, followed by cavaletti, were extremely good for him, first in walk and later in a good rounding trot. The fact that a horse has to focus on these little obstacles helps to ensure more throughness but, being a clever horse, when it came to riding him on the flat again, some of the snaking returned.

It was only after he was coming together behind and I could really feel his hind legs pushing under me that I decided I would try the deep method. This stallion took to it very happily and was capable of offering confident rounding downwards almost immediately. This was naturally helped by the fact that there had been plenty of early stretching down in the walk on a long rein. Gradually, his back and hocks had strengthened as a result of the collected exercises in walk, while the circles and serpentines had helped to increase suppleness. Hacking out and a little jumping had made him eager and forward going and, with his natural uphill sense of balance, there was no reason why he would not be an ideal candidate.

By extending and opening his frame in the deep work, while still keeping the withers up and the legs pushing under, all the blocks which had allowed his energy to escape around the shoulder area were rapidly unscrambled. He loved the work, became much more confident in his working and medium gaits and, at times, amplified the movement so much that it was as though we were floating on air. Never once did I feel him leaning on my hand; I knew then that this method could be used to enhance my horse with surprising effect; obviously this could not have happened had not the basics been there in the first place.

The next horse was decidedly hollow throughout. Broken too young; pushed into a severe bit and taught tricks such as Spanish walk before his back was connecting his hind end to his front, the head and neck were held artificially high. He had to be remouthed and taken back to square one. I remember reading somewhere that Rembrandt also had a very weak topline and that the reason Nicole Uphoff had developed the deep method for him was because it enabled her to strengthen him through the entire frame. With my horse, the stretching down seemed very difficult at first. We spent many weeks perfecting it in walk and, even then, he required me to be very light with my seat although I used a mild spur to encourage him to respond more attentively to my leg. With my hands deep but without losing the projecting feeling through my waist, he gradually came down to follow my hand without dropping his back.

Now he is working superbly in a deep rounded outline in trot and canter without either backing off the hand or dropping through the forehand. It has taken over two years of patient work but it has not only helped his back, it has subsequently eradicated much of the resistance in his mouth and neck. Even now, however, I never ask him to do this exercise without thoroughly preparing him. Each horse is a little different but in his case I prepare him by stretching him forward in free walk on a long rein at the onset of exercise, then bringing him together with some collection for the turns and lateral work in walk, followed by a good brisk working canter and only then progressing to the deep work before starting the work proper. At other times, I may leave the deep work until later on in our programme.

Deep work should certainly never be considered the answer to everything. There will be days when the horse really seems to need it; others when it can be counter-productive. As always, every horse is different and with some horses it clearly should not be asked for at all.

There's a little rhyme I made up to help riders to think more about how to use the hands for both collected and deep work. It goes like this:

> *Hands together and your horse comes together*
> *Hands apart, and you'll send him more apart;*
> *If you want him deep, then your hands must be deep*
> *But wherever your hands are; ride him forward from the start!*

As I said before, there is a great deal of logic to riding.

CHAPTER 17

Restoring nobility to the horse and to ourselves

People speak of the Dark Ages, a time when men were barbaric and so much of the anterior ancient classical world had been destroyed and vandalised. The Middle Ages, too, were not renowned for their enlightenment, particularly where the treatment of animals and the sick and the vulnerable was concerned. Yet I believe there have always been cruel, unthinking people at all stages of history, including our own, and, sadly, the shadow of the Dark Ages looms perilously close at times in this supposedly civilised society as we head towards the year 2000.

For those of us who love the horse, and it is my belief that there are far more people who seriously respect and want the best for their animals than those who don't, it is important now to find the courage to change attitudes before, indeed, we do return to the dark times of the Hun and the Vandal. Now that so many animal rights groups wait in the wings, impatiently flexing the muscles of political correctness, it is important that the sporting bodies themselves cleanse their image before others distort the picture and irretrievably change it for them. All horse lovers, therefore, have a responsibility to bring to public attention any harsh, cruel procedure which may bring a particular discipline into disrepute.

Accordingly, we must learn to overcome our natural reticence to interfere and open our eyes to some of the unacceptable practices still passed off in the name of training in certain jumping, racing, showing and dressage yards. Thankfully, the rack for humans may have passed into history, but for horses there are always new instruments of torture, worse by far than the bearing rein against which Anna Sewell campaigned so successfully in *Black Beauty*.

Just one such example is the appearance on many yards of a new machine designed to fix nosebands into place on the soft nose of a dressage horse. The flash noseband, an acceptable aid if properly used, can now be mechanically winched to reach the desired degree of tightness which the human hand has failed to achieve. As a result, it has now been necessary to market a liner for these nosebands to help, in the words of one manufacturer, 'to prevent permanent scarring'. Words like this should chill the blood, yet one may hear them on the lips of people who profess to love horses.

Then there are the spikes and weights to encourage higher action in gaited horses, the pumping of steroids into show horses, the overfeeding and underexercising of small laminitic ponies, and the use of certain 'incentives' to achieve greater height and accuracy over poles in some showjumping yards. The Victorian fashion for high heads in carriage horses has been replaced by a desire for low, overbent ones in dressage but the pain level, whether from the bearing rein or the draw rein, remains about the same.

Some countries allow the shooting of horses from helicopters; in others they have been driven over cliffs or simply left in corrals to starve. In more clinical and supposedly humane conditions, certain horses are cooped up like battery hens to produce hormones for ageing humans. Where there is money to be made or to be saved, the inhumanity of man to the horse denigrates us all. It is my opinion that militant action is not the answer. Only with courage, speaking out, providing an alternative and appealing to the best in people can we redress the balance.

One used to believe that the abuse of horses went hand in hand with poverty. This is certainly the case in those countries where the equine is still a beast of burden but, through the resources of international charities, the British International League for the Protection of Horses, the Ada Cole Memorial Stables and the Brooke Hospital in Cairo being the forerunners, education is leading to happier times for many animals in the less developed world.

Ironically, it is where high finance plays a major part in our sporting activities that we often find the worst instances of abuse. Yet it was not always that way. Kings and rulers of great wealth were generally the first to introduce centres of learning and culture at their courts. Those academies which exerted the greatest influence on a more humane approach to training the horse emanated out of the wealth of the rich and powerful Habsburg dynasty and also from the courts of Hanover, Versailles, St James, Copenhagen and Lisbon.

It was not only in the last three centuries that men learned to treat the horse with respect. Compared to some modern attitudes, those of certain twelfth- and thirteenth-century horsemen of education appear positively saintlike. We know from ancient chroniclers that many of the knights who followed the Crusades loved their horses and made every possible provision for them. Men like Jordanus Ruffus, chief stablemaster and compatriot to Kaiser Friedrich I, who presided at an élite Christian court in Sicily in the first half of the thirteenth century, was a latter-day Xenophon, although at that time the work of the Greek commander had not been translated or published in Europe so he would have had no knowledge of him.

Following in the traditions of his royal master, a great falconer and lover of the countryside, Jordanus studied and wrote about veterinary science, the breeding of horses and how to train them. After a life of freedom in the mountains as a weanling, the young three year old was to be gently introduced to life with man. Headcollars made from wool were preferred to hemp, for they were softer; the horse was to be gently touched all over and encouraged to follow his handler, voluntarily and in hand until he had total confidence. Only then would the backing process begin. When it came to choosing a bit, we are advised: 'only the lightest you can find. When you first put it on, smear honey or other sweet juices on it'. Finally, when mounted, 'ride without excitement without noise and without spurs as carefully as you possibly can. Ride in slow walk on the right and on the left hand. Change the rein often and while doing so, stroke along the neck'.

Such enlightened advice is too often lacking in the most up-to-date yards. Could this be caused by a lack of imagination, by a lack of understanding, or from sheer greed to get everything done as quickly as possible, as economically as possible without thought for how it was done? In this last chapter, we shall be examining what motivates a rider and will consider the role of imagination in our work with horses.

For a long time now I have felt that it is only the constant striving for perfection, stretching far above all attainable goals, which can lend true awareness and integrity to our relationship with the horse. Without this burning desire for self-improvement, it is too easy to lapse, to allow our human weaknesses to dishonour the horse, even to abuse him. Being the way we are, we cannot therefore afford to put our personal considerations or ambitions first; we have, first and foremost, to ride for love if we are to be creative and restore the horse to his natural potential.

It is all too easy to rob a horse of his allure, presence and beauty, to enslave him and to produce a tick-tock machine, a dull robot which bears little relation to the magical creature of speed, grace and light with which we have been blessed. One of the reasons why people shy away from riding mares is not because they are cussed or stupid, but because of their sensitive mercurial nature which takes time and trouble to understand. Yet, as the Spanish say, there is nothing better to ride than a noble mare, but for us to bring out the best in them, we ourselves have to learn to be noble.

I admit I did not always think like this. Like most, I suspect, I rarely examined my motives for many years, but gradually I came to appreciate that the desire to win or to be seen to be successful can be a very different matter from the pursuit of excellence. It shames me now that there must have been times when, unwittingly, I subjected my horses to mental pressures which were not deserved. I remember once, on hard ground, kicking my own lovely mare ungratefully when she recovered herself from almost falling on a particularly slippery corner in order to prevent her doing it again. It was only later, watching the video, that I realised how close she had been to falling and how gallantly she had saved us both and how unfair it was to ask any horse to go out and 'do dressage' in such conditions. I would never have worked her like this at home in my right mind; how could I have expected a performance of any kind on a pitted, unlevel field in August with the grass burnt to a cinder? From then on, I never competed again except on proper surfaces.

We have all enjoyed the thrill of winning something at some stage in our lives. We have all dreamed of rising to new heights, of appearing at or qualifying for a specific occasion which is considered prestigious. When a rider can honestly participate in this way without compromising their horse, that is highly laudable. While there will always be results which are well deserved and well won, there is sometimes another side to the coin.

I was very impressed by a story told to me recently by a successful dressage rider from the north east of the country, whose constant winning powers actually led to her giving up competing, an unusual reason nowadays but which makes it all the more recountable. It happened that she and her Dutch-bred horse had won several championships in a row; had achieved more points in the listings than anyone else in the area and their work had been highly commended by more than one international dressage judge who had sat in on her Prix St Georges winning tests.

The crunch came on one particular occasion when she knew she had not done well. Her horse had not appeared to concentrate, it had acted mechanically and was dully submissive, and she finished her test knowing the partnership, the lightness and the joy had all been missing. Afterwards, she handed the horse over to a helper and hastened back to the arena to watch the next few tests. The competitor whom she rightly considered her most formidable opponent was just riding in. She watched spellbound. A beautiful flowing test unfolded; the horse was correct, the expression was there and the two worked in harmony; it was a lovely overall picture. My friend knew she had been fairly and squarely beaten.

At prize giving, a curious thing happened; she looked at the scoreboard and could not believe her eyes. She had been placed first. How could this be? Her rival, something of an unknown, was lying third. She was sure the

We really owe it to the horse to ride him forward, up, round, light and together as nature made him. Everything should flow for there is nothing jagged or fractured in equine locomotion.

(Photo: Bob Langrish)

mistake would soon be rectified. The results and the ribbons were given in reverse order. The moment she could have intervened passed by as in a dream. Finally, while tussling within herself, she heard her name called out to go to receive the cup and walked forward to take the honour. There had been no mistake – at least not in the mind of the judges. For her personally, however, it was all a terrible mistake. In her heart she knew they had given her the trophy because of who she was, not because of what she had achieved on that particular day.

'As I went up to take the accolade', she told me, 'I felt terrible. I wanted to hand the cup to the other girl and say, "You deserve this!" but I couldn't. Something stopped me. I just could not bring myself to make a scene and do the right thing. I regret it terribly. It's something I've got to learn to live

Mares, through their sensitivity, will become very close if we allow them. This is Andorinha, a pure-bred Alter Real Lusitano, who probably knows me better than any of my friends.
(Photo: courtesy *Horse & Rider Magazine*)

with for the rest of my life.' From that day on, she never competed again.

Yet competition need not deter the thinking rider. Competition is healthy but it must be seen to encourage far more than mechanical perfection and to reject enslaved performance. More credit should be given to harmonious displays when an obviously happy horse works with his rider rather than in spite of his passenger. Empathetic, quiet and clearly correct riding must be rewarded. Horses which can only perform to a constantly flailing spur should be penalised. Judges must be encouraged to look more at the overall picture as well as mentally measuring strides or footfalls. Those judges who are brave enough to send out of the arena a competitor who is misusing their horse must be more supported and applauded by all concerned.

The idea of showing your horse in dressage should not be so far removed from the Iberian idea of taking your horse to the fair or fiesta. When I lived in Portugal there were three major horse events per year to which all the traditional country riders aspired. These were real festivals of the horse, running over a number of days and offering something for everyone. They were held at Vila Franca, Santarem and Golegã, towns set deep in the horsebreeding areas of the Tagus Valley, where Lusitanos have been bred since the time of the Romans who organised the first equestrian events. Here the humblest mingled with the mightiest in the land but, whatever your horse, the self-set criterion was the same for every combination.

This was that you only appeared in the ridden classes or in the parade when you and the horse had reached a certain standard of excellence and you were confident of going out there and showing him before friends and neighbours to his very best advantage. The more handsome the combination, the more vibrant, natural and alive the horse looked under his rider, the higher he was acclaimed by all around.

I am not suggesting that technical virtuosity should be overlooked; this will and must always take precedence. But there is a lesson to be learned from the atmosphere of the fairground. Those silent centaurs that thrill the crowds as they pass by, stallion next to stallion, suspended in space in effortless animation, show an exuberance which should not be quenched. As they merge with the crowds, twirling and skirting the liquor and the hot chestnut stalls with the careful grace of ballet dancers, then flamboyantly parading past fire-crackers, shouts, bands and whistles – that for me sums up the spirit of the art of riding. There can be no art without total confidence – rider in the horse and horse in the rider. If we could bring back a little of that willing trusting partnership to our dressage arenas, competition would attract far more enthusiasts than it does today.

When competition becomes the motivation instead of the result of motivation, then there is something seriously wrong. Before the time of the car, motivation to ride might well have come from the need to travel from place to place. Today, there has to be something lacking in our relationship with the horse if motivation does not come from love. As Nuno Oliveira wrote, 'without love there can be no art'. I have often thought there can be no love without imagination.

Material success rarely brings lasting satisfaction. Somehow it falls short of edifying the soul. Riding for the sake of riding and not for what it may bring is the only way to ensure real success. Once we have understood the purpose of schooling, learning the step-by-step process of suppling the horse through gymnastic exercise and taking delight in its effects, the fascination of the work is irresistible and becomes even more important than the end product.

Noble dreams can be dreamt on a noble horse. My late husband, Henry Loch, riding at Golegã, 1974 and showing how round and light a horse can be.

It is rather like writing a book. Although there is a huge sense of achievement when the finished volume is unwrapped from its parcel and there is one's name on the cover, while the carefully chosen title beams out at you, there is an unreal quality as you handle the crisp, ink-scented pages, still pristine fresh off the press. You cannot quite believe the book is really yours – it is finished. Somehow you have lost that warm rapport, the intimate partnership, the constant beckoning of the growing *oeuvre*, calling you sometimes in the small hours of dawn, like a baby waiting to be nurtured and cherished. All at once, the goal, the result, however glorious, is now public property. The real thrill was in the writing, the quiet, sometimes laborious moments, coupled with the flights of the imagination. Consummation comes from the day-to-day creation of a piece of work.

So it is with horses. Working alone for the pure pleasure of teaching, schooling, educating a willing or even not so willing equine partner is intimate, special and very personal. To do it properly requires all one's concentration, the heart and soul must be involved and there is no room for other matters for that short period in time when he is yours and you are his. He knows your voice, your hand, your every move, your inconsistencies, your strengths; he knows each flexion of your back, the embrace of your thighs, the pressure of your knees and, if you have done your work well, he will also know your mind. Once again we are reminded of that famous saying of R. S. Surtees: 'There is no secret so fine as that between a horseman and his horse.' To share such secrets with a noble creature who willingly makes himself our servant and friend is a privilege which should humble us and, above all, motivate us each time we place our foot in the stirrup. Without thought for any manmade goal, our inspiration should come from the knowledge that here is our pristine canvas and we have the opportunity to make art.

I know I am not alone in feeling like this. Talking or corresponding with others who share the same idealism, the struggle to find a purer way of riding, it has been heartening to note the parallels which can be drawn, to learn of the shared hopes and desires and, in particular, to glimpse the excitement, inspiration and enthusiasm which radiates from all who embark on the quest for further knowledge and greater understanding. For the real challenge lies not in personal success but in mastering the techniques required to elevate and enhance the horse through empathetic and creative equitation. However expert the rider and however young the horse, each partnership not only affords us a sense of participation and discovery in a wonderful science, it also leads us to a deeper self-awareness. As the way ahead unfolds and lightens up before us, it is the path itself, with all its myriad perceptions and treasures, which becomes the goal.

The last time I voiced these thoughts before an audience was at a demonstration I gave with three of my Lusitano horses at Harwood Hall in Essex. At the end of the evening, it was time for questions. A man stood up and announced, 'You are a master of Zen.' It was a statement, not a question, and I felt reluctant to deflate the note of triumph and certainty in his voice when I shook my head and said, 'Sadly, I have to contradict you. I know nothing about Zen.' (It was only after this pronouncement that I obtained a book on the subject to see what he had meant.)

Perhaps this little anecdote only goes to show that, whatever the discipline, be it the martial arts, poetry, sculpture or riding, those who open and devote themselves to a life of scholarship without hope of material reward, only of increased understanding, will find themselves much more able to manage whatever trials come one's way – not necessarily in one's riding but in life itself. Material goals so often disappoint; no one, not even fortune itself, can shut the door on your quest for greater knowledge, for being at one with your horse.

People often say, 'You've had such an interesting life; you seem to have been very lucky in everything you've done.' Lucky with home and family and being born at a wonderful time when, thankfully, the war was just over and there was a huge spirit of optimism about and at a time when faith in God, king and country and a certain sense of duty were ingrained into every school child, yes, I agree, I was extremely fortunate. As for work, career and situation, I am not sure whether luck is the right word. I do know I have always had to work very hard, and still do, which involves making certain personal sacrifices and more self-discipline than one might care to admit. While I set myself goals, such as writing an article, embarking on a book, accepting a horse to school, etc., I am not unrealistic. I don't think I set out to make new things happen, but if an idea presents itself – as it often does – I try to make the most of it at that point in time and go with the flow as best one can.

Friends are something else – some, even those far from home, are amazing in their goodness and generosity; others let you down. Sometimes those who seem the closest or for whom you have tried the hardest can be the ones who kick you in the teeth. I have learned that the more you do for people, the less you should ever expect back. Then no one should feel owed anything by anyone else. Life does not work that way and there are people who cannot handle being in someone's debt, however small.

Animals are so very different from humans for they are not worried about their ego, which is wonderful. No doubt that is why so many of us love them and rely on them so much. They are rarely fickle, jealous, resentful or ungrateful. They are invariably polite and are not afraid to show delight in one's company and are unreservedly forgiving and pleased to see you, whatever the circumstances, whatever the weather, whatever the state of the art. My own horses are just as loving as my dogs, movingly so, and it would be untruthful to deny that they are a constant source of inspiration and renewed faith in the innate goodness of the Creation.

For this reason, I am not particularly interested in what they bring, over and above our work together, their personality and friendship. It is the partnership which counts and that is what their education, schooling and refinement are all about. Apart from certain successes at our own breed shows, we have never got into a situation where prestigious prizes in the form of huge trophies or having one's photograph on the front cover of *Horse and Hound* become the objective. How disappointing if it did not work out! I suppose if ever I had a horse who subscribed to everyone's idea of the perfect international dressage horse, it might be nice one day to aim to ride for one's country, but so far this has not happened and it is not very likely. In the meantime, one can reach out across the continents in other ways and I feel blessed that this has been possible.

If recognition is sometimes unexpected, and certainly unasked for, the following amusing but actually heartwarming incident, which happened in Portugal, says it all. I had been invited to be President of Show at Golegã, something which sounds very grand but is, in reality, very much a courtesy thing, providing a very good excuse for the Portuguese to strengthen their ties with other countries and, in particular, to lavish on others the abundant hospitality for which they are so famous. In this context, the Portuguese have always, culturally and historically, maintained very close links with Great Britain.

The Golegã Show for the Lusitano Horse runs over an entire week around Martinmas or the Festival of San Martinho, a time when country fairs used to be celebrated all over Europe, particularly during the Middle Ages in England. Newcomers to Golegã are always struck by the air of antiquity and the total rurality about the occasion. Well attended by visiting Brazilians and the Spanish from just across the border, it is first and foremost a very Iberian and colourful event with many haphazard and delightful displays of horsemanship going on behind the scenes of the main event which takes place in the town's market square.

When my late husband and I first started attending Golegã back in the very early seventies, the number of non-Latin faces one would encounter in the crowds could probably be counted on the fingers of one hand. Nowadays, as its fame has spread, hundreds of dedicated horsefolk fly in

Today, Nicole Uphoff-Becker still rides Lusitanos. This beautiful picture of the former world champion, mounted on Sultão, the palomino which appeared at the Royal Horse Gala, has a timeless quality about it. (Photo: courtesy Nicola Ensinger-Dannar)

from the USA, Australia, Germany, Switzerland, France and the UK to indulge in a week of non-stop activity and Lusitano horses *ad infinitum*.

On this particular occasion (it was November 1990), I was told by someone in the secretary's office that Nicole from Germany was looking for me; apparently she had read my book *The Royal Horse of Europe* and wanted my autograph. Would I make myself available to her? 'Who is this Nicole?' I asked, imagining it to be someone I had never heard of.

'You know – Nicole,' they all said in a low-key sort of way. 'Nicole, the dressage rider. The German one who won at Seoul!'

'Nicole Uphoff!' I asked incredulously.

'That's her! She wants your autograph.'

Later we met at an official lunch organised by Arsenio Raposo Cordeiro, a dear friend and at that time President of the Portuguese Stud Book. We sat one on each side of him and he introduced us. I was immediately struck by her sweet smile and total lack of self-importance. After the usual small talk, the subject of my book came up and I told her it should have been me asking her for *her* autograph. She just grinned and said no, no, she'd really enjoyed my book and wanted it signed. I thought then how rare it is to meet someone at the pinnacle of their career who is not only modest but also generous and, even more special than that, completely open about all breeds of horse and always looking to know more. Later I saw her happily ensconced in a bullfighting saddle with a flat black Portuguese hat on her head, joining in the parade on one of the top breeder's most prized horses. She was grinning from ear to ear.

The one thing horses should teach above all else is flexibility. As we have already remarked, every horse is different and if we are to learn from each new experience our desires must be directed to his well-being, his comfort and his understanding of us. This requires adaptability of the mind, the ability to admit mistakes, change course, sometimes to backtrack and reconsider. Far from raising traits of weakness, such attitudes show signs of strength. Thus our quest to find a true and just rapport with every horse we ride enables us, through perseverance and versatility, to be enriched. The struggle for purity of form, of marrying movement and balance, helps us in turn to grow more wholesome and balanced as people. It also empowers us with a deeper sense of fortitude and purpose, although sometimes this has to be tempered with humility.

Not long ago I was discussing all this with a friend and one-time pupil of may late husband, who is now a knowledgeable trainer in her own right in Europe. In many ways, her life has been similar to my own. Born of hardworking Scottish and English stock who worked abroad like my own family, she has been with horses and teaching since her teenage years and spent several years riding at a prestigious national academy in Europe. After many years of freelance teaching all over the world, she had enrolled on a course with Michel Henriquet, advisor to the Cadre Noir at Saumur and a friend and disciple of the late Nuno Oliveira. Author of many highly regarded dressage books, he is also the trainer of French Olympic rider, Catherine Durant, now Madame Henriquet.

By coincidence, and quite separately, I had visited Michel only a few weeks before my friend, staying as a guest in his beautiful house at the edge of the Versailles Chateau estates just outside Bailly to research my last book. He was kind enough to offer me a few lessons at the end of my visit.

Not knowing of each other's experiences until years later, both my friend and I were to receive a dose of humility at Michel's school. Tough to take at the time, as we were both well established in our own right by then, we are equally thankful for that interlude. Today we are able to agree how it has helped us on our own personal paths of learning as well as in our teaching.

Although we had never admitted it to each other, I think both she and I had expected an easy ride while in France. Michel knew of our previous scholarship, even giving me valuable support over the three-point seat controversy when I was under attack with my second book. For both of us, however, the first lesson on his school horses came as a shock. M. Henriquet is a task master of the old school and from the moment you enter the *manège* he finds fault. By the time you have ridden one circuit of the track, four or five criticisms will have been fired off in quick succession. Within minutes, you are totally demoralised. By the end of the lesson you are a quivering wreck and feel you know nothing, and in this way he imparts a few salient points which you never forget for the rest of your life.

Although things improved, I still felt pretty mortified as I left his yard, scarcely comforted when, with the glimmer of a twinkle in his eyes, he kissed me goodbye and commented drily: 'Pour une anglaise, tu montes assez bien.' From an instructor who only deals in perfection, it helped a little but did not detract from the important lesson I had learned.

Driving back to England, circumventing the Paris ring road, I began to realise and appreciate what he had done for me; he had made me humble. He had also made me think and, by verbally chastising me, he had corrected a fault which previously I had not even considered a fault. This concerned the height of my hands and the length of the rein which, for him, was clearly too long. Michel wanted my hand more into the base of the horse's neck as though pushing it forward and away from me; not floating in mid-air on a contact which neither gave nor received with sufficient finesse. Since then I have noticed that this is the position taken by the riders of the Spanish Riding School of Vienna and some of the more empathetic competition riders such as Kyra Kyrkland, Pia Laus and our own Carl Hester, but by no means everyone.

Old habits die hard but Michel had changed my thinking around and I acted upon his advice and very soon learned how right he was! When I returned to my own horses I learned the value of the hand *in place* with scarcely a hair's breadth between the horse's skin and one's own. Words of writers like Jousseaume[1] ('think of the neck like a rudder, the more it is straight and rigid, the more the leg action will be efficient on the hindquarters') or of Seunig[2] ('the supple horse reaches for the *sustaining* hand and adapts to the bit') now made so much more sense.

Needless to say, I have never forgotten that lesson in France and it has made all the difference in the world to all the horses I have ridden since. I gladly acknowledge that the fruits of my humbling are still with me today.

Comparing notes years later with my friend, who prefers to remain anonymous, she too learned much from her experiences in that small intimate yard near Versailles. I never asked what her particular fault was, but she reported being taken to task and feeling greatly humiliated at the time. Yet, from a similar demoralised state, she too absorbed the sound advice and, like myself, now acknowledges that everything she learned with M. Henriquet was a necessary part of her own progress towards the light.

A nice follow-up to the story was that neither of us was very surprised when, later, Michel's protegée and partner, Catherine, went to the Barcelona Olympics and was rated the highest-ranking dressage team rider in France. I should point out that it had taken around twenty years of his careful tuition for him to allow her to perform in public!

In a strange way it has been experiences like these which have not only strengthened my commitment to teaching but led to a revitalising of my faith which had lapsed during the early Portuguese years. In common with so many young people, life in the sun encouraged a fairly hedonistic selfish existence. I had arrived in Portugal at the end of the swinging sixties and, although thankfully never attracted by drugs, one was constantly joining up with those whose main purpose in life was to have fun. The so-called beautiful people were often deeply materialistic and idle and the message which pumped out from the all-pervading popular music was to go with the swing, let destiny take you, you are not responsible for your own actions, let it all hang out.

Curiously, there was never a word about putting something back into the

---

[1] *Progressive Dressage* by André Jousseaume.
[2] *Horsemanship* by Waldemar Seunig.

melting pot, self-denial or modesty. In between work, riding and beach parties, I read the fashionable novels of the time and was attracted to, but could not quite equate my own philosophy with that of those writers who seemed to take the view that to be your own person there is little need to submit to any form of moral code or natural discipline.

Years later I rejected such a stance completely but it took the harsh reality of serious work with horses to strengthen my Christian faith and clarify my beliefs. Obviously not everyone is going to view life in the same light; nevertheless, I believe that if one is not prepared to acknowledge and bow to certain moral codes and disciplines within nature itself, we are left meandering, without direction and powerless to act positively. Only with principles can we ride horses; only with formulas can we build houses or aeroplanes; only with logic can we form philosophies, but before we can understand or begin to appreciate any of this, we also need faith and imagination.

The following passage, written by the poet Robert Lynd in 1933 as a preface to *An Anthology of Modern Verse*, somehow says it all.

> We often speak of the imagination as though it were a brilliant faculty of lying; on the contrary, it is a faculty by which not only do we see and hear things that the eye cannot see or the ear hear, but which enables the eye to see and the ear to hear things that they did not see or hear before. To scorn the imagination is to be a blind man deliberately refusing the miracle of sight. It is imagination that cleanses the scales from our eyes and awakens our senses to the real things that surround us. We cannot fall in love without imagination, or become good citizens conscious of our citizenship, or enjoy the song of a robin, or the beauty of a rose. . . . Where there is no imagination, there is cruelty, selfishness, death. We can see the results of the lack of imagination in the cruelty with which nation treats nation and class treats class. To treat a child without imagination is to treat it without love. To Blake imagination seemed to be another word for the Holy Ghost.

This latter pronouncement really made me think. William Blake was a man whose views on life and religion were often extremely unorthodox and rocked the establishment thinking of his day. Nevertheless, his great hymn 'Jerusalem' is nowadays played at the most prestigious official occasions. It evokes more love, passion and religious fervour than perhaps any hymn or tune of modern times. The words and music seize the imagination and have the capacity to move people to tears. It is chosen by people to play at weddings, funerals, important events, any occasion when we need to get back inside ourselves and remember who we are.

Riding and verse have a natural correlation. The rhythm of a horse, the beat of his hooves, is not unlike the tick-tock stanza of a rhyme. These

Dreams and myths have been woven around the horse. He exists in all our psyches.

(Photo: courtesy Italian State Tourist Office)

sounds, these images arouse the senses. Poetry shows glimpses of the fantastical, the magical; it shows us what life can be as well as what life is, and the horse plays a major role. The horse – whether the 'Ride a Cock horse to Banbury Cross' or 'This is the way the Ladies Ride' or 'All the King's Horses and all the Kings's Men' – it doesn't matter too much. Alongside the unicorn, the horse has always been there in our nursery rhymes, our dreams and our psyche; he is a mythical fairytale creature, loved by poets, painted by artists. The dreamlike horse appeals to the psychologist in us all. Yet it is his flesh and blood and thunder side, his rhythm and his power, which bring us back to our roots, connecting us to Mother Earth.

To be an empathetic rider, I believe imagination plays an important role. As a teenager studying for A Level English, I had been deeply attracted by the ethos of the romantic poets. Around the same time I discovered that my surname, Cameron, was an anagram of the word 'romance'. Perhaps I should not have been surprised. As children, we had grown up on stories of proud Scottish ancestors fighting for a glorious cause, and had worn our Highland kilts with pride. The work of English poets like Bryon, Shelley, Keats and Wordsworth might seem light years away from those tales of noble pursuit and spilt blood in the heather, yet I felt a common bond. Like the anagram of our name, all had been charged by a sense of high romance. This, in turn, affected me. I determined that if ever I had a daughter she would be called Allegra after Bryon's lovely daughter whom Shelley wrote about with such affection in his autobiography.

There was one particular verse from Bryon which I particularly remember for it seemed to encapsulate the spirit of that poetic age with its deep reverence for nature. I came across it again the other day as I was finishing this book. Indeed, it sums up a great deal of what I thought then, and what I still think today, concerning all creation, including the role of the horse.

There is a pleasure in the pathless woods
There is a rapture on the lonely shore
There is society, where none intrudes
By the deep sea and music in its roar;
I love not man the less, but Nature more,
From these interviews, in which I steal
From all I may be, or have been before,
To mingle with the Universe, and feel
What I can ne'er express, yet cannot all conceal.

Not long ago I was talking to an English friend in Spain about how every horse you work with makes you feel more humble, but at the same time gives one an ennobling experiences.

'Of course!' was her surprising response, for she was always rather a dry and abrupt person. 'This is recognised here by all horsemen and women. The Spanish call it "nobre". It's a word that means much more than in English since it is not just the horse that is noble; people recognise that he gives something back to you. That is "nobre", and it's not just in your riding but in everything you do. For example, through horses I have come to appreciate the countryside out here. Now, I am learning about the olive tree; and the olive tree is rather like the horse, the more you learn, the more you realise how little you know, and the more you want to know. I doubt if I would have wanted to know these things or recognised the wonder of it all, had it not been for my horses.'

'But this is what I've found!' I replied, heartened and excited. 'Thoughts like these have made me want to write this book. Once you start the quest, once you look beyond the obvious, once you engage your mind, use your imagination and get inside your subject – whatever subject, the more you want to discover about everything.

'And suddenly, everything comes towards you! You find other similar-minded people not because you go out and look for them, but they come forward. Special situations seem to present themselves. This, in turn, leads to the most amazing things happening which you never dreamed could have happened.'

I have discussed this, too, with my husband, an environmental lawyer who is deeply committed to his subject. Yet, even in his steadfast dedication, as an adviser, lecturer and writer, to raising environmental operational standards worldwide he is still incredibly interested in other things. While attending international seminars, many of which he chairs or treading the corridors of power as he advises ministers at the heart of foreign government, he still finds the time and energy to visit that country's art galleries or opera houses. Naturally suspicious of accepted dogma, particularly within his own profession, he opens himself to other, less fickle influences. Good sport, a trilogy of plays at Stratford, music at Bayreuth, fine architecture in a Victorian railway station in some forgotten colonial outpost, everything which subscribes to a particular discipline and a striving for excellence motivates and stimulates him. Far from channelling or narrowing the mind in one particular way, specialisation should stretch us all, allowing a more far-reaching, percipient awareness of everything within the Creation. It certainly also puts things back in perspective and is pretty humbling.

In this way, over many years and throughout many experiences, I have come to discover that equitation is just one segment of a mighty wheel. A vibrant, turning, changing wheel, every spoke of that wheel is important to the whole, and, despite the downsides, the whole is a mere part of a greater plan. The more we look, the more we find, the more we learn, the more amazing and fulfilling life can be but we have to *want* it; nothing comes by chance alone.

I find it very stimulating when one can recognise the same influences working within people from completely different disciplines. I remember being deeply moved for days after seeing the documentary film *Gorillas in the Mist* about the life work of Diane Fosse in Tanzania, who was murdered for trying to protect her beloved gentle giant primate friends. As I was finishing this chapter, my daughter, now thirteen and growing up fast, went to stay with friends and saw the same film. She told me how she cried and described it all with such feeling and such compassion that I felt greatly lifted. Clearly the young care as much as we do and for those who have that imagination to feel and to want to make things better in this world of often sad people and sad or endangered animals, there is still hope for the future.

One day I was driving home from giving a dressage clinic in North Wales and tuned into Radio 2. It was that time in the afternoon when, on long drives, one has to be careful not to get sleepy. I had been busy thinking about how the clinic had gone, only half-listening to the programme, when my attention was alerted. The subject was the whale and the wife of zoologist, writer James Harold was being interviewed. The way she spoke about their joint love of the whale impressed me; it also impressed me when she said that as she began to understand the whale, so she wanted to know more about the tides, the way the sun rises, the influences on the creatures of the deep of the moon and the stars, how learning about the rhythms of this huge mammal in its natural habitat awakened her to the movement of dolphins, how both creatures sing and tend their young and how magical and miraculous it all became for her once she made the time to study.

Past attractions, material values pale into insignificance as we embrace a subject with our whole being; the psyche enters a deeper phase of understanding and a leap of faith is made when one goes public; one speaks or writes of one's beliefs, wanting to share them with others. Once that is accomplished you bare your soul and there is no going back.

Suddenly I felt elated. I was not alone! It was not just inspirational horse people like the great Podhajsky, or Henriquet in France, my Portuguese friends and mentors, Belasik in America, Henry's old pupil in Spain and all the many wonderful students I have had the privilege to teach over the past many years. The same emotions which I had felt and found hard sometimes

Deeply concentrating, straight as an arrow, the classical rider makes his final salute after a
display of Lusitano horses at Addington CDI in 1996. Here Mestre João de Portugal
Trigueiros de Aragão demonstrates total oneness with the horse.

(Photo: courtesy Elizabeth Furth)

to put into words were felt by others. For me it was the horse; for my husband, Wagner; for my daughter, her cat; for my mother, her poetry; for Diana, her gorillas; for Ms Harold it was the whale. For others it might be a lump of clay and the potter's wheel, a piece of fine leather, a bed of poppies or the sound of birdsong in the meadow. What mattered was we felt it, and others could feel it too.

When we allow imagination, education, humility and love to enter the picture, all things can be changed. I truly believe there is a new spirit about and that all things are possible. Most people who ride today do love their horses; they love their horses far more than they love rosettes but sometimes they need someone to remind them of that. If people can listen to their souls, adhere to their secret beliefs, follow their good and natural instincts, then there is hope for horses.

A horse is a gift from Creation. He is here to serve but not to be enslaved. He is lent to us and we in our ignorance cannot afford to abuse him for in so doing we deny and abuse ourselves. There is a wonderful passage from the American natural history writer Henry Beston who was born in 1888 and who published his important book *The Outermost House* in 1928. Although the following excerpt was not written specifically about horses, it is so beautiful, so profound, and sums up so very much of what the true student of classical riding feels about the world we live in and the animals with which we work, that I have chosen it to end this book.

We patronise them for their incompleteness, for their tragic fate of having taken form so far below ourselves. And therein do we err. For the animals shall not be measured by man. In a world older and more complete than ours they move finished and complete, gifted with extensions of the senses we have lost or never attained, living by voices we shall never hear. They are not brethren, they are not underlings; they are other nations, caught with ourselves in the net of life and time, fellow prisoners of the splendour and the travail of the earth.

Equestrian bibliography

In the pursuit and study of classical riding over a period of some three decades, I have read and enjoyed more books on the subject than I could probably begin to number. For the purpose of clarity, however, I have only listed below those authors who are directly referred to from a training point of view in the text of this book. In the same way that exclusion from this bibliography does not necessarily denote a lack of appreciation, neither does inclusion necessarily infer that every book below absolutely reflects my own views. Nevertheless, all books, included or excluded, have given much food for thought.

Albrecht, Brigadier General Kurt, *Principles of Dressage*, translated by Nicole Bartle, J.A. Allen, London, 1993
  A Dressage Judge's Handbook, J.A. Allen, 1988
Astley, Philip, *Astley's System of Equestrian Education*, London, 1801
Baucher, François, *The Principles of Horsemanship*, Vinton & Co., London, 1919
  Dictionnaire d'Equitation, Emile Hazan, Paris, 1966
Belasik, Paul, *Riding Towards the Light*, J.A. Allen, London, 1990
  Exploring Dressage Technique, J.A. Allen, London, 1994
Beudant, Etienne, *Exterieure et Haute Ecole*, Amat, Paris, 1923
Berenger, *A New System of Horsemanship from the French of Monsieur Bourgelat*, Henry Woodfall, London, 1754
Blaque-Belair, Lt Col. *Cavalry Horsemanship*, translated by John Swire, Vinton & Co., London, 1919
Bourgelat (see Berenger)
Burger, Udo, *The Way to Perfect Horsemanship*, translated by Nicole Bartle, J.A. Allen, London, 1986
Cavendish, William, Duke of Newcastle, *Methode et Invention Nouvelle de Dresser les Chevaux*, Antwerp, 1658
  A General System of Horsemanship in All its Branches, modern facsimile from the 1743 English edition
Decarpentry, General Albert, *Academic Equitation*, translated by Nicole Bartle, J.A. Allen, London, 1971
  Piaffer and Passage, translated by Patricia Galvin, J.A. Allen, London, 1971
de Kunffy, Charles, *Creative Horsemanship*, A.S. Barnes & Co., New Jersey, 1975
  The Athletic Development of the Dressage Horse, Howell Book House, USA, 1992
  The Ethics and Passions of Dressage, Half Halt Press, USA, 1993
  Training Strategies for Dressage Riders, Howell Book House, USA, 1994

Dwyer, Francis, *On Seats and Saddles*, William Blackwood & Sons, Edinburgh and London, 1869

Guérinière, Sieur François Robichon de la, *Ecole de Cavalierie*, Paris, 1733; translated as *Schools of Horsemanship* by Tracy Boucher, J.A. Allen, London, 1994

Handler, Col. Hans, *The Spanish Riding School in Vienna*, Thames & Hudson, London, 1972

Hayes, Captain Horace, FRCVS, *Illustrated Horse Breaking*, Hurst & Blackett, London, 1905

Henriquet, Michel, *A la Recherche de l'Equitation*, Crepin Leblond, Paris, 1968

    L'Equitation, un Art, une Passion, Editions du Seuil, Paris, 1973

    Gymnase et Dressage, Editions Maloine, Paris, 1991

Herbermann, Erik F. *The Dressage Formula*, J.A. Allen, 1980

Herbert, Henry, 10th Earl of Pembroke, *Military Equitation*, London, 1778

Jousseaume, André, *Progressive Dressage*, translated by Jeanette Vigneron, J.A. Allen, London, 1978

Klimke, Dr Reiner, *Alerich, The Making of a Dressage World Champion*, Merehurst Press, London, 1987

    Basic Training of the Young Horse, J.A. Allen, London, 1985

Licart, Commandant Jean, *Basic Equitation*, J.A. Allen, London, 1966

Littauer, Captain V.S., *The Forward Seat*, Hurst & Blackett, London, New York, 1947

    Commonsense Horsemanship, Arco, New York, 1976

    The Development of Modern Riding, J.A. Allen, London

Loch, Sylvia, *The Royal Horse of Europe*, J.A. Allen, London, 1986

    The Classical Seat, D.J. Murphy, Haslemere, Surrey, GU27 2PE, 1987

    Dressage, The Art of Classical Riding, The Sportsman's Press, London, 1990

Marialva, Marquess of, this Portuguese maestro inspired *Arte da Cavallaria*, written by his ecuyer, Manuel Carlos Andrade, published Lisbon, 1790

Mairinger, Franz, *Horses are made to be Horses*, Rigby Publishers, Sydney, 1983

Müseler, Wilhelm, *Riding Logic*, Eyre Methuen, London, 1965

Oliveira, Nuno, *Alta Escola, Haute Ecole*, J.A. Allen, London, 1965

    Reflections on Equestrian Art, J.A. Allen, London, 1976

    Memorias e Trabalhos de Meio Seculo dum Cavaleiro Portugues, Lisbon, 1981

    Notes and Reminiscences of a Portuguese Rider, Howley & Russell, Caramut, Australia, 1982

    Classical Principles of the Art of Training Horses, Howley & Russell, Caramut, Australia, 1983

    From an Old Master Trainer to Young Trainers, Howley & Russell, Caramut, Australia, 1986

    Horses and Their Riders, Howley & Russell, Caramut, Australia, 1988

Paillard, Commandant Jean Saint-Fort, *Understanding Equitation*, Pitman Publishing Ltd, London, 1975

Paterson, Major T.S., MC 19th Lancers, *Sympathetic Training of Horse and Man*, H.F. & G. Witherby, London, 1925

Pembroke, Henry Earl of, *Military Equitation, or A Method of Breaking Horses and Teaching Soldiers to Ride designed for the Use of the Army*, London, 1778

Peters, Colonel J.G., *A Treatise on Equitation*, Whittaker & Co., London, 1835

Podhajsky, Colonel Alois, *My Dancing White Horses*, Harrap, London, 1964

    The Complete Training of Horse and Rider, Harrap, London, 1967

    My Horses, My Teachers, Harrap, London, 1969

    The Art of Dressage: Basic Principles of Riding and Judging, Harrap, London, 1979

The White Stallions of Vienna, The Sportsman's Press, London, 1985

Racinet, Jean-Claude, *Another Horsemanship*, publ. 1091 Mountain Spring Road, Anderson, SC 29621, USA, 1991

Ruffus, Jordanus, *The Book of Jordanus Ruffus*, approx. AD 1250

Seunig, Waldemar, *Horsemanship*, Doubleday, New York, 1974 translated from the German by Leonard Mins. Robert Hale & Company, London, 1976

Stecken, Fritz, *Training the Horse and Rider*, Arco Publishing, New York, 1977

Steinbrecht, Gustav, *Le Gymnase du Cheval*, Epiac, Paris, 1963

Surtees, R.S., *Mr Sponge's Sporting Tour*, 1853

Swift, Sally, *Centred Riding*, The Kingswood Press, London, 1985

Timmis, Colonel Reginald S., *Modern Horse Management*, Cassell & Co., London, Toronto, 1915

Vezzoli, Gary C., *Superior Horsemanship*, A.S. Barnes & Co., New York, 1978

Watjen, Richard L., *Dressage Riding*, J.A. Allen, London, 1979

Wright, Gordon, *The Cavalry Manual of Horsemanship & Horsemastership, Education of the Rider*, Wiltshire Book Company, USA, 1977

Wynmalen, Henry, *Equitation*, Country Life Publications, London, 1946

   Dressage, A Study of the Finer Points of Riding, Museum Press, London, 1953

   The Horse in Action, Harold Starke Ltd, London 1964

Xenophon, General, *The Art of Horsemanship*, translated by M.H. Morgan, J.A. Allen, London, 1962

National Manuals

The Manual of Horsemanship of the British Horse Society and the Pony Club, published by The British Horse Society, National Equestrian Centre, Kenilworth, Warwicks 1961, 1993 editions

Advanced Techniques of Riding, The Official Instruction Handbook of the German National Equestrian Federation, Threshold Books, London, 1986

The Official Manual of the US Cavalry School at Fort Riley edited for today's Civilian Riders, see Wright, Gordon

Index